THE NOVEL TODAY

Malcolm Bradbury was born in Sheffield in 1932. He was educated at University College of Leicester, Queen Mary College, London, and Manchester University, and at Indiana University and Yale University. He was Staff Tutor in Literature and Drama, Department of Adult Education, University of Hull from 1959-61 and then became Lecturer in English Language and Literature at Birmingham University. In 1966 he went to the University of East Anglia where he was Lecturer, Senior Lecturer and then Reader in English and American Literature. In 1970 he became Professor of American Studies.

His books of criticism include *Evelyn Waugh* (1962), *What is a Novel?* (1969), *The Social Context of Modern English Literature* (1971) and *Possibilities: Essays on the State of the Novel* (1972), and his novels are *Eating People is Wrong* (1959), *Stepping Westward* (1965) and *The History Man* (1975).

D0488645

THE NOVEL TODAY

*Contemporary Writers on
Modern Fiction*

EDITED BY
MALCOLM BRADBURY

Fontana/Collins

First published in Fontana 1977

Made and printed in Great Britain by
William Collins Sons & Co. Ltd, Glasgow

Contents

Introduction MALCOLM BRADBURY 7

Against Dryness IRIS MURDOCH 23

Writing American Fiction PHILIP ROTH 32

The Novel as Research MICHEL BUTOR 48

Some Notes on Recent American Fiction SAUL BELLOW 54

The Literature of Exhaustion JOHN BARTH 70

The Novelist at the Crossroads DAVID LODGE 84

The House of Fiction FRANK KERMODE 111

Notes on an Unfinished Novel JOHN FOWLES 136

Introduction to *Aren't You Rather Young to be Writing Your Memoirs?* B. S. JOHNSON 151

Preface to *The Golden Notebook* DORIS LESSING 169

Scheherezade runs out of plots, goes on talking; the King, puzzled, listens: an Essay on New Fiction PHILIP STEVICK 186

The Myth of the Postmodernist Breakthrough GERALD GRAFF 217

Bibliography 250

Notes on Authors 254

MALCOLM BRADBURY

Introduction

I began to write fiction on the assumption that the true
enemies of the novel were plot, character, setting and
theme, and having once abandoned these familiar ways of
thinking about fiction, totality of vision or structure was
really all that remained. And structure – verbal and
psychological coherence – is still my largest concern
as a writer.

JOHN HAWKES (1965)

Fabulation, then, means a return to a more verbal kind of
fiction. It also means a return to a more fictional kind.
By this I mean a less realistic and more artistic kind of
narrative: more shapely, more evocative; more concerned
with ideas and ideals, less concerned with things.

ROBERT SCHOLES (1967)

The use of words like 'material' and 'chapters' already
makes me feel like a novelist, that is, a man who creates
a time-continuum with words. How difficult that is! And
how loathsome!

ALFRED ANDERSCH (1967)[1]

I

This is an anthology of essays by and interviews with some
of the most important novelists, English, American and
European, who are writing today, together with a few
articles by critics who seem to me to have written broadly,
sympathetically and well about the situation and character
of fiction now. The statements are all reprinted from elsewhere; some are fairly well known, some much less so;
some come from sources that the interested reader would
find hard to trace. They are very various statements, as you
might expect from a wide range of novelists of different
kinds, from different age-groups and from different countries. But they seem to me, taken together, to display an

important, fascinating critical debate that has grown up, inside and around the novel, in recent years. We live in an age in which fiction has conspicuously grown more provisional, more anxious, more self-questioning, than it was a few years ago. Looking about us at the novel now, it must seem that many questions about the nature of fictionality and about its constituent parts – the role of plot and story, the nature of character, the relationship between realism and fantasy or fabulation – have come to the forefront of attention. Indeed, ideas about what the novel is, and what it might be, have shifted so markedly in recent years that we might well judge that a serious aesthetic shift is taking place; that, in fact, there are signs of a distinctive new era of style.

This is something that happens from time to time in fiction, as part of the novel's ongoing business, its development. And so in many respects the present debate, though it is intensified, is not original. Most of the questions and issues in discussion go right back to the novel's full emergence as a form in the seventeenth and eighteenth centuries, when the novel was indeed novel, when it evolved as a distinct species and as a significant social institution, and when its nature was much considered. And they especially bear on polar distinctions that have long been made – between, on the one hand, the novel's propensity toward realism, social documentation and interrelation with historical events and movements, and on the other with its propensity toward form, fictionality, and reflexive self-examination. The novel has always had two reputations – as a relatively innocent affair, an instrument for expressing our pleasure in tale and our delight in social fact through the one literary language, prose, that we all speak and write; and as a complex verbal invention, in which the ambiguities of narrative, the complexities of structure-making, the problems of making a grammar for experience, the perplexities of creating a sense of truth from falsehood, have been explored. The two reputations have both contested and consorted with each other, and helped make the novel the very various form it is: a form highly implicated in history, much concerned with representation, yet with an essential bias toward self-questioning and 'reflexiveness'. In some periods the one side of fiction has been emphasized, in some the other. But in our century the process of oscillation has been very much sharper, and in this process there have been two key periods: at the beginning of the century, and since the war.

'It has arrived, in truth, the novel, late at self-consciousness; but it has done its utmost ever since to make up for lost opportunities,' wrote Henry James, eyeing the future of fiction, in an essay written on the century's turn.[2] James saw a split growing up between the popular and the aesthetic functions of the novel, and sensed great changes, the opportunity for the novel to become more itself. And indeed, in the following years, up to the 1920s, a great reappraisal of the novel occurred; we call this modernism. In some ways it was a realization of the poetic and symbolist potential of fiction, but it was also a kind of crisis. The modern novelist had lost something of the nineteenth-century confidence in reality, in progressive sequence, in the natural growth of relationship between individuals and their moral and social progress. So the novel, in a world in which these essential relationships had become provisional, turned inward to examine, not just the symbolic and mythic resources of fiction, but also the complexities and anxieties of creative consciousness, the angle of vision, the point of view, the grammar of presentation. It went deep into the flow of individual or collective consciousness, with its altered structure of relationship, its changed temporality; it also looked outward at a less substantial and solid material world, at a chaotic history and a troubled social order; it emphasized the ambiguous connections of the inner and the outer life. In this it was consistent with new philosophy and psychology, new convictions of the plurality of worldviews that made up our sense of experience and reality. To James, and to many modern novelists, the novel thus could become the essential modern form; and become that in proportion as it attended to the anxieties of creation, the problems of writing a fiction at all in such a world. The novel was both dying and being reborn; and what was needed, as James rightly stressed, was a new poetics of fiction, a new understanding of its procedures. This was at first largely an affair of practitioners only; James attempted to provide much of this himself, in his own great prefaces and essays. Indeed, it was not really until after the Second World War that criticism began to grant the novel the greatness and centrality James had claimed for it; but then, until the present time, the novel does indeed seem to have become, in criticism, the exemplary literary object, displacing the poem, and, to a lesser extent, the play, as the type of literary experience, an ultimate example of what we do when we tell a story, report a fact, devise an order for events.

By this time, it seemed, much of the impetus of the modern movement had been exhausted; the postwar years saw the revival of the liberal and realist novel. The writers who emerged after 1945 are, of course, very much *our* novelists, and their development is very much related to our development, our contemporary history. After 1945 the novel showed every sign of reasserting its realistic potential, its moral and social concern, its sense of life as progress. The lessons of the great moderns – Dostoevsky and Mann, Joyce and Proust, Musil and Kafka, Faulkner and Virginia Woolf – had been taken, but they were assimilated back into a spirit of relative realism, and technical and epistemological questions were not strongly pressed; the novel was the book of life, the quintessence of experience. But as the revived liberal and historical hopes of the 1950s began to falter in the 1960s, the mood began to change. Formal and epistemological questions about the novel began to reassert themselves; many of the novelists who had begun writing after the war began to change in manner; and certain constituents of the modernist impulse, especially its tendency toward play and game, its stress on art as forgery, and its surreal and fabulous dimension, began to appear significant again. Again a stress on the insubstantiality or corruptibility of history became evident, the problems of establishing solid character, in a world in which humanism was threatened, in which man was held by many to be the sum of his roles, was felt, and the idea of the novel as realistic tale was challenged. Some writers systematically and self-consciously elaborated the referential character of the novel, using the modes of reportage, documentary, and journalism, as in the non-fiction novel; others emphasized the one-dimensionality of character and the flattening of plot by apeing popular forms or inventing the technetronic novel; others insisted on the elusiveness or the unreliability of text, creating novels where the dominant narrator asserting the truth of

what is realism? — a representation of
life? But we want a creation of life.

his tale either disappeared from sight into text or reappeared
in the overt guise of the game-player or impresario, display-
ing the lie he had made, the fictionality he commanded. In
general, then, the realistic centre tended to disappear; the
stable text lost its stability; the reader was invited into the
novel in novel ways. These developments appeared to occur,
at roughly the same rhythm, on an international scale; and
even in England, where the realistic and the liberal tradition
in fiction has been notably strong, the consequences have
been striking.

Indeed, one might note, among practitioners and critics
alike, a growing fascination with the *idea* of the novel; this
is one reason for the intensification of the debate surround-
ing it. In criticism, as I have said, the novel threw off its
status as a lowly or an upstart form, and came in for much
attention; theories and histories of the novel and of narrative began to abound. The first really innovative studies
appeared in the forties and fifties, with books like F. R.
Leavis's *The Great Tradition* (1948) and Ian Watt's *The Rise
of the Novel* (1957), books that paralleled the interest of
contemporary novelists in the realism and the moral re-
source of fiction. Following on from Mark Schorer's seminal
essay of 1948. 'Technique as Discovery', other critics came
to question the notion that the novel was essentially composed of plot, character and description, and recognized that
it was also structure, pattern, form. They saw that it was
more than a representation of life but a making of life, a
verbal fiction, analogous to all the other fictions we construct when we offer to organize and explain experience, to
define reality. In the sixties there were a number of important studies of this kind – Wayne Booth's *The Rhetoric of
Fiction* (1961), David Lodge's *Language of Fiction* (1966), and
Robert Scholes's and Robert Kellogg's *The Nature of Narrative* (1966), among others – and increasingly studies focused
on modes and typologies of narrative, taking the novel as a
sample case of self-conscious organization of experience,
Frank Kermode's *The Sense of an Ending* (1967) being perhaps the most remarkable instance.[3] The lore of structuralism and of formalism was increasingly applied, as well as
sophisticated techniques of Marxist analysis, and now a bulk
of theory, taking the novel as a narratological phenomenon
in culture, has come into being. These notions clearly affect

what contemporary novelists are doing, though they do not precisely mesh with it; it is important to remember that the obligations of the critic and the writer are very different. The critic's task is to explore the history of a form, the character of its cultural existence, the typologies of creation; the novelist's obligation is to make himself a stylistic and experiential citizen of a world that does not fully exist for him until he has done this; he has to invent the possibility of a book in a world he sees as not yet fully named. He does this both within a convention, the convention of the novel, and against it; he repeats but also remakes the form; he exercises options in a particular historical and cultural situation, but keeps attempting, afresh, to distil this as a signed and personal authenticity.

This is why – although there is a distinct debate and a movement toward something like a period of style – we find it hard to give a quasi-historical definition of what is happening. There have been attempts at this, as some of the essays here show; writers like William H. Gass, Robert Scholes and Raymond Federman have provided us with terms like 'meta-fiction' and 'surfiction' to describe the character of the contemporary experimental novel, while other critics, like Ihab Hassan and Leslie Fiedler, have proposed a larger, period stylistic entity they call 'postmodernism', by which they hope to define the contemporary cultural situation.[4] What these critics suggest is that, just as modernism required a breakdown of the traditional vocabulary of fictional criticism before it could be fully understood, so today we need a new terminology and a new kind of critical practice to cope with contemporary fiction. These are, indeed, important steps towards comprehension; but they run the risk of authenticating a particular part of a somewhat larger tendency. There is a debate, an international one, in which the business of the novel is put under questioning, and in which certain preoccupations are evident: with, for example, the primary fictiveness of fictions; with the role of narrative and the problems of the narrator and the authority he might claim for his text; with the relationship between fictional structures and other structural types of prose-writing, like history-writing, autobiography, reportage, confession; with the unteleological fiction, the text that is simply satisfied to be, without insisting on its meaning; with the sense of a world rendered not as causal but simply as experiential; with pastiche and parody, and the interlocking of different mannerisms and styles; with the power of plots and plotters, the temptations and coercions of endings, the threat and the possibility of code and design; with the question of whether the novel bears the power to distil meaning or simply to design chance logics. It is certainly not a single debate, and as in many stylistic regimes the striking feature is not ultimately the singleness of a style but the way in which many varied mannerisms, emerging from very different needs and preoccupations among the writers who produce them, seem to connect.

In compiling this anthology, then, I have tried to suggest my sense that there is a debate, something like a phase of style; and also that the debate is very various, broad, and international, and takes in many diverse phenomena. The aesthetic scene in fiction today ranges very widely. It reaches from the fictions of Borges, preoccupied with the status of imaginary acts and the relation between the orders of the mind and the orders of the universe, through Nabokov's massive inventions of fictional worlds which, though unhoused from reality, separated from rooted language, seen through mirrors and shimmers, nonetheless afford butterfly glimpses of a symbolist revelation, to Samuel Beckett's linguistic minimalism, his philosophical reduction of language to utterance. It ranges from the vestigial, comic characters of Thomas Pynchon or William Gaddis, swamped in a technological universe coded through and through with plots, yet experiencing entropy, to the strange tropisms of feeling that replace character in the anti-anthropomorphic universe of Alain Robbe-Grillet or Nathalie Sarraute, to the contingent, undefined characters of Iris Murdoch, who finally discover in the dances of love and power a certain self-definition. It stretches from the fictional and fabulous worlds of Italo Calvino, created from the 'combinatorial game' we play with the history of story, through John Barth's modernizations of the narrative stock bequeathed to us by old acts of narration (Greek myths, the Arabian Nights) to Donald Barthelme's narrative fragments, scraps of stories that run away into their own incompleteness; from Raymond Queneau's parodies, which turn writing into an endless multiplation of texts, through Angus Wilson's high mimicry and many-voiced narrations, to John Fowles's pastiche of nine-teenth-century realism as practised by the writer who knows himself to be the stylistic contemporary of Roland Barthes and Alain Robbe-Grillet. It includes William Burroughs's cut-up, fold-in, drugged method of composition and the intense fantasies of John Hawkes; the decomposed confessional cry of Philip Roth's later novels and the exposed modern con-sciousness of the psycho-historical novelist Norman Mailer.

The contemporary novel is a broad community that must reasonably count among its significant citizens Günter Grass and Max Frisch, Saul Bellow and Bernard Malamud, Richard Brautigan, Robert Coover and Kurt Vonnegut, Muriel Spark, Doris Lessing and B. S. Johnson, Claude Simon, Michel Butor and Philippe Sollers, as well as many more. It is profitably seen in the comparative gaze, so that the connections can be better examined. Part of the problem is that current discussion has, as John Fletcher notes, been largely confined to the more strident elements in the present avant-garde; the difficult task is to bring the more extra-ordinary bedfellows – he names Allen Ginsberg and Muriel Spark – into significant relation.[5] We live in an age in which style is more than national, and when comparable historical pressures shape form in many countries. The purpose of the essays selected here is to see this matter under the inter-national gaze. There is also another purpose: to emphasize what is not, I think, sufficiently recognized, that in this broad stylistic evolution the contemporary English novel is substantially implicated, and has played a relevant and significant part.

II

The stylistic changes that have taken place in the recent novel have, in fact, occurred in a number of different coun-tries, and this means that they have inevitably occurred inside different traditions of critical discourse, arisen from different assumed histories of the novel, and have within themselves different ideologies, different views of man. There are certain broad elements that are worth distinguish-ing to suggest a present mood: one of them is that many novelists today have become uneasy with the code of old fictional expectations, with the established history of the novel, and have sought to re-experience and remake the form by enquiring into its essentials. As for these codes, they have come from two main sources. One is the realistic aesthetics of the nineteenth-century novel, aesthetics which emphasized the referential and historical expressiveness of fiction, and revealed themselves in a working discourse of 'plot' and 'character'. The other is the modernist aesthetics of the earlier part of this century, which emphasized the formal and symbolist resources of the novel, and expressed itself in an aesthetics in which 'pattern', 'form', and 'myth' assumed a paramount importance. To many contemporary writers both of these aesthetics have become historical; and in a world of changed human and epistemological relationships, of high technology and strange and distorted history, of extravagant individual consciousness and a disoriented sense of human purpose, they have tried to redefine the fictional act in altered ways. One distinguishing mark of the alteration is a shift in attention away both from the referential business of the novel and from neo-epic formalism and experimental inclusiveness. And two particular consequences have become notable. One is the tendency of fiction to withdraw both from referential composition, realism, *and* from schematic formal organization, from designs of point of view, systems of interlocking consciousness, toward the presentation of the lexical surface of the text itself : a text which is a product of authorial consciousness, but exists provisionally, dominated not by characters, designed perspectives, or systems of values and sympathy, but by the rhythm of composition itself. The text becomes the sufficient event. The second, related phenomenon is a fascination with the fictional process as a parody of form – it becomes a game-like construct with which permutations can be played. The alliance of writer, character, plot and reader becomes part of the subject of the novel, and fiction becomes the instrument by which the contingency of experience can be playfully ordered, given or not given significance, defined or not defined as 'reality'.

According to which contemporary national tradition we look at, we shall come to emphasize some of these features over others. The French *nouveau roman* is, as Roland Barthes has noted, a state of affairs in which language acts lexically, foregrounding certain elements in the text, certain states of mind, certain objects of description – to the point where those states of mind or those objects exceed their apparent function, and conventional literary space is redefined.[6] The contemporary American novel, rather less solemn in its approach to contingency, inclined to absurdist comedy rather than absurdist philosophy, as Saul Bellow's essay here suggests, has tended to emphasize the fictive, the inherent *as if* of fiction, so that processes of narration are put before us with emphasis; thus the novels of Nabokov and Barth. Between the *nouveau roman* and the contemporary American novel of, say, Barth and John Hawkes and Jerzy Kosinski, certain obvious resemblances do occur; states of mind are foregrounded, the process of accumulating text is offered as phenomenon without necessary order – or, if order or code is given, it is once again signalled and foregrounded. Other novelists, both in America (Norman Mailer, Kurt Vonnegut, Truman Capote) and perhaps more especially in Germany (Günter Grass, Alfred Andersch, Heinrich Böll), have emphasized the referential aspects of fiction, in works we define as reportage or non-fiction novels; while this may seem a derivative of realism, it depends on attending to the point where a 'real' or historical situation interacts with the process of making; again history or reality becomes a contingency structured by an elected narrative act, as Vonnegut's *Slaughterhouse-5* conspicuously suggests. Thus, again, if David Lodge is right in arguing, in his essay 'The Novelist at the Crossroads', reprinted here, that today there seem to be paths leading in different directions away from the road of realism, one toward fictiveness and fantasy, one toward documentary, the paths seem to meet together again further on. The fiction of the matt surface, of reportage and fictiveness, share in common a curiosity about the real and an introverted fascination with the means of getting there: that fascination tends to desert or to parody the traditional substance of fiction.

The conventional account of these matters is that the new developments came from two primary sources – from France, where the *nouveau roman* began to be talked about from around 1953, and from the United States, where a fascination with the status of fictionality grew evident at the end of the 1950s, and intensified during the later 1960s. Increasingly, certain developments in Germany and Italy have been admitted to the scene, but on the whole the English novel has been regarded as isolated, provincial, and more or less untouched by these tendencies. This is, I think, a somewhat misleading history. For one thing, the developments were clearly partly shaped by the previous evolution of the novel tradition in the different countries. The French *nouveau roman* has been deeply conditioned by the belief that the French novel changed scarcely at all since Flaubert; and certain developments stressed by Robbe-Grillet and Sarraute, for example, would seem reasonably commonplace to a writer trained in the tradition of Joyce, Gertrude Stein, and Virginia Woolf. In America, the novel-tradition was deeply influenced by the marked persistence of naturalism in American writing, which sustained itself with a vigour considerably greater than that in European countries, with the possible exception of Russia; this, in turn, came under question in the postwar period. In England, the considerable impact of modernist writing in the twenties and thirties undoubtedly helped to bring back the liberal revival of the 1950s, at a time when experimentalism seemed to have exhausted itself in latter-day Bloomsbury. However, it now seems more important to stress that many of the best English writers of the 1950s were not intrinsically anti-experimental; more often they were simply defined as such by the critics who read them.

As a result, a somewhat unreliable orthodoxy seems to have grown up about the character of the postwar English novel. It is thus significant that Raymond Federman's useful and exciting collection of essays, *Surfiction: Fiction Now and Tomorrow* (1975), which explores the new fiction which 'exposes the fictionality of reality' and which disestablishes 'all distinctions between the real and the imaginary, between the conscious and the subconscious, between the past and the present', functions on a basically French-American axis, with some reference to German and Italian writing, but none to English.[7] This is consistent with a now prevalent, but I think misleading, view. Most of the books about postwar English fiction are by American critics, a sad reflection on our own refusal to attend critically to our most interesting writers; nearly all of these – Frederick R. Karl's *A Reader's Guide to the Contemporary English Novel* (1959: rev. 1963), James Gindin's *Postwar British Fiction: New*

Accents and Attitudes (1962), and Rubin Rabinovitz's significantly titled *The Reaction Against Experiment in the English
Novel: 1950–1960* (1967) – have, through their choice of
authors, and the realistic emphasis of their criticism, defined
a version of current English fiction which ignores a considerable part of its development. This partly reflects the time
at which the books were written, but it also is part of an
interest in reading English writing as sociological writing, a
way into an account of current English culture. And, though
Bernard Bergonzi's more recent, and also more sensitive and
subtle, study *The Situation of the Novel* (1970) does help to
complicate the picture, it, too, notes that the English novel
is 'no longer novel' and affords 'predictable pleasures'; it
also observes that English novelists seem to have retained
the liberal ideology longest, and therefore have avoided the
literature of extremity practised, with considerable experimental excitement, elsewhere.

There is an element of justice in the emphasis; there is
also a considerable falsification. It was to the taste of
English critics in the 1950s to associate together writers as
various as Kingsley Amis, John Wain, John Braine, David
Storey, Angus Wilson and Iris Murdoch as 'angry young
men', novelists of social realism; but it was far from true
then, and it totally mislays the significance of the subsequent careers of a number of them. If it is reasonable
enough to note, in contemporary English fiction, a certain
persistence of the liberal novel, an attempt to sustain the
idea of character and to redeem elements of realism, this
has been done in the context of a climate of anxious experiment, and a deep working curiosity has grown up in English
fiction, among some of the best practitioners, about the
fictional constituents of the novel. Among the most important of these writers are Angus Wilson, Iris Murdoch, Muriel
Spark, David Storey, B. S. Johnson and John Fowles, all of
whom have speculated much about the value of realism, the
relationship of writer to text, the coerciveness of plot, the
substance of character, the onerousness of form and endings.
Angus Wilson's early novels were praised for their panoramic view of English life and Anglo-Saxon attitudes; they
attended to a complex web of society, to the moral growth
of individuals, the crises of liberal values. But they were
also much perplexed about the status of text, the nature of

the literary imagination, and the tendency of art to falsify.
When these preoccupations surfaced most strongly, in *No
Laughing Matter* (1967), a panoramic novel about English
life from 1912 to the 1950s which is presented not as
realism but through the distorting mirrors of pastiche and
parody of other writers, through mimicry of characters,
through a constant questioning of the solid substantiality of
personality, many readers were baffled, though the book
was very consistent with Wilson's development. Iris Murdoch's first novel, *Under the Net* (1954), was, at the time
of publication, mistakenly read as a work in the angry
young man manner. It was in fact considerably influenced
by Sartre, Beckett, and Raymond Queneau, to whom it is
dedicated; it was not a tale about an alienated young man
but a quest into the nature of language and art, into the
falsifications we produce by naming things, into the relation
between contingency and design, and the function of love
and of silence. It laid down the themes of a highly complex
literary career that, by the sixties, had become much more
mythic than realistic – Robert Scholes rightly identifies Iris
Murdoch as one of the modern 'fabulators'[8] – and in which
questions of form and the reality of character played a
central part.

Indeed, by the sixties much of the realistic emphasis of
the 1950s was beginning to fade in the English novel, for
reasons resembling those that affected writers in other countries. As Angus Wilson's novels probed the ways of pastiche
and parody, and Iris Murdoch's became a mythic enquiry
into the status of character, so Muriel Spark's middle work
turned into an economical, clean analysis of the relationship
of novelist to agent, a fight for the driver's seat, and an
exemplary exposure of the power and pull of endings, the
author's right to impose the 'inevitable'. David Storey's
novels plumbed extreme psychological depths; B. S. Johnson
and John Berger experimented with disordered narrative;
John Fowles examined the magicality of invention, and the
possibility of granting his characters the existential freedom
to choose beyond the limits of his own plotting imagination. It is certainly possible to discern, in the English novel
more than in the bulk of novels in France or the United
States, an attempt to salvage a modern humanism, to maintain the idea of character against the swamping text; but a

sense of inevitable pressures has promoted a strong experimental disposition. All this is visible in Iris Murdoch's essay of 1961, 'Against Dryness', an important statement reprinted here, which defends a respectful but modern contingency against the 'dry' consolations of form or an over-indulged absurdism. But the essay also emphasizes, from a post-existential position, that we are not isolated free choosers, that we live in a universe itself contingent and therefore brute and nameless, from which we urge order only through comprehension and love; to these matters the novelist must attend. And in general, and despite the realistic bias of much contemporary literary reviewing in England, which has limited the fictional debate, the experimental potential of the novel has been strongly emphasized by contemporary English novelists, and has markedly intensified in the later 1960s and early 1970s.

The important thing, then, is that these fictional developments be seen in the context of a novel form significantly evolving and changing, if with somewhat different weights and preoccupations in different countries; that is the assumption of this anthology. 'I presume that the movement of fiction should always be in the direction of what we sense as real,' says one 'postmodern' American novelist, Ronald Sukenick, who entitled one of his books, distilling the appropriate paradox, *The Death of the Novel and Other Stories* (1969). 'Its forms are expendable. The novelist accommodates the ongoing flow of experience, smashing anything that impedes his sense of it, even if it happens to be the novel.' The novel now, with its shifted range of possibilities, from the phantasmagoric to the realistic, from the inert text to the text that painstakingly signals its structure and mode, is in a profitable ferment under precisely that impetus. If the theorizing of novelists, those front-line performers, sometimes seems larger and more exciting than some of their production, that is a risk. But in the end the theorizing is about a central form of our literary experience, and the task ends on the pages of novels themselves, where finally we must test it and enjoy, or not, as the case may be.

NOTES

1. John Hawkes, interviewed by J. J. Enck in *Wisconsin Studies in Contemporary Literature*, vi, 2 (Summer 1964), reprinted in L. S. Dembo and Cyrena N. Pondrom (eds.), *The Contemporary Writer* (Madison, Wis., 1972); Robert Scholes, *The Fabulators* (New York and London, 1967); Alfred Andersch, *Efraim's Book* (London, 1967).

2. Henry James, 'The Future of the Novel' (1899), reprinted in Henry James, *The Future of the Novel* (New York, Vintage, 1956), edited by Leon Edel.

3. A fuller and more detailed list of important modern studies of the novel is given in the bibliography at the end of this book.

4. William H. Gass, *Fiction and the Figures of Life* (New York, 1971), p. 25. Robert Scholes, 'Metafiction', *Iowa Review*, 1,4 (Fall 1970), pp. 109–15; Scholes defines 'metafiction' as a fiction which 'assimilates all the perspectives of criticism into the fictional process itself'. Raymond Federman, 'Prefatory Note' to Federman (ed.), *Surfiction: Fiction Now and Tomorrow* (Chicago, Swallow Press, 1975); 'surfiction' is 'the kind of fiction that tries to explore the possibilities of fiction; the kind of fiction that challenges the tradition that governs it; the kind of fiction that constantly renews our faith in man's imagination and not in man's distorted vision of reality – that reveals man's irrationality rather than man's rationality'. Leslie Fiedler, 'Cross the Border – Close That Gap: Postmodernism', in *Sphere History of Literature in the English Language, Vol. 9: American Literature Since 1900* (London, Barrie and Jenkins, 1975), ed. Marcus Cunliffe. Ihab Hassan, *Paracriticisms: Seven Speculations of the Times* (Chicago, University of Illinois Press, 1975).

5. John Fletcher, *Claude Simon and Fiction Now* (London, Calder and Boyars, 1975); this useful book is part of an important series, 'Critical Appraisals', devoted to contemporary writers.

6. Roland Barthes, 'Objective Literature: Alain Robbe-Grillet', reprinted as an introductory essay to *Two Novels by Robbe-Grillet* (New York, Grove, 1965). The accompanying essay by Bruce Morrissette, 'Surfaces and Structures in Robbe-Grillet's Novels', offers a useful counterweight, suggesting that there are distinct structural-formal elements in Robbe-Grillet's works.

7. Raymond Federman, 'Prefatory Note' to *Surfiction*, cited above.

8. Robert Scholes, op. cit.

IRIS MURDOCH

Against Dryness
A Polemical Sketch

(reprinted with permission from *Encounter*, January 1961)

The complaints which I wish to make are concerned primarily with prose, not with poetry, and primarily with novels, not with drama; and they are brief, simplified, abstract, and possibly insular. They are not to be construed as implying any precise picture of 'the function of the writer'. It is the function of the writer to write the best book he knows how to write. These remarks have to do with the background to present-day literature, in Liberal democracies in general and Welfare States in particular, in a sense in which this must be the concern of any serious critic.

We live in a scientific and anti-metaphysical age in which the dogmas, images, and precepts of religion have lost much of their power. We have not recovered from two wars and the experience of Hitler. We are also the heirs of the Enlightenment, Romanticism, and the Liberal tradition. These are the elements of our dilemma: whose chief feature, in my view, is that we have been left with far too shallow and flimsy an idea of human personality. I shall explain this.

Philisophy, like the newspapers, is both the guide and the mirror of its age. Let us look quickly at Anglo-Saxon philosophy and at French philosophy and see what picture of human personality we can gain from these two depositories of wisdom. Upon Anglo-Saxon philosophy the two most profound influences have been Hume and Kant: and it is not difficult to see in the current philosophical conception of the person the work of these two great thinkers. This conception consists in the joining of a materialistic behaviourism with a dramatic view of the individual as a solitary will. These subtly give support to each other. From Hume through Bertrand Russell, with friendly help from mathematical logic and science, we derive the idea that reality is finally a quantity of material atoms and that significant discourse must relate itself directly or indirectly to reality so conceived. This position was most picturesquely summed up in Wittgenstein's *Tractatus*. Recent philosophy, especially the later work of Wittgenstein and the work of Gilbert Ryle derivative therefrom, alters this a little. The atomic Humian picture is abandoned in favour of a type of conceptual analysis (in many ways admirable) which emphasizes the structural dependence of concepts upon the public language in which they are framed. This analysis has important results in the philosophy of mind, where it issues in modified behaviourism. Roughly : my inner life, for me just as for others, is identifiable as existing only through the application to it of public concepts, concepts which can only be constructed on the basis of overt behaviour.

This is one side of the picture, the Humian and post-Humian side. On the other side, we derive from Kant, and also Hobbes and Bentham through John Stuart Mill, a picture of the individual as a free rational will. With the removal of Kant's metaphysical background this individual is seen as alone. (He is in a certain sense alone on Kant's view also, that is : not confronted with real dissimilar others.) With the addition of some utilitarian optimism he is seen as eminently educable. With the addition of some modern psychology he is seen as capable of self-knowledge by methods agreeable to science and common sense. So we have the modern man, as he appears in many recent works on ethics and I believe also to a large extent in the popular consciousness.

We meet, for instance, a refined picture of this man in Stuart Hampshire's book *Thought and Action*. He is rational and totally free except in so far as, in the most ordinary law-court and commonsensical sense, his degree of self-awareness may vary. He is, morally speaking, monarch of all he surveys and totally responsible for his actions. Nothing transcends him. His moral language is a practical pointer, the instrument of his choices, the indication of his preferences. His inner life is resolved into his acts and choices, and his beliefs, which are also acts, since a belief can only be identified through its expression. His moral arguments are references to empirical facts backed up by decisions.

The only moral word which he requires is 'good' (or 'right'), the word which expresses decision. His rationality expresses itself in awareness of the facts, whether about the world or about himself. The virtue which is fundamental to him is sincerity.

If we turn to French philosophy we may see, at least in that section of it which has most caught the popular imagination, I mean in the work of Jean-Paul Sartre, essentially the same picture. It is interesting how extremely Kantian this picture is, for all Sartre's indebtedness to Hegelian sources. Again, the individual is pictured as solitary and totally free. There is no transcendent reality, there are no degrees of freedom. On the one hand there is the mass of psychological desires and social habits and prejudices, on the other hand there is the will. Certain dramas, more Hegelian in character, are of course enacted within the soul; but the isolation of the will remains. Hence *angoisse*. Hence, too, the special anti-bourgeois flavour of Sartre's philosophy which makes it appeal to many intellectuals: the ordinary traditional picture of personality and the virtues lies under suspicion of *mauvaise foi*. Again the only real virtue is sincerity. It is, I think, no accident that, however much philosophical and other criticism Sartre may receive, this powerful picture has caught our imagination. The Marxist critics may plausibly claim that it represents the essence of the Liberal theory of personality.

It will be pointed out that other phenomenological theories (leaving aside Marxism) have attempted to do what Sartre has failed to do, and that there are notable philosophers who have offered a different picture of the soul. Yes; yet from my own knowledge of the scene I would doubt whether any (non-Marxist) account of human personality has yet emerged from phenomenology which is fundamentally unlike the one which I have described and can vie with it in imaginative power. It may be said that philosophy cannot in fact produce such an account. I am not sure about this, nor is this large question my concern here. I express merely my belief that, for the Liberal world, philosophy is not in fact at present able to offer us any other complete and powerful picture of the soul. I return now to England and the Anglo-Saxon tradition.

The Welfare State has come about as a result, largely, of

socialist thinking and socialist endeavour. It has seemed to
bring a certain struggle to an end; and with that ending has
come a lassitude about fundamentals. If we compare the
language of the original Labour Party constitution with that
of its recent successor we see an impoverishment of thinking and language which is typical. The Welfare State is the
reward of 'empiricism in politics'. It has represented to us
a set of thoroughly desirable but limited ends, which could
be conceived *in non-theoretical terms*; and in pursuing it, in
allowing the idea of it to dominate the more naturally
theoretical wing of our political scene, we have to a large
extent lost our theories. Our central conception is still a
debilitated form of Mill's equation: happiness equals freedom equals personality. There should have been a revolt
against utilitarianism; but for many reasons it has not taken
place. In 1905 John Maynard Keynes and his friends wel-
comed the philosophy of G. E. Moore because Moore re-
instated the concept of experience. Moore directed attention
away from the mechanics of action and towards the inner
life. But Moore's 'experience' was too shallow a concept;
and a scientific age with simple, attainable, empirical aims
has preferred a more behaviouristic philosophy.

What have we lost here? And what have we perhaps
never had? We have suffered a general loss of concepts, the
loss of a moral and political vocabulary. We no longer use
a spread-out substantial picture of the manifold virtues of
man and society. We no longer see man against a background of values, of realities, which transcend him. We
picture man as a brave naked will surrounded by an easily
comprehended empirical world. For the hard idea of truth
we have substituted a facile idea of sincerity. What we have
never had, of course, is a satisfactory Liberal theory of
personality, a theory of man as free and separate and
related to a rich and complicated world from which, as a
moral being, he has much to learn. We have bought the
Liberal theory as it stands, because we have wished to
encourage people to think of themselves as free, at the cost
of surrendering the background.

We have never solved the problems about human personality posed by the Enlightenment. Between the various
concepts available to us the real question has escaped: and
now, in a curious way, our present situation is analogous

to an eighteenth-century one. We retain a rationalistic optimism about the beneficent results of education, or rather, technology. We combine this with a romantic conception of 'the human condition', a picture of the individual as stripped and solitary: a conception which has, since Hitler, gained a peculiar intensity.

The eighteenth century was an era of rationalistic allegories and moral tales. The nineteenth century (roughly) was the great era of the novel; and the novel throve upon a dynamic merging of the idea of person with the idea of class. Because nineteenth-century society was dynamic and interesting and because (to use a Marxist notion) the type and the individual could there be seen as merged, the solution of the eighteenth-century problem could be put off. It has been put off till now. Now that the structure of society is less interesting and less alive than it was in the nineteenth century, and now that Welfare economics have removed certain incentives to thinking, and now that the values of science are so much taken for granted, we confront in a particularly dark and confusing form a dilemma which has been with us implicitly since the Enlightenment, or since the beginning, wherever exactly one wishes to place it, of the modern Liberal world.

If we consider twentieth-century literature as compared with nineteenth-century literature, we notice certain significant contrasts. I said that, in a way, we were back in the eighteenth century, the era of rationalistic allegories and moral tales, the era when the idea of human nature was unitary and single. The nineteenth-century novel (I use these terms boldly and roughly: of course there were exceptions) was not concerned with 'the human condition', it was concerned with real various individuals struggling in society. The twentieth-century novel is usually either crystalline or journalistic; that is, it is either a small quasi-allegorical object portraying the human condition and not containing 'characters' in the nineteenth-century sense, or else it is a large shapeless quasi-documentary object, the degenerate descendant of the nineteenth-century novel, telling, with pale conventional characters, some straightforward story enlivened with empirical facts. Neither of these kinds of literature engages with the problem that I mentioned above.

It may readily be noted that if our prose fiction is either

crystalline or journalistic, the crystalline works are usually the better ones. They are what the more serious writers want to create. We may recall the ideal of 'dryness' which we associate with the symbolist movement, with writers such as T. E. Hulme and T. S. Eliot, with Paul Valéry, with Wittgenstein. This 'dryness' (smallness, clearness, self-containedness) is a nemesis of Romanticism. Indeed it *is* Romanticism in a later phase. The pure, clean, self-contained 'symbol', the exemplar incidentally of what Kant, ancestor of both Liberalism and Romanticism, required art to be, is the analogue of the lonely self-contained individual. It is what is left of the other-worldliness of Romanticism when the 'messy' humanitarian and revolutionary elements have spent their force. The temptation of art, a temptation to which every work of art yields except the greatest ones, is to console. The modern writer, frightened of technology and (in England) abandoned by philosophy and (in France) presented with simplified dramatic theories, attempts to console us by myths or by stories.

On the whole : his truth is sincerity and his imagination is fantasy. Fantasy operates either with shapeless day-dreams (the journalistic story) or with small myths, toys, crystals. Each in his own way produces a sort of 'dream necessity'. Neither grapples with reality : hence 'fantasy', not 'imagination'.

The proper home of the symbol, in the 'symbolist' sense, is poetry. Even there it may play an equivocal role since there is something in symbolism which is inimical to words, out of which, we have been reminded, poems are constructed. Certainly the invasion of other areas by what I may call, for short, 'symbolist ideals', has helped to bring about a decline of prose. Eloquence is out of fashion; even 'style', except in a very austere sense of this term, is out of fashion.

T. S. Eliot and Jean-Paul Sartre, dissimilar enough as thinkers, both tend to undervalue prose and to deny it any *imaginative* function. Poetry is the creation of linguistic quasi-things; prose is for explanation and exposition, it is essentially didactic, documentary, informative. Prose is ideally transparent; it is only *faute de mieux* written in words. The influential modern stylist is Hemingway. It would be almost inconceivable now to write like Landor.

Most modern English novels indeed are not *written*. One feels they could slip into some other medium without much loss. It takes a foreigner like Nabokov or an Irishman like Beckett to animate prose language into an imaginative stuff in its own right.

Tolstoy who said that art was an expression of the religious perception of the age was nearer the truth than Kant who saw it as the imagination in a frolic with the understanding. The connection between art and the moral life has languished because we are losing our sense of form and structure in the moral world itself. Linguistic and existentialist behaviourism, our Romantic philosophy, has reduced our vocabulary and simplified and impoverished our view of the inner life. It is natural that a Liberal democratic society will not be concerned with techniques of improvement, will deny that virtue is knowledge, will emphasize choice at the expense of vision; and a Welfare State will weaken the incentives to investigate the bases of a Liberal democratic society. For political purposes we have been encouraged to think of ourselves as totally free and responsible, knowing everything we need to know for the important purposes of life. But this is one of the things of which Hume said that it may be true in politics but false in fact; and is it really true in politics? We need a post-Kantian unromantic Liberalism with a different image of freedom.

The technique of becoming free is more difficult than John Stuart Mill imagined. We need more concepts than our philosophies have furnished us with. We need to be enabled to think in terms of degrees of freedom, and to picture, in a non-metaphysical, non-totalitarian, and non-religious sense, the transcendence of reality. A simple-minded faith in science, together with the assumption that we are all rational and totally free, engenders a dangerous lack of curiosity about the real world, a failure to appreciate the difficulties of knowing it. We need to return from the self-centred concept of sincerity to the other-centred concept of truth. We are not isolated free choosers, monarchs of all we survey, but benighted creatures sunk in a reality whose nature we are constantly and overwhelmingly tempted to deform by fantasy. Our current picture of freedom encourages a dream-like facility; whereas what we require is a renewed sense of the difficulty and complexity of the moral life and the opacity of persons. We need more concepts in terms of which to picture the substance of our being; it is through an enriching and deepening of concepts that moral progress takes place. Simone Weil said that morality was a matter of attention, not of will. We need a new vocabulary of attention.

It is here that literature is so important, especially since it has taken over some of the tasks formerly performed by philosophy. Through literature we can re-discover a sense of the density of our lives. Literature can arm us against consolation and fantasy and can help us to recover from the ailments of Romanticism. If it can be said to have a task, that surely is its task. But if it is to perform it, prose must recover its former glory, eloquence and discourse must return. I would connect eloquence with the attempt to speak the truth. I think here of the work of Albert Camus. All his novels were *written*; but the last one, though less striking and successful than the first two, seems to me to have been a more serious attempt upon the truth: and illustrates what I mean by eloquence.

It is curious that modern literature, which is so much concerned with violence, contains so few convincing pictures of evil.

Our inability to imagine evil is a consequence of the facile, dramatic and, in spite of Hitler, optimistic picture of ourselves with which we work. Our difficulty about form, about images – our tendency to produce works which are either crystalline or journalistic – is a symptom of our situation. Form itself can be a temptation, making the work of art into a small myth which is a self-contained and indeed self-satisfied individual. We need to turn our attention away from the consoling dream necessity of Romanticism, away from the dry symbol, the bogus individual, the false whole, towards the real impenetrable human person. That this person is substantial, impenetrable, individual, indefinable, and valuable is after all the fundamental tenet of Liberalism.

It is here, however much one may criticize the emptiness of the Liberal idea of freedom, however much one may talk in terms of restoring a lost unity, that one is forever at odds with Marxism. Reality is not a given whole. An understanding of this, a respect for the contingent, is essential to imagination as opposed to fantasy. Our sense of form, which is an aspect of our desire for consolation, can be a danger to our sense of reality as a rich receding background. Against the consolations of form, the clean crystalline work, the simplified fantasy-myth, we must pit the destructive power of the now so unfashionable naturalistic idea of character.

Real people are destructive of myth, contingency is destructive of fantasy and opens the way for imagination. Think of the Russians, those great masters of the contingent. Too much contingency of course may turn art into journalism. But since reality is incomplete, art must not be too much afraid of incompleteness. Literature must always represent a battle between real people and images; and what it requires now is a much stronger and more complex conception of the former.

In morals and politics we have stripped ourselves of concepts. Literature, in curing its own ills, can give us a new vocabulary of experience, and a truer picture of freedom. With this, renewing our sense of distance, we may remind ourselves that art too lives in a region where all human endeavour is failure. Perhaps only Shakespeare manages to create at the highest level both images and people; and even *Hamlet* looks second-rate compared with *Lear*. Only the very greatest art invigorates without consoling, and defeats our attempts, in W. H. Auden's words, to use it as magic.

PHILIP ROTH

Writing American Fiction

(reprinted with permission from *Reading Myself and Others*,
Farrar, Straus and Giroux, 1975)

Several winters back, while I was living in Chicago, the
city was shocked and mystified by the death of two teenage
girls. So far as I know, the populace is mystified still; as for
the shock, Chicago is Chicago, and one week's dismemberment fades into the next's. The victims this particular year
were sisters. They went off one December night to see an
Elvis Presley movie, for the sixth or seventh time we are
told, and never came home. Ten days passed, and fifteen
and twenty, and then the whole bleak city, every street and
alley, was being searched for the missing Grimes girls, Pattie
and Babs. A girl friend had seen them at the movie, a group
of boys had caught a glimpse of them afterwards getting
into a black Buick, another group said a green Chevy, and
so on and so forth, until one day the snow melted and the
unclothed bodies of the two girls were discovered in a road-
side ditch in a forest preserve west of Chicago. The coroner
said he didn't know the cause of death, and then the newspapers took over. One paper ran a drawing of the girls on
the back page, in bobby socks and Levi's and babushkas:
Pattie and Babs a foot tall, and in four colours, like Dixie
Dugan on Sundays. The mother of the two girls wept herself
right into the arms of a local newspaper lady, who apparently set up her typewriter on the Grimeses' front porch
and turned out a column a day, telling us that these had
been good girls, hard-working girls, average girls, church-
going girls, et cetera. Late in the evening one could watch
television interviews featuring schoolmates and friends of
the Grimes sisters: the teenage girls look around, dying to
giggle, the boys stiffen in their leather jackets. 'Yeah, I
knew Babs, yeah, she was all right, yeah, she was popular
. . .' On and on, until at last comes a confession. A skid-
row bum of thirty-five or so, a dishwasher, a prowler, a
no-good named Benny Bedwell, admits to killing both girls,
after he and a pal cohabited with them for several weeks in

various flea-bitten hotels. Hearing the news, the weeping
mother tells the newspaper lady that the man is a liar – her
girls, she insists now, were murdered the night they went
off to the movie. The coroner continues to maintain (with
rumblings from the press) that the girls show no signs of
having had sexual intercourse. Meanwhile, everybody in
Chicago is buying four papers a day, and Benny Bedwell,
having supplied the police with an hour-by-hour chronicle
of his adventure, is tossed in jail. Two nuns, teachers of the
girls at the school they attended, are sought out by the
newspapermen. They are surrounded and questioned, and
finally one of the sisters explains all. 'They were not
exceptional girls,' the sister says, 'they had no hobbies.'
About this time, some good-natured soul digs up Mrs Bedwell, Benny's mother, and a meeting is arranged between
this old woman and the mother of the slain teenagers. Their
picture is taken together, two overweight, overworked
American ladies, quite befuddled but sitting up straight for
the photographers. Mrs Bedwell apologizes for her Benny.
She says, 'I never thought any boy of mine would do a thing
like that.' Two weeks later, maybe three, her boy is out on
bail, sporting several lawyers and a new one-button-roll suit.
He is driven in a pink Cadillac to an out-of-town motel
where he holds a press conference. Yes, he is the victim of
police brutality. No, he is not a murderer; a degenerate
maybe, but even that is changing. He is going to become
a carpenter (a carpenter!) for the Salvation Army, his
lawyers say. Immediately, Benny is asked to sing (he plays
the guitar) in a Chicago night spot for two thousand dollars
a week, or is it ten thousand? I forget. What I remember
is that suddenly, into the mind of the onlooker, or newspaper reader, comes The Question : is this all public relations? But of course not – two girls are dead. Still, a song
begins to catch on in Chicago, 'The Benny Bedwell Blues'.
Another newspaper launches a weekly contest : 'How Do
You Think the Grimes Girls Were Murdered?' and a prize
is given for the best answer (in the opinion of the judges).
And now the money begins to flow; donations, hundreds
of them, start pouring in to Mrs Grimes from all over
the city and the state. For what? From whom? Most
contributions are anonymous. Just the dollars, thousands
and thousands of them – the *Sun-Times* keeps us informed

T.N.T. – B

of the grand total. Ten thousand, twelve thousand, fifteen thousand. Mrs Grimes sets about refinishing and redecorating her house. A stranger steps forward, by the name of Shultz or Schwartz – I don't really remember – but he is in the appliance business and he presents Mrs Grimes with a whole new kitchen. Mrs Grimes, beside herself with appreciation and joy, turns to her surviving daughter and says, 'Imagine me in that kitchen!' Finally, the poor woman goes out and buys two parakeets (or maybe another Mr Shultz presents them as a gift); one parakeet she calls Babs, the other Pattie. At just about this point, Benny Bedwell, doubtless having barely learned to hammer a nail in straight, is extradited to Florida on the charge of having raped a twelve-year-old girl there. Shortly thereafter I left Chicago myself, and so far as I know, though Mrs Grimes hasn't her two girls, she has a brand-new dishwasher and two small birds.

And what is the moral of the story? Simply this: that the American writer in the middle of the twentieth century has his hands full in trying to understand, describe, and then make *credible* much of American reality. It stupefies, it sickens, it infuriates, and finally it is even a kind of embarrassment to one's own meagre imagination. The actuality is continually outdoing our talents, and the culture tosses up figures almost daily that are the envy of any novelist. Who, for example, could have invented Charles Van Doren? Roy Cohn and David Schine? Sherman Adams and Bernard Goldfine? Dwight David Eisenhower?

Several months back, most of the country heard one of the candidates for the Presidency of the United States say something like, 'Now if you feel that Senator Kennedy is right, then I sincerely believe you should vote for Senator Kennedy, and if you feel that I am right, I humbly submit that you vote for me. Now, I feel, and this is certainly a personal opinion, that I am right . . .' and so on. Though it did not appear this way to some thirty-four million voters, it still seems to me a little easy to ridicule Mr Nixon, and it is not for that reason that I have bothered to paraphrase his words here. If one was at first amused by him, one was ultimately astonished. Perhaps as a satiric literary creation, he might have seemed 'believable', but I myself found that on the TV screen, as a real public figure, a political fact, my mind balked at taking him in. Whatever else the television debates produced in me, I should point out, as a literary curiosity, they also produced professional envy. All the machinations over make-up and rebuttal time, all the business over whether Mr Nixon should look at Mr Kennedy when he replied, or should look away – all of it was so beside the point, so fantastic, so weird and astonishing, that I found myself beginning to wish I had invented it. But then, of course, one need not have been a fiction writer to wish that *someone* had invented it, and that it was not real and with us.

The daily newspapers, then, fill us with wonder and awe (is it possible? is it happening?), also with sickness and despair. The fixes, the scandals, the insanity, the idiocy, the piety, the lies, the noise . . . Recently, in *Commentary*, Benjamin DeMott wrote that the 'deeply lodged suspicion of the times [is] namely, that events and individuals are unreal, and that power to alter the course of the age, of my life and your life, is actually vested nowhere'. There seems to be, said DeMott, a kind of 'universal descent into unreality'. The other night – to give a benign example of the descent – my wife turned on the radio and heard the announcer offering a series of cash prizes for the three best television plays of five minutes' duration, written by children. It is difficult at such moments to find one's way around the kitchen. Certainly few days go by when incidents far less benign fail to remind us of what DeMott is talking about. When Edmund Wilson says that after reading *Life* magazine he feels he does not belong to the country depicted there, that he does not live in this country, I understand what he means.

However, for a writer of fiction to feel that he does not really live in his own country – as represented by *Life* or by what he experiences when he steps out the front door – must seem a serious occupational impediment. For what will his subject be? His landscape? One would think that we might get a high proportion of historical novels on contemporary satire – or perhaps just nothing. No books. Yet almost weekly one finds on the best-seller list another novel which is set in Mamaroneck or New York City or Washington, with characters moving through a world of dishwashers and TV sets and advertising agencies and senatorial investigations. It all *looks* as though the writers are turning out books about our world. There is *Cash McCall* and *The Man in the Grey Flannel Suit* and *Marjorie Morningstar* and *The Enemy Camp* and *Advise and Consent*, and so on. But what is noteworthy is that these books aren't very good. Not that the writers aren't sufficiently horrified with the landscape to suit me – quite the contrary. They are generally full of concern for the world about them; finally, however, they just don't imagine the corruption and vulgarity and treachery of American public life any more profoundly than they imagine human character – that is, the country's private life. All issues are generally solvable, suggesting that they are not so much awe-struck or horror-struck as they are provoked by some topical controversy. 'Controversial' is a common word in the critical language of this literature, as it is, say, in the language of the TV producer.

It is hardly news that in best-sellerdom we frequently find the hero coming to terms and settling down in Scarsdale, or wherever, knowing himself. And on Broadway, in the third act, someone says, 'Look, why don't you just love each other?' and the protagonist, throwing his hand to his forehead, cries, 'God, why didn't *I* think of that!' and before the bulldozing action of love, all else collapses – verisimilitude, truth, and interest. It is like 'Dover Beach' ending happily for Matthew Arnold, and for us, because the poet is standing at the window with a woman who understands him. If the literary investigation of our era were to become solely the property of Wouk, Weidman, Sloan Wilson, Cameron Hawley, and Broadway's *amor-vincit-omnia* boys it would be unfortunate indeed – like leaving sex to the pornographers, where again there is more to what is happening than first meets the eye.

But the times have not yet been given over completely to lesser minds and talents. There is Norman Mailer. And he is an interesting example of a writer in whom our era has provoked such a magnificent disgust that dealing with it in fiction has almost come to seem, for him, beside the point. He has become an actor in the cultural drama, the difficulty of which is that it leaves one with less time to be a writer. For instance, to defy the civil-defence authorities and their H-bomb drills, you have to take off a morning

from the typewriter and go down and stand outside of City
Hall; then, if you're lucky and they toss you in jail, you
have to give up an evening at home and your next morning's work as well. To defy Mike Wallace, or challenge his
principle-less aggression, or simply use him or straighten
him out, you must first be a guest on his programme –
there's one night shot. Then you may well spend the next
two weeks (I am speaking from memory) disliking yourself
for having gone, and then two more writing an article
attempting to explain why you did it and what it was like.
'It's the age of the slob,' says a character in William Styron's new novel. 'If we don't watch out they're going to
drag us under . . .' And the dragging under can take many
forms. We get, from Mailer, for instance, a book like
Advertisements for Myself, a chronicle for the most part of
why I did it and what it was like – and who I have it in for:
his life as a substitute for his fiction. An infuriating, self-
indulgent, boisterous, mean book, not much worse than
most advertising we have to put up with – but, taken as a
whole, curiously moving in its revelation of despair, so great
that the man who bears it, or is borne by it, seems for the
time being to have given up on making an imaginative
assault upon the American experience, and has become
instead the champion of a kind of public revenge. However,
what one champions one day may make one its victim the
next; once having written *Advertisements for Myself*, I
don't see that you can write it again. Mailer probably now
finds himself in the unenviable position of having to put up
or shut up. Who knows – maybe it's where he wanted to be.
My own feeling is that times are tough for a fiction writer
when he takes to writing letters to his newspaper rather
than those complicated, disguised letters to himself, which
are stories.

The last is not intended to be a sententious, or a con-
descending remark, or even a generous one. However, one
suspects Mailer's style or his motives, one sympathizes with
the impulse that leads him to want to be a critic, a reporter,
a sociologist, a journalist, or even the Mayor of New York.
For what is particularly tough about the times is writing
about them, as a serious novelist or storyteller. Much has
been made, much of it by the writers themselves, of the fact
that the American writer has no status, no respect, and no

audience. I am pointing here to a loss more central to the task itself, the loss of a subject; or, to put it another way, a voluntary withdrawal of interest by the fiction writer from some of the grander social and political phenomena of our times.

Of course there have been writers who have tried to meet these phenomena head-on. It seems to me I have read several books or stories in the past few years in which one character or another starts to talk about 'The Bomb', and the conversation usually leaves me feeling less than convinced, and in some extreme instances, with a certain amount of sympathy for fallout; it is like people in college novels having long talks about what kind of generation they are. But what then? What can the writer do with so much of the American reality as it is? Is the only other possibility to be Gregory Corso and thumb your nose at the whole thing? The attitude of the Beats (if such a phrase has meaning) is not entirely without appeal. The whole thing is a joke. America, ha-ha. But that doesn't put very much distance between Beatdom and its sworn enemy, best-sellerdom – not much more than what it takes to get from one side of a nickel to the other: for is America, ha-ha, really any more than America, hoo-ray, stood upon its head?

Now it is possible that I am exaggerating the serious writer's response to our cultural predicament and his inability or unwillingness to deal with it imaginatively. There seems to me little, in the end, to prove an assertion about the psychology of a nation's writers, outside, that is, of their books themselves. In this case, unfortunately, the bulk of the evidence is not books that *have* been written but the ones that have been left unfinished, and those that have not even been considered worth the attempt. Which is not to say that there have not been certain literary signs, however, certain obsessions and innovations, to be found in the novels of our best writers, supporting the notion that the social world has ceased to be as suitable or as manageable a subject as it once may have been.

Let me begin with some words about the man who, by reputation at least, is *the* writer of the age. The response of college students to the work of J. D. Salinger indicates that perhaps he, more than anyone else, has not turned his back on the times but, instead, has managed to put his finger on whatever struggle of significance is going on today between self and culture. *The Catcher in the Rye* and the recent stories in *The New Yorker* having to do with the Glass family surely take place in the immediate here and now. But what about the self, what about the hero? The question is of particular interest here, for in Salinger, more than in most of his contemporaries, the figure of the writer has lately come to be placed directly in the reader's line of vision, so that there is a connection, finally, between the attitudes of the narrator as, say, brother to Seymour Glass, and as a man who writes by profession.

And what of Salinger's heroes? Well, Holden Caulfield, we discover, winds up in an expensive sanitarium. And Seymour Glass commits suicide finally, but prior to that he is the apple of his brother's eye – and why? He has learned to live in this world – but how? By not living in it. By kissing the soles of little girls' feet and throwing rocks at the head of his sweetheart. He is a saint, clearly. But since madness is undesirable and sainthood, for most of us, out of the question, the problem of how to live *in* this world is by no means answered; unless the answer is that one cannot. The only advice we seem to get from Salinger is to be charming on the way to the loony bin. Of course, Salinger is under no obligation to supply advice of any sort to writers or readers – still, I happen to find myself growing more and more curious about this professional writer, Buddy Glass, and how *he* manages to coast through life in the arms of sanity.

There is in Salinger the suggestion that mysticism is a possible road to salvation; at least some of his characters respond well to an intensified, emotional religious belief. Now my own reading in Zen is minuscule, but as I understand it from Salinger, the deeper we go into this world, the further we can get away from it. If you contemplate a potato long enough, it stops being a potato in the usual sense; unfortunately, however, it is the usual sense that we have to deal with from day to day. For all his loving handling of the world's objects there seems to me, in Salinger's Glass family stories as in *The Catcher*, a spurning of life as it is lived in the immediate world – this place and time is viewed as unworthy of those few precious people who have been set down in it only to be maddened and destroyed.

A spurning of our world – though of a different order – occurs in the work of another of our most gifted writers, Bernard Malamud. Even when Malamud writes a book about baseball, *The Natural*, it is not baseball as it is played in Yankee Stadium but a wild, wacky game, where a player who is instructed to knock the cover off the ball promptly steps up to the plate and does just that : the batter swings and the inner core of the ball goes looping out to centre field, where the confused fielder commences to tangle himself in the unwinding sphere; then the shortstop runs out and, with his teeth, bites the centre fielder and the ball free from one another. Though *The Natural* is not Malamud's most successful book, it is at any rate our introduction to his world, which is by no means a replica of our own. There are really things called baseball players, of course, and really things called Jews, but there much of the similarity ends. The Jews of *The Magic Barrel* and the Jews of *The Assistant* are not the Jews of New York City or Chicago. They are Malamud's invention, a metaphor of sorts to stand for certain possibilities and promises, and I am further inclined to believe this when I read the statement attributed to Malamud which goes, 'All men are Jews.' In fact, we know this is not so; even the men who are Jews aren't sure they're Jews. But Malamud, as a writer of fiction, has not shown specific interest in the anxieties and dilemmas and corruptions of the contemporary American Jew, the Jew we think of as characteristic of our times. Rather, his people live in a timeless depression and a placeless Lower East Side; their society is not affluent, their predicament is not cultural. I am not saying – one cannot, of Malamud – that he has spurned life or an examination of its difficulties. What it is to be human, and to be humane, is his deepest concern. What I do mean to point out is that he does not find – or has not yet found – the *contemporary* scene a proper or sufficient backdrop for his tales of heartlessness and heartache, of suffering and regeneration.

Now, Malamud and Salinger cannot, of course, be considered to speak for all American writers, and yet their fictional response to the world about them – what they choose to emphasize or to ignore – is of interest to me simply because they are two of the best. Of course there are plenty of other writers around, capable ones too, who do not travel the same roads; however, even among these others, I wonder if we may not be witnessing a response to the times, less apparently dramatized perhaps than the social detachment in Salinger and Malamud, but there in the body of the work nonetheless.

Let us take up the matter of prose style. Why is everybody so bouncy all of a sudden? Those who have been reading Saul Bellow, Herbert Gold, Arthur Granit, Thomas Berger, and Grace Paley will know to what I am referring. Writing recently in *The Hudson Review*, Harvey Swados said that he saw developing 'a nervous muscular prose perfectly suited to the exigencies of an age which seems at once appalling and ridiculous. These are metropolitan writers, most of them are Jewish, and they are specialists in a kind of prose-poetry that often depends for its effectiveness as much on how it is ordered, or how it looks on the printed page, as it does on what it is expressing. This is risky writing . . .' Swados added, and perhaps it is in its very riskiness that we can discover some kind of explanation for it. I'd like to compare two short descriptive passages, one from Bellow's *The Adventures of Augie March*, the other from Gold's new novel, *Therefore Be Bold*, in the hope that the differences revealed will be educational.

As numerous readers have already pointed out, the language of *Augie March* combines literary complexity with conversational ease, joins the idiom of the academy with the idiom of the streets (not all streets – certain streets); the style is special, private, energetic, and though it can at times be unwieldy, it generally serves Bellow brilliantly. Here, for instance, is a description of Grandma Lausch:

> With the [cigarette] holder in her dark little gums between which all her guile, malice, and command issued, she had her best inspirations of strategy. She was as wrinkled as an old paper bag, an autocrat, hard-shelled and jesuitical, a pouncy old hawk of a Bolshevik, her small ribboned grey feet immobile on the shoekit and stool Simon had made in the manual-training class, dingy old wool Winnie [the dog] whose bad smell filled the flat on the cushion beside her. If wit and discontent don't

necessarily go together, it wasn't from the old woman that I learned it.

Herbert Gold's language has also been distinctly special, private, energetic. One notices in the following passage from *Therefore Be Bold* that here too the writer begins by recognizing a physical similarity between the character to be described and some unlikely object, and from there, as in Bellow's Grandma Lausch passage, attempts to wind up, via the body, making a discovery about the soul. The character described is named Chuck Hastings.

In some respects he resembled a mummy – the shrivelled yellow skin, the hands and head too large for a wasted body, the bottomless eye sockets of thought beyond the Nile. But his agile Adam's apple and point-making finger made him less the Styx-swimmer dog-paddling toward Coptic limbos than a high-school intellectual intimidating the navel-eyed little girls.

First, the grammar itself has me baffled : ' . . . bottomless eye sockets of thought beyond the Nile'. Is the thought beyond the Nile, or the eye sockets? What does it mean to be beyond the Nile anyway? These grammatical difficulties have little in common with the ironic inversion with which Bellow's description begins : 'With the holder in her dark little gums between which all her guile, malice, and command issued . . .' Bellow goes on to describe Grandma Lausch as an 'autocrat', 'hard-shelled', 'jesuitical', 'a pouncy old hawk of a Bolshevik' – imaginative certainly, but tough-minded, *exact*, not primarily exhibitionistic. Of Gold's Chuck Hastings, however, we learn, 'His agile Adam's apple and point-making finger made him less the Styx-swimmer dog-paddling toward Coptic limbos', etc. . . . Language in the service of the narrative, or literary regression in the service of the ego? In a recent review of *Therefore Be Bold*, Granville Hicks quoted this very paragraph in praise of Gold's style. 'This is high-pitched,' Mr Hicks admitted, 'but the point is that Gold keeps it up and keeps it up.' I take it the sexual pun is not deliberate; nevertheless, it might serve as a reminder that showmanship and passion are not one and the same. What we have here is not stamina or vitality but reality taking a back seat to personality – and not the personality of the imagined character, but of the writer who is doing the imagining. Bellow's description seems to arise out of a writer's firm grasp of his character: Grandma Lausch *is*. Behind the description of Chuck Hastings there seems to me something else that is being said: Herbert Gold is. Look at me, I'm writing.

Now, I am not trying to sell selflessness here. Rather, I am suggesting that this nervous muscular prose that Swados talks about may perhaps have something to do with the unfriendly relations that exist between the writer and the culture. The prose suits the age, Swados suggests, and I wonder if it does not suit it, in part, because it rejects it. The writer thrusts before our eyes – it is in the very ordering of his sentences – *personality*, in all its separateness and specialness. Of course, the mystery of personality may be nothing less than a writer's ultimate concern; and certainly when the muscular prose is revealing of character and evocative of an environment – as in *Augie March* – it can be wonderfully effective; at its worst, however, as a form of literary onanism, it seriously curtails the fictional possibilities, and may perhaps be thought of as a symptom of the writer's loss of the community – or what is *outside* himself – as subject.

True, the bouncy style can be understood in other ways as well. It is not surprising that most of the practitioners Swados points to are Jewish. When writers who do not feel much of a connection to Lord Chesterfield begin to realize that they are under no real obligation to try and write like that distinguished old stylist, they are likely enough to go out and be bouncy. Also, there is the matter of the spoken language which these writers have heard, as our statesmen might put it, in the schools, the homes, the churches and the synagogues of the nation. I would even say that when the bouncy style is not an attempt to dazzle the reader, or one's self, but to incorporate into American literary prose the rhythms, nuances, and emphases of urban and immigrant speech, the result can sometimes be a language of new and rich emotional subtleties, with a kind of backhanded charm and irony all its own, as in Grace Paley's book of stories *The Little Disturbances of Man*.

But whether the practitioner is Gold, Bellow, or Paley,

there is a further point to make about the bounciness: it is an expression of pleasure. However, a question: If the world is as crooked and unreal as it feels to me it is becoming, day by day; if one feels less and less power in the face of this unreality; if the inevitable end is destruction, if not of all life, then of much that is valuable and civilized in life – then why in God's name is the writer pleased? Why don't all our fictional heroes wind up in institutions, like Holden Caulfield, or suicides, like Seymour Glass? Why is it that so many of them – not just in books by Wouk and Weidman but in Bellow, Gold, Styron, and others – wind up affirming life? For surely the air is thick these days with affirmation, and though we shall doubtless get our annual editorial this year from *Life* calling for affirmative novels, the fact is that more and more books by serious writers seem to end on a note of celebration. Not just the tone is bouncy, the moral is bouncy too. In *The Optimist*, another of Gold's novels, the hero, having taken his lumps, cries out in the book's last line, 'More. More. More! More! More!' Curtis Harnack's novel, *The Work of an Ancient Hand*, ends with the hero filled with 'rapture and hope' and saying aloud, 'I believe in God.' And Saul Bellow's *Henderson the Rain King* is a book given over to celebrating the regeneration of the heart, blood, and general health of its hero. Yet it is of some importance, I think, that the regeneration of Henderson takes place in a world that is thoroughly and wholly imagined, *but that does not really exist*. It is not the tumultuous Africa of the newspapers and the United Nations discussions that Eugene Henderson visits. There is nothing here of nationalism or riots or apartheid. But why should there be? There is the world, and there is also the self. And the self, when the writer turns upon it all his attention and talent, is revealed to be a most remarkable thing. First off, it exists, it's real. *I am*, the self cries out, and then, taking a nice long look, it adds, *and I am beautiful.*

At the conclusion to Bellow's book, his hero, Eugene Henderson, a big, sloppy millionaire, is returning to America, coming home from a trip to Africa, where he has been plague fighter, lion tamer, and rainmaker; he is bringing back with him a real lion. Aboard the plane he befriends a small Persian boy, whose language he cannot understand.

Still, when the plane lands at Newfoundland, Henderson takes the child in his arms and goes out onto the field. And then :

> Laps and laps I galloped around the shining and riveted body of the plane, behind the fuel trucks. Dark faces were looking from within. The great, beautiful propellers were still, all four of them. I guess I felt it was my turn to move, and so went running – leaping, leaping, pounding, and tingling over the pure white lining of the grey Arctic silence.

And so we leave Henderson, a very happy man. Where? In the Arctic. This picture has stayed with me since I read the book a year ago : of a man who finds energy and joy in an imagined Africa, and celebrates it on an unpeopled, icebound vastness.

Earlier I quoted from Styron's new novel, *Set This House on Fire*. Now Styron's book, like Bellow's, also tells of the regeneration of an American who leaves his own country and goes abroad for a while to live. But where Henderson's world is wildly removed from our own, Kinsolving, Styron's hero, inhabits a place we immediately recognize. The book is thick with detail that twenty years from now will probably require extensive footnotes to be thoroughly understood. The hero is an American painter who has taken his family to live in a small town on the Amalfi coast. Cass Kinsolving detests America, and himself. Throughout most of the book he is taunted, tempted, and disgraced by Mason Flagg, a fellow countryman, who is rich, boyish, naïve, licentious, indecent, cruel, and stupid. Kinsolving, by way of his attachment to Flagg, spends most of the book choosing between living and dying, and at one point, in a tone that is characteristic, says this about his expatriation :

> . . . the man I had come to Europe to escape [why he's] the man in all the car advertisements, you know, the young guy waving there – he looks so beautiful and educated and everything, and he's got it *made*, Penn State and a blonde there, and a smile as big as a billboard. And he's going places. I mean electronics. Politics. What they

call communication. Advertising. Saleshood. Outer space. God only knows. And he's as ignorant as an Albanian peasant.

However, despite all his disgust with what American public life can do to a man's private life, Kinsolving, like Henderson, comes back to America at the end, having opted for existence. But the America that we find him in seems to me to be the America of his childhood, and (if only in a metaphoric way) of everyone's childhood : he tells his story while he fishes from a boat in a Carolina stream. The affirmation at the conclusion is not as go-getting as Gold's 'More! More!' or as sublime as Harnack's 'I believe in God,' or as joyous as Henderson's romp on the Newfoundland airfield. 'I wish I could tell you that I had found some belief, some rock . . .' Kinsolving says, 'but to be truthful, you see, I can only tell you this : that as for being and nothingness, the only thing I did know was that to choose between them was simply to choose being . . .' Being. Living. Not where one lives or with whom one lives – but *that* one lives.

And what does all of this add up to? It would, of course, drastically oversimplify the art of fiction to suggest that Saul Bellow's book or Herbert Gold's prose style arise ineluctably out of our distressing cultural and political predicament. Nonetheless, that the communal predicament *is* distressing weighs upon the writer no less, and perhaps even more, than upon his neighbour – for to the writer the community is, properly, both subject and audience. And it may be that when this situation produces not only feelings of disgust, rage, and melancholy, but impotence too, the writer is apt to lose heart and turn finally to other matters, to the construction of wholly imaginary worlds, and to a celebration of the self, which may, in a variety of ways, become his subject, as well as the impetus that establishes the perimeters of his technique. What I have tried to point out is that the vision of self as inviolable, powerful, and nervy, self-imagined as the only seemingly real thing in an unreal-seeming environment, has given some of our writers joy, solace, and muscle. Certainly to have come through a serious personal struggle intact, simply to have survived, is nothing to be made light of, and it is for just this reason that Styron's hero manages to engage our sympathies right down to the end. Still, when the survivor cannot choose but be ascetic, when the self can only be celebrated as it is excluded from society, or as it is exercised and admired in a fantastic one, we then do not have much reason to be cheery. Finally, for me there is something unconvincing about a regenerated Henderson up on the pure white lining of the world dancing around that shining airplane. Consequently, it is not with this scene that I should like to conclude, but instead with the image of his hero that Ralph Ellison presents at the end of *Invisible Man*. For here too the hero is left with the simple stark fact of himself. He is as alone as a man can be. Not that he hasn't gone out into the world; he has gone out into it, and out into it, and out into it – but at the end he chooses to go underground, to live there and to wait. And it does not seem to him a cause for celebration either.

The Novel as Research

(reprinted with permission from *Inventory: Essays,*
Jonathan Cape, 1970; Simon and Schuster, 1968)

I

The novel is a particular form of narrative.

And narrative is a phenomenon which extends considerably beyond the scope of literature; it is one of the essential
constituents of our understanding of reality. From the time
we begin to understand language until our death, we are
perpetually surrounded by narratives, first of all in our
family, then at school, then through our encounters with
people and reading.

Other people, for us, are not only what we have seen of
them with our own eyes, but also what they have told us
about themselves, or what others have told us about them.
They are not only the people we have seen, but also all
those we have been told about by others.

This is true not only of human beings, but of things
themselves, and of places, for example, where we have
never been but which have been described to us.

This narrative in which we are steeped takes the most
varied forms, from family tradition, or the news we
exchange at dinner about what we have done during the
day, to journalistic reports or historical works. Each of these
forms links us to a particular segment of reality.

All these veracious narratives have one characteristic in
common : they are always, in principle, verifiable. I should
be able to check what someone has told me by information
from another source, and so on indefinitely; otherwise, I
am dealing with a mistake or a fiction.

Among all these narratives by which a large share of our
daily world is constituted, there may be some which are
deliberately invented. If, in order to avoid any misunder-
standing, we assign to the events which are recounted to us
certain characteristics which immediately distinguish them
from those we usually see with our own eyes, we are dealing with a literature of fantasy, myths, tales, and so on. The

novelist, on the other hand, presents us with events that resemble everyday events; he wants to give them as much as possible the appearance of reality, and this can even go to the point of staging a hoax (Defoe).

But what the novelist tells us is not verifiable, and, as a consequence, what he says about it must suffice to give it that appearance of reality. If I meet a friend and he gives me some surprising piece of news, in order to convince me of its truth he can always resort to telling me that such and such people were also witnesses, that all I have to do is check the story with them. On the other hand, from the moment a writer puts the word *novel* on the cover of his book, he declares that it is useless to seek this kind of confirmation. It is only by what he tells us about his characters, and by this alone, that they can convince us, can live, even if they have actually existed in reality.

Suppose we were to discover a letter writer of the nineteenth century telling his correspondent that he knew Père Goriot very well, that he was nothing at all like the man Balzac has described, and that on such and such a page there are even enormous errors of fact; this would obviously have no importance for us. Père Goriot is what Balzac tells us about him (and what we can go on to say about him after that); I may consider Balzac mistaken in his judgements of his own creation, I may even decide that the character eludes him, but to justify my position I shall have to rely on the very sentences of Balzac's text; I cannot invoke any other witness.

Even though veracious narrative always has the support, the last resort, of external evidence, the novel must suffice to create what it tells us. That is why it is the phenomenological realm par excellence, the best possible place to study how reality appears to us, or might appear; that is why the novel is the laboratory of narrative.

II

Work on the form of novel, therefore, assumes a major importance.

For veracious narratives, by becoming public and historic, are gradually stabilized, classified and grouped according to certain principles (in fact the principles of what is today known as the traditional novel, the novel which raises no questions). Our primitive understanding is replaced by another, much more impoverished one which systematically rejects certain aspects; it gradually disguises the real experience, substitutes itself for it, ultimately achieving a generalized hoax. Exploration of the different forms of the novel reveals what is contingent in the form we are used to, unmasks it, releases us from it, allows us to rediscover beyond this fixed narrative everything it camouflages or passes over in silence: that fundamental narrative in which our whole life is steeped.

Further, it is obvious that since form is a principle of choice (and style in this regard appears as one of the aspects of form, being the way in which the details of the language are actually linked together, the thing that determines the choice of one word or turn of phrase rather than another), new forms will reveal new things in reality, new connections, and naturally, the more the internal coherence of these new forms is stressed in relation to others, the more rigorous they will be.

Inversely, different forms of narrative correspond to different realities. Now, it is clear that the world in which we live is being transformed with great rapidity. Traditional narrative techniques are incapable of integrating all the new relations thus created. There results a perpetual uneasiness; it is impossible for our consciousness to organize all the information which assails it, because it lacks adequate tools.

The search for new novelistic forms with a greater power of integration thus plays a triple role in relation to our consciousness of reality: unmasking, exploration, and adaptation. The novelist who refuses to accept this task, never discarding old habits, never demanding any particular effort of his reader, never obliging him to confront himself, to question attitudes long since taken for granted, will certainly enjoy a readier success, but he becomes the accomplice of that profound uneasiness, that darkness, in which we are groping for our way. He stiffens the reflexes of our consciousness even more, making any awakening more difficult; he contributes to its suffocation, so that even if his intentions are generous, his work is in the last analysis a poison.

Formal invention in the novel, far from being opposed to realism as shortsighted critics often assume, is the *sine qua non* of a greater realism.

III

But the novel's relationship to the reality which surrounds us is not confined to the fact that what it describes is presented as an illusory fragment of that reality, a very isolated, pliable fragment which it is then possible to study at close range. The difference between the events of a novel and those of life does not lie only in the fact that we can verify the latter while the former can be reached only through the text which creates them. For the events of a novel are also, to use the common expression, more 'interesting' than real ones. The emergence of these fictions corresponds to a need, fulfils a function. Imaginary characters fill the gaps in reality and enlighten us about it.

Not only the creation but also the reading of a novel is a kind of waking dream. It is thus susceptible to psycho-analysis in the broad sense. Further, if I want to explain a given theory, whether psychological, sociological, ethical or whatever, it is often convenient to take a fictitious example. The characters of a novel will play this part to perfection; and I will recognize these characters in my friends and acquaintances, I will elucidate the conduct of the latter by relying on the adventures of the former, and so on.

This application of the novel to reality is extremely complex, and the novel's 'realism', the fact that it is presented as an illusory fragment of daily life, is only one particular aspect of it, the one which allows us to isolate it as a literary genre.

I call the 'symbolism' of a novel the sum of the relation-ships of what it describes to the reality we experience.

These relationships are not the same in all novels, and it seems to me that the critic's essential undertaking is to unravel them, to illuminate them so that we can extract from each particular work its entire lesson.

But since, in the creation of a novel and in that re-creation which is attentive reading, we are exposed to a complex system of relationships of extremely varied signifi-cance. If the novelist sincerely tries to share his experience, if his realism is carried far enough, if the form he employs is sufficiently integrative, he will necessarily be led to account for these diverse types of relationships within his work itself. The external symbolism of a novel tends to be reflected in an internal symbolism, certain portions playing in relation to the whole the same part that the whole plays in relation to reality.

IV

This general relationship of the 'reality' described by the novel to the reality which surrounds us is, obviously, the relationship which determines what is commonly called the novel's theme or subject, which appears as a response to a certain state of consciousness. But this theme, this subject, as we have seen, cannot be separated from the way in which it is presented, from the form in which it is expressed. A new state of consciousness, a new awareness of what a novel is, of its relationships to reality, of its status, corresponds to new subjects, to new forms on every level – language, style, technique, composition, structure. Inversely, the search for new forms, revealing new subjects, reveals new relationships.

After a certain degree of reflection, realism, formalism, and symbolism in the novel appear to constitute an indissoluble unity.

The novel tends naturally towards its own elucidation, and so it should; but we know that there are certain states of consciousness characterized by an incapacity to reflect upon themselves, states which subsist only by the illusion they maintain, and to these states of consciousness correspond those works in which that indissoluble unity cannot appear, those attitudes of novelists who refuse to question themselves about the nature of their work and the validity of the forms they employ: those forms which could not be reflected upon without immediately revealing their inadequacy, their untruthfulness, those forms which give us an image of reality in flagrant contradiction to the reality which gave them birth and which they are concerned to pass over in silence. These are impostures which it is the duty of criticism to expose; for such works, for all their charms and merits, preserve and deepen the darkness, imprison consciousness in its contradictions, in its blindness, which risks leading it into the most fatal disorders.

The consequence of all this is that any genuine transformation of the novel's form, any fruitful research in this realm, can be situated only within a transformation of the concept of the novel itself, which evolves very slowly but inevitably (all the great novels of the twentieth century attest to the fact) toward a new kind of poetry at once epic and didactic, within a transformation of the very notion of literature, which begins to appear no longer as a simple pastime or luxury, but in its essential role within the workings of society, and as a systematic experiment.

translated by Gerald Fabian

SAUL BELLOW

Some Notes on Recent American Fiction

(reprinted with permission from *Encounter*, 1963)

Gertrude Stein is supposed to have explained to Hemingway that 'remarks are not literature'. Here I am offering some remarks, and I make no claim for them whatever. A writer's views on other writers may have a certain interest, but it should be clear that he reads what they write almost always with a special attitude. If he should be a novelist, his own books are also a comment on his contemporaries and reveal that he supports certain tendencies and rejects others. In his own books he upholds what he deems necessary, and usually by the method of omission he criticizes what he understands as the errors and excesses of others.

I intend to examine the view taken by recent American novelists and short-story writers of the individual and his society, and I should like to begin with the title of the new book by Wylie Sypher: *Loss of the Self in Modern Literature and Art*. I do not propose to discuss it; I simply want to cite the title, for in itself it tells us much about the common acceptance of what the Spanish critic Ortega y Gasset described some years ago as 'the dehumanization of the arts'. One chapter is devoted to the Beats, but, for the most part, Sypher finds, as we might have expected, that the theme of annihilation of Self, and the description of an 'inauthentic' life which can never make sense, is predominantly European and particularly French. The names he most often mentions are those of André Gide, Sartre, Beckett, Sarraute, and Robbe-Grillet: writers whose novels and plays are derived from definite theories which make a historical reckoning of the human condition and are peculiarly responsive to new physical, psychological, and philosophical theories. American writers, when they are moved by a similar spirit to reject and despise the Self, are seldom encumbered by such intellectual baggage, and this fact pleases their European contemporaries, who find in them a natural, that is, a brutal or violent acceptance of the new universal truth by minds free from intellectual preconceptions.

In the early twenties D. H. Lawrence was delighted to discover a blunt, primitive virtue in the first stories of Ernest Hemingway, and twenty years later André Gide praised Dashiell Hammett as a good barbarian.

European writers take strength from German phenomenology and from the conception of entropy in modern physics in order to attack a romantic idea of the Self, triumphant in the nineteenth century but intolerable in the twentieth. The feeling against this idea is well-nigh universal. The First World War with its millions of corpses gave an aspect of the horrible to romantic over-valuation of the Self. The leaders of the Russian Revolution were icy in their hatred of bourgeois individualism. In the communist countries millions were sacrificed in the building of socialism, and almost certainly the Lenins and the Stalins, the leaders who made these decisions, serving the majority and the future, believed they were rejecting a soft, nerveless humanism which attempted in the face of natural and historical evidence to oppose progress.

A second great assault on the separate Self sprang from Germany in 1939. Just what the reduction of millions of human beings into heaps of bone and mounds of rag and hair or clouds of smoke betokened, there is no one who can plainly tell us, but it is at least plain that something was being done to put in question the meaning of survival, the meaning of pity, the meaning of justice and of the importance of being oneself, the individual's consciousness of his own existence.

It would be odd, indeed, if these historical events had made no impression on American writers, even if they are not on the whole given to taking the historical or theoretical view. They characteristically depend on their own observations and appear at times obstinately empirical.

But the latest work of writers like James Jones, James Baldwin, Philip Roth, John O'Hara, J. F. Powers, Joseph Bennett, Wright Morris and others shows the individual under a great strain. Labouring to maintain himself, or perhaps an idea of himself (not always a clear idea), he feels the pressure of a vast public life, which may dwarf him as an individual while permitting him to be a giant in hatred or fantasy. In these circumstances he grieves, he complains, rages, or laughs. All the while he is aware of his lack of power, his inadequacy as a moralist, the nauseous pressure of the mass media and their weight of money and organization, of cold war and racial brutalities.

Adapting Gresham's theorem to the literary situation one might say that public life drives private life into hiding. People begin to hoard their spiritual valuables. Public turbulence is largely coercive, not positive. It puts us into a passive position. There is not much we can do about the crises of international politics, the revolutions in Asia and Africa, the rise and transformation of masses. Technical and political decisions, invisible powers, secrets which can be shared only by a small elite. render the private will helpless and lead the individual into curious forms of behaviour in the private sphere.

Public life, vivid and formless turbulence, news, slogans, mysterious crises, and unreal configurations dissolve coherence in all but the most resistant minds, and even to such minds it is not always a confident certainty that resistance can ever have a positive outcome. To take narcotics has become in some circles a mark of rebellious independence, and to scorch one's personal earth is sometimes felt to be the only honourable course. Rebels have no bourgeois certainties to return to when rebellions are done. The fixed points seem to be disappearing. Even the Self is losing its firm outline.

One recent American novel deals openly and consciously with these problems : *The Thin Red Line* by James Jones, a book which, describing the gross and murderous conditions of jungle combat, keeps a miraculously sensitive balance and does not weary us with a mere catalogue of horrors. What Mr Jones sees very precisely is the fluctuation in the value of the life of the individual soldier. Childhood in some cases ends for the fighting man as he accepts the lesson of realism. The attitude of Storm, one of the older soldiers, towards Fife, a younger man, is described as follows : 'He [Fife] was a good enough kid. He just hadn't been away from home long enough. And Storm, who had started off bumming during the Depression when he was only fourteen, couldn't find kids like that very interesting.' Storm, the mess sergeant, tolerates the inexperienced Fife, but First Sergeant Welsh has no such tolerance. He cannot abide softness and the lack of realism, and he cruelly and punitively teaches the hard lesson to his undeveloped subordinates. Real knowledge as he sees it is brutal knowledge and it must be painfully and brutally learned. The heart of the lesson, as Welsh understands it, is that it matters little – it matters, therefore, not at all – whether any single man survives or falls. Welsh offers no indulgence to anyone and asks none for himself. His message to mankind is that you must cast the cold eye on life, on death.

Mr Jones shrewdly understands that the philosophy of Welsh is not ultimately hard. Towards himself the sergeant is not fanatically severe, and his toughness betrays a large degree of self-pity. What Jones describes here is the casting off of a childish or feminine or false virtue, despised because it cannot meet the test of survival. In apprehending what is real, Jones's combat soldiers learn a bitter and levelling truth and in their realism revenge themselves on the slothful and easy civilian conception of the Self. The new idea cruelly assails the old, exposing its conventionality and emptiness. Young Fife, after he has gone the rugged course, kills like the rest, becomes quarrelsome, drinks and brawls, and casts off his hesitant, careful, and complaining childishness.

A very different sort of novel, in a peaceful sphere far removed from the explosions and disembowellings of Guadalcanal, is J. F. Powers's *Morte d'Urban*, which does not so much study as brood over the lives of priests belonging to the Order of St Clement. Father Urban, a well-known preacher and a man of some talent, is transferred for reasons not clearly understood from Chicago, where he has worked effectively, to a new Foundation of the Order in Duesterhaus, Minnesota. To Urban, a sociable and civilized priest, this transfer can only be seen as a mysterious banishment, and he is described by Mr Powers looking from the train windows at the empty country beyond Minneapolis.

. . . flat and treeless, Illinois without people. It didn't attract, it didn't repel. He saw more streams than he'd see in Illinois, but they weren't working. November was winter here. Too many white frame farmhouses, not new and not old, not at all what Father Urban would care to come to for Thanksgiving or Christmas. Rusty implements. Brown dirt. Grey skies. Ice. No snow. A great deal of talk about this on the train. Father Urban dropped entirely out of it after an hour or so. The Voyageur arrived in Duesterhaus a few minutes before eleven that morning, and Father Urban was the only passenger to get off.

In more ways than one, Father Urban is viewed as the only passenger. At the new Foundation he is, without complaint, in a solitary situation. In charge of the Duesterhaus Foundation is Father Wilfred '. . . who, on account of his broad nose and padded cheeks, had been called Bunny in the Novitiate. Bunny Bestudik.' Father Wilfred's concerns are all of a practical nature. His interests are the interests of any Midwestern American who has to run a place efficiently; he watches the fuel bills, thinks about the pick-up truck and its rubber, the cost of paint, and is anxious to have good public relations. This religious Order is described as a community of consumers. It is the American and average character of activities whose ultimate aim is religious that Mr Powers wants to describe. His tone is dry and factual and he tells of the discussions of the Fathers who have to heat, paint, and renovate their buildings, sand the floors, tear up old linoleum, lay new tiles in the bathrooms, and this light and dry comedy cannot be maintained through such a long account of the effort to fill up a great emptiness with activity which is insufficiently purposeful. The religion of Father Urban is expressed in steadiness and patience, in endurance, not in fiery strength. His resistance to the prolonged barrenness and vacant busyness of this thoroughly American Order is made in a spirit of mild and decent martyrdom. Indeed, the only violent and passionate person in the book is a certain Billy Cosgrove. Billy is rich and generous. He gives lavishly to the Order but he expects also to have his way. He and Father Urban eat shish kebab and drink champagne, play golf and go fishing. With Billy one talks of cars and sailing boats. Urban gets along rather well with spoiled and boisterous Billy until Billy tries to drown a deer in the water of Bloodsucker Lake. Billy has been fishing and is in an ugly mood because his luck has been bad. Seeing a swimming deer, he decides to seize it by the antlers and hold its head under water. As hungry for trophies as the soldiers in *The Thin Red Line*, Billy wants those antlers. Father Urban, who cannot bear his cruelty, starts up the motor of the boat, and Billy falls into the water. For this outrage Billy will never forgive him.

What Father Urban had been thinking just before the appearance of the deer was that in the Church there was perhaps too great an emphasis on dying for the faith and winning the martyr's crown.

How about living for the faith? Take Lanfranc and William the Conqueror – of whom it was written (in the Catholic Encyclopædia and Father Urban's notes on a book he might write some day): 'He was mild to good men of God and stark beyond all bounds to those who withsaid his will.'

Billy Cosgrove turns out to occupy the position of the Conqueror. He is stark beyond all bounds, and Urban is never again to see his face. Nor does Urban seem destined to write his book. He goes to the Novitiate of the Order as Father Provincial, there to deal with practical matters to the best of his ability. But he appears to be succumbing to a brain injury he received while playing golf. He had been struck on the head by a golf ball in Minnesota and is now subject to fits of dizziness. A martyr's crown seems to be waiting Urban as the book ends.

Powers does not look at the issue of the single Self and the multitude as nakedly as Jones does, and it is a pity that he chose not to do so, for he might have been able to offer us a more subtle development of the subject. He would have been examining what Mr Sypher calls 'Loss of the Self' from the point of view of a Christian, that is, from the point of view of one who believes in the existence of something more profound than the romantic or secular idea of Self-hood, namely, a soul. But there is curiously little talk of souls in this book about a priest. Spiritually, its quality is very thin. That perhaps is as Mr Powers meant it to be. Even at play Father Urban is serving the Church, and, if he is hit on the head by a golf ball, we can perhaps draw our own conclusions from that about the present age viewed as a chapter in the spiritual history of mankind. Here great things will only be dimly apprehended even by the most willing servant of God. Still this seems to me unsatisfactory, and I am not sure that I can bring myself to admire such meekness. A man might well be meek in his own interests, but furious at such abuses of the soul and eager to show what is positive and powerful in his faith. The lack of such power makes faith itself shadowy, more like obscure tenacity than spiritual conviction. In this sense Mr Powers's book is disappointing.

The individual in American fiction often comes through to us, especially among writers of 'sensibility', as a colonist who has been sent to a remote place, some Alaska of the soul. What he has to bring under cultivation, however, is a barren emptiness within himself. This is, of course, what writers of sensibility have for a long time been doing and what they continue to do. The latest to demonstrate his virtuosity with exceptional success is John Updike, who begins the title story of his new collection, *Pigeon Feathers*, 'When they moved to Firetown, things were upset, displaced, rearranged.' The rearrangement of things in new and hostile solitude is a common theme with writers of sensibility. David, the only child of a family which has moved to the country, is assailed by terror when he reads in H. G. Wells's *The Outline of History* that Jesus was nothing more than a rather communistic Galilean, '. . . an obscure political agitator, a kind of hobo in a minor colony of the Roman Empire'. The effect of this is to open the question of death and immortality. David is dissatisfied with answers given by the Reverend Dobson and by his parents. He cannot understand the pleasure his mother takes in her solitary walks along the edge of the woods. '. . . to him the brown stretches of slowly rising and falling land expressed only a huge exhaustion.'

' "What do you want Heaven to be?" ' asks David's mother. 'He was becoming angry, sensing her surprise at him. She had assumed that Heaven had faded from his head long ago. She had imagined that he had already entered in the secrecy of silence, the conspiracy that he now knew to be all around him.'

Young David in the end resolves the problem for himself aesthetically. Admiring the beauty of pigeon feathers he feels consoled by the sense of a providence. '. . . the God who had lavished such craft upon these worthless birds would not destroy His whole Creation by refusing to let David live forever.' The story ends with a mild irony at the expense of the boy. Nevertheless, there is nothing to see here but the writer's reliance on beautiful work, on an aesthetic discipline and order. And sensibility, in such forms, incurs the dislike of many because it is perceptive inwardly, and otherwise blind. We suspect it of a stony heart because it functions so smoothly in its isolation. The writer of sensibility assumes that only private exploration and inner development are possible, and accepts the opposition of public and private as fixed and indissoluble.

We are dealing with modern attitudes towards the ancient idea of the individual and the many, the single Self in the midst of the mass or species. In modern times the idea of the unique Self has become associated with the name of Rousseau. Nietzsche identified the Self with the God Apollo, the god of light, harmony, music, reason and proportion, and the many, the tribe, the species, the instincts and passions, with Dionysus. Between these two principles, the individual and the generic, men and civilizations supposedly work out their destinies. It is to Nietzsche, too, that we owe the concept of the 'last man'. His 'last man' is an obituary on the unitary and sufficient Self produced by a proud bourgeois and industrial civilization. Dostoevsky's Underground Man is an analogous figure. Atheism, rationalism, utilitarianism, and revolution are signs of a deadly sickness in the human soul, in his scheme of things. The lost Selves whose souls are destroyed he sees as legion. The living soul clearly discerns them. It owes this illumination to Christ the Redeemer. More optimistically, an American poet like Walt Whitman imagined that the single Self and the democratic mass might complement each other. But on this side of the Atlantic, also, Thoreau described men as leading lives of quiet desperation, accepting a deadly common life: the individual retires from the community to define or re-define his real needs in isolation beside Walden Pond.

Still later a French poet tells us '*Je est un autre.*' Rimbaud and Jarry launch their bombs and grenades against the tight little bourgeois kingdom of the Self, that sensitive sovereign.

Darwin and the early anthropologists unwittingly damage his sovereignty badly. Then come the psychologists, who explain that his Ego is a paltry shelter against the unendurable storms that rage in outer reality. After them come the logicians and physical scientists who tell us that 'I' is a grammatical expression. Poets like Valéry describe this Self as a poor figment, a thing of change, and tell us that consciousness is interested only in what is eternal. Novelists like Joyce turn away from the individualism of the romantics and the humanists to contemplate instead qualities found in dreams and belonging to the entire species – Earwicker is everybody. Writers like Sartre, Ionesco, and Beckett or like our own William Burroughs and Allan Ginsberg are only a few of the active campaigners on this shrinking front against the Self. One would like to ask these contemporaries, 'After nakedness, what?' 'After absurdity, what?'

But, on the whole, American novels are filled with complaints over the misfortunes of the sovereign Self. Writers have inherited a tone of bitterness from the great poems and novels of this century, many of which lament the passing of a more stable and beautiful age demolished by the barbarous intrusion of an industrial and metropolitan society of masses or proles who will, after many upheavals, be tamed by bureaucracies and oligarchies in brave new worlds, human anthills.

These works of the first half of our century nourish the imagination of contemporary writers and supply a tonal background of disillusion or elegy.

There are modern novelists who take all of this for granted as fully proven and implicit in the human condition and who complain as steadily as they write, viewing modern life with a bitterness to which they themselves have not established clear title, and it is this unearned bitterness that I speak of. What is truly curious about it is that often the writer automatically scorns contemporary life. He bottles its stinks artistically. But, seemingly, he does not need to study it. It is enough for him that it does not allow his sensibilities to thrive, that it starves his instincts for nobility or for spiritual qualities.

But what the young American writer most often appears

to feel is his *own* misfortune. The injustice is done to *his* talent if life is brutish and ignorant, if the world seems overcome by Spam and beer, or covered with detergent lathers and poisonous monoxides. This apparently is the only injustice he feels. Neither for himself nor for his fellows does he attack power and injustice directly and hotly. He simply defends his sensibility.

Perhaps the reason for this is the prosperity and relative security of the middle class from which most writers come. In educating its writers it makes available to them the radical doctrines of all the ages, but these in their superabundance only cancel one another out. The middle-class community trains its writers also in passivity and resignation and in the double enjoyment of selfishness and goodwill. They are taught that they can have it both ways. In fact they are taught to expect to enjoy everything that life can offer. They can live dangerously while managing somehow to remain safe. They can be both bureaucrats and bohemians, they can be executives but use pot, they can raise families but enjoy bohemian sexuality, they can observe the laws while in their hearts and in their social attitudes they may be as subversive as they please. They are both conservative and radical. They are everything that is conceivable. They are not taught to care genuinely for any man or any cause.

A recent novel like Philip Roth's *Letting Go* is a consummate example of this. Roth's hero, Gabriel, educated to succeed in this world and to lead a good life come hell or high water, is slightly uncomfortable in his selfishness. But nevertheless he wants his, as the saying goes, and he gets his. But he feels obscurely the humiliation of being a private bourgeois Self, the son of an unhappy but prosperous dentist, and he senses that a 'personal life' with its problems of personal adjustment and personal responsibility and personal happiness, its ostensibly normal calculations of profit and loss, safety and danger, lust and prudence is a source of shame. But Gabriel's middle-class parents sent him into life to make the grade and that is precisely, with tough singlemindedness, what he does. His shame therefore becomes a province of his sensibility, and it is something he can be rather proud of as he does what he was going to do anyway.

Roth's hero clings to the hope of self-knowledge and personal improvement, and he concludes that, with all his faults, he loves himself still. His inner life, if it may be called that, is a rather feeble thing of a few watts. Conceivably it may guide him to a more satisfactory adjustment but it makes me think of the usher's flashlight in the dark theatre guiding the single ticket-holder to his reserved seat. We are supposed to feel that Gabriel is unusually sensitive, but what we find is that he is a tough young man who cannot be taken in and who will survive the accidents of life that madden or kill genuinely sensitive young men.

I would like now to list the categories suggested by my reading of current novels: the documentation of James Jones, the partially Christian approach of Powers, the sensibility of Updike, and the grievance of Philip Roth. I do not retract my earlier statement that in American novels – for I have decided rather arbitrarily to limit myself to examining these – the tone of complaint prevails. The public realm, as it encroaches on the private, steadily reduces the powers of the individual; but it cannot take away his power to despair, and sometimes he seems to be making the most of that. However, there are several other avenues commonly taken: stoicism, nihilistic anger, and comedy. Stoicism and comedy are sometimes mixed, as in the case of the late German dramatist Bertolt Brecht, but our own contemporary American stoicism comes from Hemingway, and its best American representative at present is John O'Hara.

O'Hara is properly impatient with people who suffer too intensely from themselves. The characters in his latest collection of stories, *The Cape Cod Lighter*, for whom he shows a decided preference, appear to be bluff, natural people, who know how to endure hurt and act with an elementary and realistic sense of honour. When Ernest Pangborn in the story 'The Professors' learns that he has misjudged his colleague Jack Veech and understands at last that Veech's behaviour has been decent and manly, he is moved to say something to him but does not know what to say.

A compliment would be rejected, and a word of pity would be unthinkable. Indeed the compliment was being paid to Pangborn; Veech honoured him with his confidence and accorded him honour more subtly, more truly, by asking no further assurances of his silence.

The emotion we feel here is made possible by long reticence, by the deep burial of self-proclamation or self-assertion. We recall the pure decencies of schooldays, and the old chivalrous or military origins of these. These, surely, are virtues of silence and passivity. We endure. We are rewarded by a vision of one another's complexities, but there is no possibility of a flourish, or of rhetoric, or anything that would make an undue personal claim.

This is no longer the sovereign Self of the Romantics, but the decent Self of Kipling whose great satisfaction it is to recognize the existence of a great number of others. These numerous others reduce personal significance, and both realism and dignity require us to accept this reduction. Such stoicism of separateness is the opposite of sensibility with its large claims for the development of internal riches.

But the O'Haras are curiously like the Updikes in at least one respect. They are scrupulous craftsmen and extraordinarily strict about their writing. Nothing unrealistic, unnatural, or excessive (as they define those qualities) is suffered to appear. O'Hara insists upon a hard literalness in his language which reminds one of the simple crystalline code of his characters. There is a roughness in O'Hara which may make the writer of sensibility feel like a dude. O'Hara's self-identification is obviously with the workman, with the average, with plain people. Or perhaps he feels himself to be a part of the majority, which is to say, of the crowd. Certainly he does not merely react against what he judges an incorrect definition of the individual; he hates it violently. And conceivably he hates it in himself. His view of sensibility or of an intricate and conceivably self-indulgent privacy is, like Hemingway's (in *The Sun Also Rises*, for instance), entirely negative. He sees the romantic Self with the eyes of the crowd. And the crowd is a leveller. The average it seeks is anything but Whitman's divine average.

The absolute individualism of the Enlightenment has fallen. Contemporary writers like Brecht, or Beckett, or the Beats, and recently and most atrociously William Burroughs in his *Naked Lunch*, have repudiated it in a spirit of

T.N.T. – C

violence. Some have been violently comic at its expense, others ruthlessly nihilistic and vengeful. Among them there are some who gather unto themselves more and more and more power only to release it destructively on this already discredited and fallen individualism. In this they seem at times to imitate the great modern consolidations of power, to follow the example of parties and states and their scientific or military instruments. They act, in short, like those who hold the real power in society, the masters of the Leviathan. But this is only an imitation of the real power. Through this imitation they hope perhaps to show that they are not inferior to those who lead the modern world. Joint Chiefs or Pentagons have power to do as they will to huge populations. But there are writers who will not reckon themselves among these subordinate masses and who aim to demonstrate an independent power equal to the greatest. They therefore strike one sometimes as being extra-ordinarily eager to release their strength and violence against an enemy, and that enemy is the false conception of Self created by Christianity and by Christianity's successors in the Enlightenment. Modern literature is not satisfied simply to dismiss a romantic, outmoded conception of the Self. In a spirit of deepest vengefulness it curses it. It hates it. It rends it, annihilates it. It would rather have the maddest chaos it can invoke than a conception of life it has found false. But after this destruction, what?

I have spoken of complaint, stoicism, sensibility, and nihilistic rage, and I would like to touch now on recent American writers who have turned to comedy. It is obvious that modern comedy has to do with the disintegrating outline of the worthy and humane Self, the bourgeois hero of an earlier age. That sober, prudent person, the bourgeois, although he did much for the development of modern civilization, built factories and railroads, dug canals, created sewage systems, and went colonizing, was indicted for his shallowness and his ignoble and hypocritical ways. The Christian writer (see Dostoevsky's portrait of Luzhin in *Crime and Punishment*) and the revolutionary (see Mangan in Shaw's *Heartbreak House*) repudiated him and all his works. The First World War dealt a blow to his prestige from which it never recovered. Dada and surrealism raised a storm of laughter against him. In the movies René Clair and Charlie Chaplin found him out. He became the respectable little person, the gentlemanly tramp. Poets of the deepest subversive tendencies came on like bank clerks in ironic masquerade.

The trick is still good, as J. P. Donleavy has lately shown in his novel *The Ginger Man*. His hero, Sebastian Dangerfield, a free-wheeling rascal and chaser, presents himself with wickedly comic effect as an ultra-respectable citizen with an excellent credit rating, one who doesn't know what it is to hock other people's property for the price of a drink, the gentlemanly sack-artist.

The private and inner life which was the subject of serious books until very recently now begins to have an antique and funny look. The earnestness of a Proust towards himself would seem old-fashioned today. Indeed, Italo Svevo, a contemporary of Proust, in *The Confessions of Zeno*, made introspection, hypochondria, and self-knowledge the subjects of his comedy. *My* welfare, *my* development, *my* advancement, *my* earnestness, *my* adjustment, *my* marriage, *my* family – all that will make the modern reader laugh heartily. Writers may not wholly agree with Bertrand Russell that 'I' is no more than a grammatical expression, but they do consider certain claims of the 'I' to be definitely funny. Already in the nineteenth century Stendhal became bored with the persistent 'I-I-I' and denounced it in characteristic terms.

Perhaps the change that has occurred can be clearly illustrated by a comparison of Thomas Mann's *Death in Venice* with Nabokov's *Lolita*. In both stories an older man is overcome by sexual desire for a younger person. With Mann, however, this sad occurrence involves Apollo and Dionysus. Gustave von Aschenbach, an overly civilized man, an individual estranged from his instincts which unexpectedly claim their revenge, has gone too far, has entered the realm of sickness and perversity and is carried away by the plague. This is a typically Nietzschean theme. But in *Lolita* the internal life of Humbert Humbert has become a joke. Far from being as Aschenbach, a great figure of European literature, he is a fourth- or fifth-rate man of the world and is unable to be entirely serious about his passion. As for

Lolita's mother, the poor thing only makes him laugh when she falls in love with him – a banal woman. To a very considerable extent Humbert's judgement of her is based on the low level of her culture. Her banality makes her a proper victim. If her words about love and desire had not come out of a bin in which the great American public finds suitable expressions to describe its psychological and personal needs, she might have been taken more seriously. The earnestness of Mann about love and death might be centuries old. The same subject is sadly and maliciously comical in *Lolita*. Clare Quilty cannot be made to take even his own death seriously and while he is being murdered by Humbert, ridicules his own situation and Humbert's as well, losing at last a life that was not worth having anyway. The contemporary Aschenbach does not deny his desires, but then he is without the dignity of the old fellow and is always on the verge of absurdity. Wright Morris in his new novel *What a Way to Go* explicitly makes comedy of the *Death in Venice* theme. His American professors in Venice, discussing *Death in Venice* all the while, seem to feel that there is small hope for them. They decline to view themselves with full seriousness. They believe their day is over. They are unfit, and dismiss themselves with a joke.

We must carefully remind ourselves that, if so many people today exist to enjoy or deplore an individual life, it is because prodigious public organizations, scientific, industrial, and political, support huge populations of new individuals. These organizations both elicit and curtail private development. I myself am not convinced that there is less 'Selfhood' in the modern world. I am not sure anyone knows how to put the matter properly. I am simply recording the attitudes of modern writers, including contemporary Americans, who are convinced that the jig of the Self is up.

What is the modern Self in T. S. Eliot's *Waste Land*? It is the many, crossing the bridge in the great modern city, who do not know that death has already undone them; it is the 'clerk carbuncular' taking sexual liberties of brief duration with the 'lovely lady' who, after she has stooped to folly, puts a record on the gramophone. What is the Self for French novelists of the first post-war era like Louis Ferdinand Céline, or for writers like Curzio Malaparte or Albert Camus in the second post-war era? Man, in a book

like *The Stranger*, is a creature neither fully primitive nor
fully civilized, a Self devoid of depths. We have come a long
way from Montaigne and his belief in a self-perfecting, self-
knowing character.

Recent American comic novels like *Lolita*, or *The Ginger
Man*, or Burt Blechman's *How Much?*, or Bruce Friedman's
first novel *Stern* examine the private life. It is as if they
were testing the saying of Socrates, that the unexamined
life was not worth living. Apparently they find the examined
life funny too. Some cannot find the life they are going to
examine. The power of public life has become so vast and
threatening that private life cannot maintain a pretence of
its importance. Our condition of destructibility is ever-
present in everyone's mind. Our submission seems required
by public ugliness in our cities, by the public nonsense of
television which threatens to turn our brains to farina
within our heads, by even such trifling things as Muzak
broadcasts in the elevators of public buildings. The Self is
asked to prepare itself for sacrifice, and this is the situation
reflected in contemporary American fiction.

As for the future, it cannot possibly shock us since we
have already done everything possible to scandalize ourselves. We have so completely debunked the old idea of the
Self that we can hardly continue in the same way. Perhaps
some power within us will tell us what we are, now that
old misconceptions have been laid low. Undeniably the
human being is not what he commonly thought a century
ago. The question nevertheless remains. He is something.
What is he?

And this question, it seems to me, modern writers have
answered poorly. They have told us, indignantly or nihilis-
tically or comically, how great our error is, but for the rest
they have offered us thin fare. The fact is that modern
writers sin when they suppose that they *know*, as they
conceive that physics *knows* or that history *knows*. The
subject of the novelist is not knowable in any such way.
The mystery increases, it does not grow less as types of
literature wear out. It is, however, Symbolism or Realism
or Sensibility wearing out, and not the mystery of mankind.

JOHN BARTH

The Literature of Exhaustion

(reprinted with permission from *Atlantic Monthly*, August 1967)

> The fact is that every writer *creates* his own precursors.
> His work modifies our conception of the past, as it will
> modify the future.
>
> JORGE LUIS BORGES, *Labyrinths*

> You who   listen   give me life   in a
> manner   of speaking.   I won't hold you respon-
> sible.   My first words weren't my first words. I wish
> I'd begun differently.
>
> JOHN BARTH, *Lost in the Fun House*

I want to discuss three things more or less together: first,
some old questions raised by the new intermedia arts;
second, some aspects of the Argentine writer Jorge Luis
Borges, whom I greatly admire; third, some professional
concerns of my own, related to these other matters and
having to do with what I'm calling 'the literature of
exhausted possibility' – or, more chicly, 'the literature of
exhaustion'.

By 'exhaustion' I don't mean anything so tired as the
subject of physical, moral, or intellectual decadence, only
the used-upness of certain forms or exhaustion of certain
possibilities – by no means necessarily a cause for despair.
That a great many Western artists for a great many years
have quarrelled with received definitions of artistic media,
genres, and forms goes without saying: pop art, dramatic
and musical 'happenings', the whole range of 'intermedia'
or 'mixed-means' art, bear recentest witness to the tradition
of rebelling against Tradition. A catalogue I received some
time ago in the mail, for example, advertises such items as
Robert Filliou's *Ample Food for Stupid Thought*, a box full
of postcards on which are inscribed 'apparently meaningless
questions', to be mailed to whomever the purchaser judges
them suited for; Ray Johnson's *Paper Snake*, a collection of

whimsical writings, 'often pointed', once mailed to various friends (what the catalogue describes as The New York Correspondence School of Literature); and Daniel Spoerri's *Anecdoted Typography of Chance*, 'on the surface' a description of all the objects that happen to be on the author's parlour table – 'in fact, however . . . a cosmology of Spoerri's existence'.

'On the surface', at least, the document listing these items is a catalogue of The Something Else Press, a swinging outfit. 'In fact, however', it may be one of their offerings, for all I know : The New York Direct-Mail Advertising School of Literature. In any case, their wares are lively to read about, and make for interesting conversation in fiction-writing classes, for example, where we discuss Somebody-or-other's unbound, unpaginated, randomly assembled novel-in-a-box and the desirability of printing *Finnegans Wake* on a very long roller-towel. It's easier and sociabler to talk technique than it is to make art, and the area of 'happenings' and their kin is mainly a way of discussing aesthetics, really; illustrating 'dramatically' more or less valid and interesting points about the nature of art and the definition of its terms and genres.

One conspicuous thing, for example, about the 'intermedia' arts is their tendency (noted even by *Life* magazine) to eliminate not only the traditional audience – 'those who apprehend the artists' art' (in 'happenings' the audience is often the 'cast', as in 'environments', and some of the new music isn't intended to be performed at all) – but also the most traditional notion of the artist : the Aristotelian conscious agent who achieves with technique and cunning the artistic effect; in other words, one endowed with uncommon talent, who has moreover developed and disciplined that endowment into virtuosity. It's an aristocratic notion on the face of it, which the democratic West seems eager to have done with; not only the 'omniscient' author of older fiction, but the very idea of the controlling artist, has been condemned as politically reactionary, even fascist.

Now, personally, being of the temper that chooses to 'rebel along traditional lines', I'm inclined to prefer the kind of art that not many people can *do* : the kind that requires expertise and artistry as well as bright aesthetic ideas and/or inspiration. I enjoy the pop art in the famous Albright-Knox collection, a few blocks from my house in Buffalo, like a lively conversation for the most part, but was on the whole more impressed by the jugglers and acrobats at Baltimore's old Hippodrome, where I used to go every time they changed shows : genuine *virtuosi* doing things that anyone can dream up and discuss but almost no one can do.

I suppose the distinction is between things worth remarking – preferably over beer, if one's of my generation – and things worth doing. 'Somebody ought to make a novel with scenes that pop up, like the old children's books,' one says, with the implication that one isn't going to bother doing it oneself.

However, art and its forms and techniques live in history and certainly do change. I sympathize with a remark attributed to Saul Bellow, that to be technically up to date is the least important attribute of a writer, though I would have to add that this least important attribute may be nevertheless essential. In any case, to be technically *out* of date is likely to be a genuine defect : Beethoven's Sixth Symphony or the Chartres Cathedral if executed today would be merely embarrassing. A good many current novelists write turn-of-the-century-type novels, only in more or less mid-twentieth-century language and about contemporary people and topics; this makes them considerably less interesting (to me) than excellent writers who are also technically contemporary : Joyce and Kafka, for instance, in their time, and in ours, Samuel Beckett and Jorge Luis Borges. The intermedia arts, I'd say, tend to be intermediary too, between the traditional realms of aesthetics on the one hand and artistic creation on the other; I think the wise artist and civilian will regard them with quite the kind and degree of seriousness with which he regards good shoptalk : he'll listen carefully, if non-committally, and keep an eye on his intermedia colleagues, if only the corner of his eye. They may very possibly suggest something usable in the making or understanding of genuine works of contemporary art.

The man I want to discuss a little here, Jorges Luis Borges, illustrates well the difference between a technically old-fashioned artist, a technically up-to-date civilian, and a technically up-to-date artist. In the first category I'd locate all those novelists who for better or worse write not as if the twentieth century didn't exist, but as if the great writers of the last sixty years or so hadn't existed (*nota bene* that our century's more than two-thirds done; it's dismaying to see so many of our writers following Dostoevsky or Tolstoy or Flaubert or Balzac, when the real technical question seems to me to be how to succeed not even Joyce and Kafka, but those who've *succeeded* Joyce and Kafka and are now in the evenings of their own careers). In the second category are such folk as an artist-neighbour of mine in Buffalo who fashions dead Winnie-the-Poohs in sometimes monumental scale out of oilcloth stuffed with sand and impaled on stakes or hung by the neck. In the third belong the few people whose artistic thinking is as hip as any French news-novelist's, but who manage nonetheless to speak eloquently and memorably to our still-human hearts and conditions, as the great artists have always done. Of these, two of the finest living specimens that I know of are Beckett and Borges, just about the only contemporaries of my reading acquaintance mentionable with the 'old masters' of twentieth-century fiction. In the unexciting history of literary awards, the 1961 International Publishers' Prize, shared by Beckett and Borges, is a happy exception indeed.

One of the modern things about these two is that in an age of ultimacies and 'final solutions' – at least *felt* ultimacies, in everything from weaponry to theology, the celebrated dehumanization of society, and the history of the novel – their work in separate ways reflects and deals with ultimacy, both technically and thematically, as, for example, *Finnegans Wake* does in its different manner. One notices, by the way, for whatever its symptomatic worth, that Joyce was virtually blind at the end, Borges is literally so, and Beckett has become virtually mute, musewise, having progressed from marvellously constructed English sentences through terser and terser French ones to the un-syntactical, unpunctuated prose of *Comment C'est* and 'ulti-mately' to wordless mimes. One might extrapolate a theore-tical course for Beckett: language, after all, consists of silence as well as sound, and the mime is still communica-tion – 'that nineteenth-century idea', a Yale student once snarled at me – but by the language of action. But the language of action consists of rest as well as movement, and so in the context of Beckett's progress, immobile, silent figures still aren't altogether ultimate. How about an empty, silent stage, then, or blank pages (an ultimacy already attained in the nineteenth century by that *avant-gardiste* of East Aurora, New York, Elbert Hubbard, in his *Essay on Silence*) – a 'happening' where nothing happens, like Cage's 4′ 33″ performed in an empty hall? But dramatic communication consists of the absence as well as the presence of the actors; 'we have our exits and our entrances'; and so even that would be imperfectly ultimate in Beckett's case. Nothing at all, then, I suppose: but Nothingness is necessarily and inextricably the background against which Being et cetera; for Beckett, at this point in his career, to cease to create altogether would be fairly meaningful: his crowning work, his 'last word'. What a convenient corner to paint yourself into! 'And now I shall finish,' the valet Arsene says in *Watt*, 'and you will hear my voice no more.' Only the silence *Molloy* speaks of, 'of which the universe is made'.

After which, I add on behalf of the rest of us, it might be conceivable to rediscover validly the artifices of language and literature – such far-out notions as grammar, punctuation . . . even characterization! Even *plot*! – if one goes about it the right way, aware of what one's predecessors have been up to.

Now J. L. Borges is perfectly aware of all these things. Back in the great decades of literary experimentalism he was associated with *Prisma*, a 'muralist' magazine that published its pages on walls and billboards; his later *Labyrinths* and *Ficciones* not only anticipate the farthest-out ideas of The Something Else Press crowd – not a difficult thing to do – but being marvellous works of art as well, illustrate in a simple way the difference between the *fact* of aesthetic ultimacies and their artistic *use*. What it comes to is that an artist doesn't merely exemplify an ultimacy; he employs it.

Consider Borges's story 'Pierre Menard, Author of the Quixote': the hero, an utterly sophisticated turn-of-the-century French Symbolist, by an astounding effort of imagination, produces – not *copies* or *imitates*, mind, but *composes* – several chapters of Cervantes's novel.

It is a revelation [Borges's narrator tells us] to compare Menard's *Don Quixote* with Cervantes's. The latter, for example, wrote (part one, chapter nine):

> . . . truth, whose mother is history, rival of time, depository of deeds, witness of the past, exemplar and adviser to the present, the future's counsellor.

Written in the seventeenth century, written by the 'lay genius' Cervantes, this enumeration is a mere rhetorical praise of history. Menard, on the other hand, writes:

> . . . truth, whose mother is history, rival of time, depository of deeds, witness of the past, exemplar and adviser to the present, the future's counsellor.

History, the *mother* of truth: the idea is astounding. Menard, a contemporary of William James, does not define history as an enquiry into reality but as its origin . . .

Et cetera. Now, this is an interesting idea, of considerable intellectual validity. I mentioned earlier that if Beethoven's Sixth were composed today, it would be an embarrassment; but clearly it wouldn't be, necessarily, if done with ironic intent by a composer quite aware of where we've been and where we are. It would have then potentially, for better or worse, the kind of significance of Warhol's Campbell's Soup ads, the difference being that in the former case a work of art is being reproduced instead of a work of non-art, and the ironic comment would therefore be more directly on the genre and history of the art than on the state of the culture. In fact, of course, to make the valid intellectual point one needn't even re-compose the Sixth Symphony any more than Menard really needed to re-create the *Quixote*. It would've been sufficient for Menard to have *attributed* the novel to himself in order to have a new work of art, from the intellectual point of view. Indeed, in several stories Borges plays with this very idea, and I can readily imagine Beckett's next novel, for example, as

Tom Jones, just as Nabokov's last was that multivolume annotated translation of Pushkin. I myself have always aspired to write Burton's version of *The 1001 Nights*, complete with appendices and the like, in twelve volumes, and for intellectual purposes I needn't even write it. What evenings we might spend (over beer) discussing Saarinen's Parthenon, D. H. Lawrence's *Wuthering Heights*, or the Johnson Administration by Robert Rauschenberg!

The idea, I say, is intellectually serious, as are Borges's other characteristic ideas, most of a metaphysical rather than an aesthetic nature. But the important thing to observe is that Borges doesn't attribute the *Quixote* to himself, much less re-compose it like Pierre Menard; instead, he writes a remarkable and original work of literature, the implicit theme of which is the difficulty, perhaps the unnecessity, of writing original works of literature. His artistic victory, if you like, is that he confronts an intellectual dead end and employs it against itself to accomplish new human work. If this corresponds to what mystics do – 'every moment leaping into the infinite', Kierkegaard says, 'and every moment falling surely back into the finite' – it's only one more aspect of that old analogy. In homelier terms, it's a matter of every moment throwing out the bath water without for a moment losing the baby.

Another way of describing Borges's accomplishment is in a pair of his own favourite terms, *algebra* and *fire*. In his most often anthologized story, 'Tlön, Uqbar, Orbis Tertius', he imagines an entirely hypothetical world, the invention of a secret society of scholars who elaborate its every aspect in a surreptitious encyclopaedia. This *First Encyclopaedia of Tlön* (what fictionist would not wish to have dreamed up the *Britannica?*) describes a coherent alternative to this world complete in every aspect from its algebra to its fire, Borges tells us, and of such imaginative power that, once conceived, it begins to obtrude itself into and eventually to supplant our prior reality. My point is that neither the algebra nor the fire, metaphorically speaking, could achieve this result without the other. Borges's algebra is what I'm considering here – algebra is easier to talk about than fire – but any intellectual giant could equal it. The imaginary authors of the *First Encyclopaedia of Tlön* itself are not artists, though their work is in a manner of speaking fictional and would find a ready publisher in New York nowadays The author of the story 'Tlön, Uqbar, Orbis Tertius', who merely *alludes* to the fascinating *Encyclopaedia*, is an artist; what makes him one of the first rank, like Kafka, is the combination of that intellectually profound vision with great human insight, poetic power, and consummate mastery of his means, a definition which would have gone without saying, I suppose, in any century but ours.

Not long ago, incidentally, in a footnote to a scholarly edition of Sir Thomas Browne (*The Urn Burial*, I believe it was), I came upon a perfect Borges datum, reminiscent of Tlön's self-realization: the actual case of a book called *The Three Impostors*, alluded to in Browne's *Religio Medici* among other places. *The Three Impostors* is a non-existent blasphemous treatise against Moses, Christ, and Mohammed, which in the seventeenth century was widely held to exist, or to have once existed. Commentators attributed it variously to Boccaccio, Pietro Aretino, Giordano Bruno, and Tommaso Campanella, and though no one, Browne included, had ever seen a copy of it, it was frequently cited, refuted, railed against, and generally discussed as if everyone had read it – until, sure enough, in the *eighteenth* century a spurious work appeared with a forged date of 1598 and the title *De Tribus Impostoribus*. It's a wonder that Borges doesn't mention this work, as he seems to have read absolutely everything, including all the books that don't exist, and Browne is a particular favourite of his. In fact, the narrator of 'Tlön, Uqbar, Orbis Tertius' declares at the end:

. . . English and French and mere Spanish will disappear from the globe. The world will be Tlön. I pay no attention to all this and go on revising, in the still days at the Adrogué hotel, an uncertain Quevedian translation (which I do not intend to publish) of Browne's *Urn Burial*.

(Moreover, on rereading 'Tlön', etc., I find now a remark I'd swear wasn't in it last year: that the eccentric American millionaire who endows the *Encyclopaedia* does so on condition that 'the work will make no pact with the impostor Jesus Christ'.)

This 'contamination of reality by dream', as Borges calls it, is one of his pet themes, and commenting upon such contaminations is one of his favourite fictional devices. Like many of the best such devices, it turns the artist's mode or form into a metaphor for his concerns, as does the diary-ending of *Portrait of the Artist as a Young Man* or the cyclical construction of *Finnegans Wake*. In Borges's case, the story 'Tlön', etc., for example, is a real piece of imagined reality in our world, analogous to those Tlönian artifacts called *hronir*, which imagine themselves into existence. In short, it's a paradigm of or metaphor for itself; not just the *form* of the story but the *fact* of the story is symbolic; 'the medium is the message'.

Moreover, like all of Borges's work, it illustrates in other of its aspects my subject: how an artist may paradoxically turn the felt ultimacies of our time into material and means for his work – *paradoxically* because by doing so he transcends what had appeared to be his refutation, in the same way that the mystic who transcends finitude is said to be enabled to live, spiritually and physically, in the finite world. Suppose you're a writer by vocation – a 'print-oriented bastard', as the McLuhanites call us – and you feel, for example, that the novel, if not narrative literature generally, if not the printed word altogether, has by this hour of the world just about shot its bolt, as Leslie Fiedler and others maintain. (I'm inclined to agree, with reservations and hedges. Literary forms certainly have histories and historical contingencies, and it may well be that the novel's time as a major art form is up, as the 'times' of classical tragedy, grand opera, or the sonnet sequence came to be. No necessary cause for alarm in this at all, except perhaps to certain novelists, and one way to handle such a feeling might be to write a novel about it. Whether historically the novel expires or persists seems immaterial to me; if enough writers and critics *feel* apocalyptical about it, their feeling becomes a considerable cultural fact, like the feeling that Western civilization, or the world, is going to end rather soon. If you took a bunch of people out into the desert and the world didn't end, you'd come home shame-faced, I imagine; but the persistence of an art form doesn't invalidate work created in the comparable apocalyptic ambience. That's one of the fringe benefits of being an artist instead of a prophet. There are others.) If you happened to be Vladimir Nabokov you might address that felt ultimacy by writing *Pale Fire*: a fine novel by a learned pedant, in the form of a pedantic commentary on a poem invented for the purpose. If you were Borges you might write *Labyrinths*: fictions by a learned librarian in the form of footnotes, as he describes them, to imaginary or hypothetical books. And I'll add, since I believe Borges's idea is rather more interesting, that if you were the author of this paper, you'd have written something like *The Sot-Weed Factor* or *Giles Goat-Boy*: novels which imitate the form of the Novel, by an author who imitates the role of Author.

If this sort of thing sounds unpleasantly decadent, nevertheless it's about where the genre began, with *Quixote* imitating *Amadis of Gaul*, Cervantes pretending to be the Cid Hamete Benengeli (and Alonso Quijano pretending to be Don Quixote), or Fielding parodying Richardson. 'History repeats itself as farce' – meaning, of course, in the form or mode of farce, not that history is farcical. The imitation (like the Dadaist echoes in the work of the 'intermedia' types) is something new and *may be* quite serious and passionate despite its farcical aspect. This is the important difference between a proper novel and a deliberate imitation of a novel, or a novel imitative of other sorts of documents. The first attempts (has been historically inclined to attempt) to imitate actions more or less directly, and its conventional devices – cause and effect, linear anecdote, characterization, authorial selection, arrangement, and interpretation – can be and have long since been objected to as obsolete notions, or metaphors for obsolete notions: Robbe-Grillet's essays *For a New Novel* come to mind. There are replies to these objections, not to the point here, but one can see that in any case they're obviated by imitations-of-novels, which attempt to represent not life directly but a representation of life. In fact such works are no more removed from 'life' than Richardson's or Goethe's epistolary novels are: both imitate 'real' documents, and the subject of both, ultimately, is life, not the documents. A novel is as much a piece of the real world as a letter, and the letters in *The Sorrows of Young Werther* are, after all, fictitious.

One might imaginably compound this imitation, and though Borges doesn't he's fascinated with the idea: one of his frequenter literary allusions is to the 602nd night of *The 1001 Nights*, when, owing to a copyist's error, Scheherezade begins to tell the King the story of the 1001 nights, from the beginning. Happily, the King interrupts; if he didn't there'd be no 603rd night ever, and while this would solve Scheherezade's problem – which is every storyteller's problem : to publish or perish – it would put the 'outside' author in a bind. (I suspect that Borges dreamed this whole thing up : the business he mentions isn't in any edition of *The 1001 Nights* I've been able to consult. Not *yet*, anyhow : after reading 'Tlön, Uqbar', etc., one is inclined to recheck every semester or so.)

Now Borges (whom someone once vexedly accused *me* of inventing) is interested in the 602nd night because it's an instance of the story-within-the-story turned back upon itself, and his interest in such instances is threefold : first, as he himself declares, they disturb us metaphysically : when the characters in a work of fiction become readers or authors of the fiction they're in, we're reminded of the fictitious aspect of our own existence, one of Borges's cardinal themes, as it was of Shakespeare, Calderón, Unamuno, and other folk. Second, the 602nd night is a literary illustration of the *regressus in infinitum*, as are almost all Borges's principal images and motifs. Third, Scheherezade's accidental gambit, like Borges's other versions of the *regressus in infinitum*, is an image of the exhaustion, or attempted exhaustion, of possibilities – in this case literary possibilities – and so we return to our main subject.

What makes Borges's stance, if you like, more interesting to me than, say, Nabokov's or Beckett's is the premise with which he approaches literature; in the words of one of his editors : 'For [Borges] no one has claim to originality in literature; all writers are more or less faithful amanuenses of the spirit, translators and annotators of pre-existing archetypes.' Thus his inclination to write brief comments on imaginary books : for one to attempt to add overtly to the sum of 'original' literature by even so much as a conventional short story, not to mention a novel, would be too presumptuous, too naïve; literature has been done long since. A librarian's point of view! And it would itself be too presumptuous, if it weren't part of a lively, passionately relevant metaphysical vision and slyly employed against itself precisely, to make new and original literature. Borges defines the Baroque as 'that style which deliberately exhausts (or tries to exhaust) its possibilities and borders upon its own caricature'. While his own work is *not* Baroque, except intellectually (the Baroque was never so terse, laconic, economical), it suggests the view that intellectual and literary history has been Baroque, and has pretty well exhausted the possibilities of novelty. His *ficciones* are not only footnotes to imaginary texts, but postscripts to the real corpus of literature.

This premise gives resonance and relation to all his principal images. The facing mirrors that recur in his stories are a dual *regressus*. The doubles that his characters, like Nabokov's, run afoul of suggest dizzying multiples and remind one of Browne's remark that 'every man is not only himself . . . men are lived over again'. (It would please Borges, and illustrate Browne's point, to call Browne a precursor of Borges. 'Every writer,' Borges says in his essay on Kafka, 'creates his own precursors.') Borges's favourite third-century heretical sect is the Histriones – I think and hope he invented them – who believe that repetition is impossible in history and therefore live viciously in order to purge the future of the vices they commit: in other words, to exhaust the possibilities of the world in order to bring its end nearer.

The writer he most often mentions, after Cervantes, is Shakespeare; in one piece he imagines the playwright on his deathbed asking God to permit him to be one and himself, having been everyone and no one; God replies from the whirlwind that He is no one either; He has dreamed the world like Shakespeare, and including Shakespeare. Homer's story in Book IV of the *Odyssey*, of Menelaus on the beach at Pharos, tackling Proteus, appeals profoundly to Borges: Proteus is he who 'exhausts the guises of reality' while Menelaus – who, one recalls, disguised his own identity in order to ambush him – holds fast. Zeno's paradox of Achilles and the Tortoise embodies a *regressus in infinitum* which Borges carries through philosophical history, pointing out that Aristotle uses it to refute Plato's theory of forms, Hume to refute the possibility of cause and effect, Lewis Carroll to refute syllogistic deduction, William James to refute the notion of temporal passage, and Bradley to refute the general

possibility of logical relations; Borges himself uses it, citing
Schopenhauer, as evidence that the world is our dream, our
idea, in which 'tenuous and eternal crevices of unreason'
can be found to remind us that our creation is false, or at
least fictive.

The infinite library of one of the most popular stories is
an image particularly pertinent to the literature of exhaustion; the 'Library of Babel' houses every possible combination of alphabetical characters and spaces, and thus every
possible book and statement, including your and my refuta-
tions and vindications, the history of the actual future, the
history of every possible future, and, though he doesn't
mention it, the encyclopaedias not only of Tlön but of
every imaginable other world – since, as in Lucretius's universe, the number of elements, and so of combinations, is
finite (though very large), and the number of instances of
each element and combination of elements is infinite, like
the library itself.

That brings us to his favourite image of all, the labyrinth,
and to my point. *Labyrinths* is the name of his most substantial translated volume, and the only full-length study of
Borges in English, by Ana Maria Barrenechea, is called
Borges the Labyrinth-Maker. A labyrinth, after all, is a place
in which, ideally, all the possibilities of choice (of direction,
in this case) are embodied, and – barring special dispensation
like Theseus's – must be exhausted before one reaches the
heart. Where, mind, the Minotaur waits with two final
possibilities: defeat and death, or victory and freedom.
Now, in fact, the legendary Theseus is non-Baroque; thanks
to Ariadne's thread he can take a shortcut through the
labyrinth at Knossos. But Menelaus on the beach at Pharos,
for example, is genuinely Baroque in the Borgesian spirit,
and illustrates a positive artistic morality in the literature
of exhaustion. He is not there, after all, for kicks (any more
than Borges and Beckett are in the fiction racket for their
health): Menelaus is *lost*, in the larger labyrinth of the
world, and has got to hold fast while the Old Man of the
Sea exhausts reality's frightening guises so that he may
extort direction from him when Proteus returns to his 'true'
self. It's a heroic enterprise, with salvation as its object –
one recalls that the aim of the Histriones is to get history
done with so that Jesus may come again the sooner, and

that Shakespeare's heroic metamorphoses culminate not merely in a theophany but in an apotheosis.

Now, not just any old body is equipped for this labour, and Theseus in the Cretan labyrinth becomes in the end the aptest image of Borges after all. Distressing as the fact is to us liberal Democrats, the commonality, alas, will *always* lose their way and their souls; it's the chosen remnant, the virtuoso, the Thesean *hero*, who, confronted with Baroque reality, Baroque history, the Baroque state of his art, need *not* rehearse its possibilities to exhaustion, any more than Borges needs actually to *write* the *Encyclopaedia of Tlön* or the books in the Library of Babel. He need only be aware of their existence or possibility, acknowledge them, and with the aid of *very special* gifts – as extraordinary as saint- or hero-hood and not likely to be found in The New York Correspondence School of Literature – go straight through the maze to the accomplishment of his work.

DAVID LODGE

The Novelist at the Crossroads

(reprinted, abridged, with permission from *The Novelist at the Crossroads*, Routledge, 1971; Cornell, 1971)

> Marvin asks Sam if he has given up his novel, and Sam says, 'Temporarily.' He cannot find a form, he explains. He does not want to write a realistic novel, because reality is no longer realistic.
>
> NORMAN MAILER: *The Man Who Studied Yoga*

Robert Scholes's recent book *The Fabulators* (OUP, 1967) has given a new impetus to the old guessing game of 'Whither the Novel?' At least, it has prompted me to try to organize my own tentative thoughts on the subject. To do this, however, and to understand *The Fabulators*, it is necessary to go back, first, to an earlier book of Mr Scholes, *The Nature of Narrative* (1966), written in collaboration with Robert Kellogg. There, the authors proposed that there are two main, antithetical modes of narrative: the *empirical*, whose primary allegiance is to the real, and the *fictional*, whose primary allegiance is to the ideal. Empirical narrative subdivides into history, which is true to fact, and what the authors call mimesis (i.e. realistic imitation), which is true to experience. Fictional narrative subdivides into romance, which cultivates beauty, and aims to delight, and allegory, which cultivates goodness and aims to instruct. This genre theory is combined with a large-scale historical scheme, according to which the primitive oral epic was a synthesis of empirical and fictional modes that under various cultural pressures (chiefly the transition from oral to written forms of communication) broke up into its component parts; and this fragmentation occurred twice – once in late classical literature, and again in the European vernacular literatures, where the different modes were developed independently, or in partial combinations. In the late Middle Ages and the Renaissance there is a perceptible movement in narrative literature towards a new synthesis of empirical and fictional modes which finally produces, in the eighteenth century, the novel. In the experiments of modern narrative writers, however, and in the advent of new media such as motion pictures, Scholes and Kellogg saw evidence that the synthesis is about to dissolve once more.

Now, while this ambitious scheme is obviously vulnerable to scholarly sniping on points of detail, it is, I think, a suggestive and useful one when we try to take an overview of the nature and development of the novel. It gives some substance, for instance, to our vague intuition that the novel stands to modern, post-Renaissance civilization as the epic did to ancient civilization. Perhaps more important, by suggesting that the novel is a new synthesis of pre-existing narrative traditions, rather than a continuation of one of them or an entirely unprecedented phenomenon, it accounts for the great variety and inclusiveness of the novel form: its capacity for being pushed, by different authors, in the directions of history (including autobiography), allegory or romance while still remaining somehow 'the novel'. It will be noticed that I do not invoke, here, the fourth of Scholes's and Kellogg's categories – what they call 'mimesis', and what I should prefer to call 'realism'. To talk of the novel 'being pushed in the direction of realism while still remaining somehow a novel' does not make immediate sense because it is difficult to conceive of there being a conflict of interests between the novel and realism – whether one uses that elastic term primarily in a formal sense (as I do), to denote a particular mode of presentation which, roughly speaking, treats fictional events as if they were a kind of history, or in a more qualitative sense, to denote a literary aesthetic of truth-telling. For most of the novel's life-span, one of these notions of realism has tended to imply the other. If realism of presentation was not actually invented by the eighteenth-century novelists and their nineteenth-century successors, it was certainly developed and exploited by them on a scale unprecedented in earlier literature; and when all the necessary exceptions and qualifications have been made, it is generally true that the major novelists of this period justified the form, and their own particular contributions to it, by appealing to some kind of 'realist' aesthetic.

Thus, if Scholes and Kellogg are right to see the novel as a new synthesis of pre-existing narrative modes, the dominant mode, the synthesizing element, is realism. It is realism which holds history, romance and allegory together in precarious synthesis, making a bridge between the world of discrete facts (history) and the patterned, economized world of art and imagination (allegory and romance). The novel, supremely among literary forms, has satisfied our hunger for the meaningful ordering of experience *without* denying our empirical observation of its randomness and particularity. It is therefore based on a kind of compromise, but one which has permitted many varieties of emphasis, on one side or the other, from Richardson and Fielding onwards, and which has survived numerous attempts to break it up. The Gothic novel was one such attempt: a revolt against realism, sponsored for the most part by second-class minds, it was by the major novelists of the nineteenth century either ridiculed out of countenance (e.g. Jane Austen) or tamed, domesticated, and assimilated into a more realistic account of experience (e.g. the Brontës). To be sure, the compromise (or synthesis) was always more stable in Europe than in America. But even in Hawthorne and Melville, writers strongly attracted to history, allegory and romance, realism exerts a strong if intermittent influence; while in *Huckleberry Finn*, the book from which Hemingway traced all significant modern American literature, we have a classic novelistic achievement: mythic and thematic interests controlled and expressed through the realistic rendering of particular experience.

If the above argument is granted, it follows that the disintegration of the novel-synthesis should be associated with a radical undermining of realism as a literary mode; and that is precisely what is claimed in *The Nature of Narrative*. Literary realism, we may say, depicts the individual experience of a common phenomenal world, and Scholes and Kellogg point out that both parts of this undertaking are under pressure in modern culture. As, influenced by developments in human knowledge, particularly in the field of psychology, the writer pursues the reality of individual experience deeper and deeper into the subconscious or unconscious, the common perceptual world recedes and the concept of the unique person dissolves: the writer finds himself in a region of myths, dreams, symbols and archetypes that demand 'fictional' rather than 'empirical' modes for their expression. 'The mimetic impulse towards the characterization of the inner life dissolves inevitably into mythic and expressionistic patterns upon reaching the citadel of the psyche.' On the other hand, if the writer persists in seeking to do justice to the common phenomenal world he finds himself, today, in competition with new media, such as tape and motion pictures, which can claim to do this more effectively.

This latter point is taken up and developed by Mr Scholes in *The Fabulators*, which is a more topical and polemical sequel to *The Nature of Narrative*:

> the cinema gives the *coup de grâce* to a dying realism in written fiction. Realism purports – has always purported – to subordinate the words themselves to their referents, to the things words point to. Realism exalts life and diminishes art, exalts things and diminishes words. But when it comes to representing *things*, one picture is worth a thousand words, and one motion picture is worth a million. In face of competition from cinema, fiction must abandon its attempt to 'represent reality' and rely more on the power of words to stimulate the imagination.

Mr Scholes's book consists largely of appreciative studies in a number of contemporary narrative writers who have, in his view, already recognized the obsolescence of realism and hence of the traditional novel, and are exploring, with modern sophistication, the purely 'fictional' modes of allegory and romance. To describe this kind of narrative he has revived the archaic word 'fabulation'. It is, as will be evident, a development he welcomes. 'The novel may be dying,' he says, 'but we need not fear for the future.'

Lawrence Durrell, Iris Murdoch, John Hawkes, Terry Southern, Kurt Vonnegut and John Barth are the writers principally discussed. Durrell's *Alexandria Quartet* is seen as a sophisticated exploitation of the labyrinthine intrigues and reversals of (appropriately) Alexandrian romance. Murdoch's *The Unicorn* is interpreted as an elaborate and multi-faceted allegory, worked out in terms of Gothic fiction, about the conflict of secular and religious attitudes. Hawkes, and the 'Black Humorists' Southern and Vonnegut, are seen as practising a surrealistic form of picaresque. Barth's *Giles*

Goat-boy, with its rich and exuberant mixture of mythic, romantic and allegorical modes, is the perfect exemplification of Scholes's theory, and his prize exhibit.

'The only legitimate way to approach "intention" in a literary work,' Mr Scholes observes, 'is through a highly discriminated sense of genre.' In this respect his explications are useful and perceptive, but as evaluations they are somewhat undiscriminating. Reading *The Unicorn* for the first time under Mr Scholes's guidance, I felt I understood what Miss Murdoch was up to more clearly than in previous readings of her novels; but whether the 'ideas' in that book, or its involved and melodramatic plot, or the process of abstracting the former from the latter, yield any great pleasure or instruction seemed to me still open to question. It is a question that Mr Scholes scarcely faces : for him the intention to reject realism in favour of fabulation is itself a guarantee of value.

In considering this point of view it behoves the English reader to proceed carefully, and with a certain self-awareness. There is a good deal of evidence that the English literary mind is peculiarly committed to realism, and resistant to non-realistic literary modes to an extent that might be described as prejudice. It is something of a commonplace of recent literary history, for instance, that the 'modern' experimental novel, represented diversely by Joyce, Virginia Woolf and D. H. Lawrence, which threatened to break up the stable synthesis of the realistic novel, was repudiated by two subsequent generations of English novelists. And, reviewing the history of the English novel in the twentieth century it is difficult to avoid associating the restoration of traditional literary realism with a perceptible decline in artistic achievement. There is a certain uncomfortable truth in Mr Rubin Rabinovitz's comments at the end of his recent book, *The Reaction Against Experiment in the English Novel 1950–1960* (Columbia UP, 1968) :

> The critical mood in England has produced a climate in which traditional novels can flourish and anything out of the ordinary is given the denigratory label 'experiment' and neglected . . . The greatest fear of the English contemporary novelist is to commit a *faux pas*; every step is taken within prescribed limits, and the result is intelli-

gent, technically competent, but ultimately mediocre . . .
The successful novelist in England becomes, too quickly,
a part of the literary establishment . . . All too often he
uses his position as a critic to endorse the type of fiction
he himself is writing and he attacks those whose approach
is different.

Though Mr Rabinovitz has little to offer that is either new
or interesting, by way of critical comment on the English
novel of the fifties, he has burrowed deep into the journalistic archives of the period and produced some interesting documentation. It is instructive, for instance, to learn
(or be reminded) that *Lord of the Flies* (1954) was reviewed
by Walter Allen in the *New Statesman* in these terms:

> *Lord of the Flies* is like the fragment of a nightmare, for
> all that it is lightly told. It commands a reluctant assent:
> yes, doubtless it could be like that, with the regression
> from choir school to Mau Mau only a step. The difficulty
> begins when one smells allegory. 'There's not a child so
> small and weak but has his little cross to take.' These
> children's crosses, it seemed to me, were altogether too
> unnaturally heavy for it to be possible to draw con-
> clusions from Mr Golding's novel, and if that is so, it is,
> however skilfully told, only a rather unpleasant and too-
> easily affecting story.

The unexamined assumptions behind this critique, that
allegory is necessarily a literary vice, because it makes the
action of the book 'unnatural', undermining the essential
criterion of 'it could be like that', without the satisfaction
of which all 'skill' is vain – these essentially realist assumptions are entirely typical of the post-war English literary
temper. It now seems fairly obvious that this was an in-
appropriate response to *Lord of the Flies* (at least Mr Allen
has acknowledged as much by his praise of the book in
Tradition and Dream [1964]), but the instance is a caution-
ary one. Most of Golding's subsequent novels have provoked
similar objections, at least initially.
  Turning to the writers Scholes holds up for admiration
we find two English novelists (Murdoch and Durrell) who
have generally enjoyed a higher reputation abroad than at

home, and whose later work has been received with less and less favour in England; and four American writers who have made comparatively little impact on English readers. Vonnegut is not widely read in England, and although Southern is well known for the scandalous *Candy*, this scarcely amounts to a literary reputation. Hawkes's novels failed disastrously in England until the determined efforts of a few admirers, notably Christopher Ricks, recently obtained for them a respectful but grudging attention. Barth's *Giles Goat-boy*, rapturously received in America, was put down by most English reviewers.

The picture we get by putting Rabinovitz's and Scholes's books together – of an incorrigibly insular England defending an obsolete realism against the life-giving invasions of fabulation – is, however, an oversimplification. For one thing, the consensus of English literary opinion as described by Mr Rabinovitz has been greatly shaken up since 1960; for another, fabulation is not the only alternative to traditional realism that is being explored by contemporary narrative writers.

I shall take the latter point first. Mr Scholes may be right to see the novel as closer to disintegration today than it has ever been in its always hectic and unstable history, but his diagnosis of its condition in *The Fabulators* is one-sided. Since, in his view, the synthesis of empirical and fictional modes is no longer worth the trouble of maintaining, he recommends that narrative should exploit the fictional modes, for which he has a personal predilection, more or less exclusively. Logic suggests, however, that it would be equally possible to move in the opposite direction – towards empirical narrative, and away from fiction. This in fact is what we find happening.

The term 'non-fiction novel' was first coined, I believe, by Truman Capote to describe his book *In Cold Blood*, an account of a brutal multiple murder committed in Kansas in 1959. Every detail of this book is 'true', discovered by painstaking research – Capote spent many hours with the murderers in prison, for instance, getting to know their characters and backgrounds. Yet *In Cold Blood* also reads like a novel. It is written with a novelist's eye for the aesthetic possibilities of his *donnée*, for the evocative and symbolic properties of circumstantial detail, for shapeliness and ironic contrast in structure. The moral protests the book provoked in some quarters – the charge, for instance, that there was something callous and inhuman about so 'literary' a treatment of experience so painfully actual and immediate – is one indication of the way the book straddles the conventional boundary between fiction and reportage.

That Norman Mailer's *The Armies of the Night* (1968) straddles this boundary is very clearly advertised by its subtitle: 'History as a Novel – The Novel as History'. The first part ('History as a Novel') of this account of the anti-Vietnam War march on the Pentagon in 1967 is a detailed account of the author's own experience of the event, from his initial, reluctant agreement to participate, through the riotous eve-of-march gathering at the Ambassador Theatre in Washington, where Mailer drunkenly insisted on chairing the proceedings, scandalizing or embarrassing most of those present, to the early stages of the March, Mailer's self-sought arrest, imprisonment, trial and release. This section is, in Mailer's words, 'nothing but a personal history which while written as a novel was to the best of the author's memory scrupulous to facts'. It is distinguished from a straight autobiographical narrative primarily by the fact that Mailer writes about himself in the third person, thus achieving an ironic distance on his own complex personality which is one of the chief delights of the book:

> 'Let's sing them a song, boys,' Mailer called out [on the bus taking arrested demonstrators to jail]. He could not help it – the mountebank in him felt as if he were playing Winston Churchill. Ten minutes ago he had been mired in long slow thoughts of four wives – now he had a stage again and felt not unheroic. 'Can it be?' he wondered to himself, 'that I have mis-spent twenty years as a novelist, and all along have been languishing as an actor?'

This self-irony enabled by the third-person narrative method also licenses Mailer to describe his fellow-participants, such as Dwight MacDonald and Robert Lowell, with a mischievous candour that might have seemed impertinent in a conventional autobiography, and to indulge in a good deal of prophetic cultural generalization about America which, like 'ideas' in a novel, we judge by their plausibility, rhetorical force and relevance to context rather than by the stricter criteria of logic and verifiability – for example:

> the American small town . . . had grown out of itself again and again, its cells travelled, worked for government, found security through wars in foreign lands, and the nightmares which passed on the winds in the old small towns now travelled on the nozzle of the tip of the flame thrower, no dreams now of barbarian lusts, slaughtered villages, battles of blood, no, nor any need for them – technology had driven insanity out of the wind and out of the attic, and out of all the lost primitive places : one had to find it now wherever fever, force, and machines could come together, in Vegas, at the race track, in pro football, race riots for the Negro, suburban orgies – none of it was enough – one had to find it in Vietnam; that was where the small town had gone to get its kicks.

It makes a significant difference to such passages if one transposes the free indirect speech into the declarative present tense of the conventional essay.

It is less easy to describe the narrative principles of the second part of *The Armies of the Night*, partly because Mailer himself seems confused about them. When, at the beginning of this section, 'The Novel as History', he speaks of 'the novelist . . . passing his baton to the Historian', he seems to mean that the narrative method of Part 1, in which events were seen from one limited point of view, in the manner of a Jamesian novel, will be exchanged for the method of the historian, who assembles and collates data from various sources and presents a coherent account of a complex sequence of events.

> The mass media which surrounded the March on the Pentagon created a forest of inaccuracy which would blind the efforts of a historian; our novel has provided us with the possibility, no, even the instrument to view our facts and conceivably study them in that light a labour of lens-grinding has produced.

I take this to mean that, both for the writer and for us

the readers, the research into the self that is carried out in Part I has exposed and purged the inevitable bias of any human report. Thus the 'novel' has given the 'history' a unique kind of reliability. About half-way through Part II, however, Mailer abandons this claim. When he gets to the point in his narrative where the massed troops and demonstrators confront each other across 'six inches of no-man's-land' he announces that Part II 'is now disclosed as some sort of condensation of a collective novel – which is to admit that an explanation of the mystery of the events at the Pentagon cannot be developed by the methods of history – only by the instincts of the novelist'. Mailer thus claims the freedom to enhance his narrative with vivid invention – for instance, the briefing he imagines the troops getting:

'Well, men,' says the major, 'our mission is to guard the Pentagon from rioters and out-of-march scale prearranged-upon levels of defacement, meaning clear? well the point to keep in mind, troopers, is those are going to be American citizens out there expressing their constitutional right to protest – that don't mean we're going to let them fart in our face – but the Constitution is a complex document with circular that is circulating sets of conditions – put it this way, I got my buddies being chewed up by V.C. right this minute maybe I don't care to express personal sentiments now, negative, keep two things in mind – those demos out there could be carrying bombs or bangelore torpedoes for all we know, and you're going out with no rounds in your carbines so thank God for the ·45. And first remember one thing more – they start trouble with us, they'll wish they hadn't left New York unless you get killed in the stampede of us to get to them. Yessir, you keep a tight asshole and the fellow behind you can keep his nose clean.'

This, certainly, uses to advantage a novelist's gift for caricature by violating the rules of modern historical method (though the convention is a very familiar one in classical historiography).

The Armies of the Night implies no disillusionment on the author's part with the novel as a literary form: on the contrary, it reaffirms the primacy of that form as a mode of exploring and interpreting experience. The non-fiction novel, however, is, like fabulation, often associated with such disillusionment. A case in point is the young English writer B. S. Johnson, whose break with the conventional novel was very explicitly made in *Albert Angelo* (1964). This, for about three-quarters of its length, is the story of a young architect who is unable to practise his profession, and is obliged to earn his living as a supply teacher in a number of tough London schools. He is a fairly familiar kind of English post-war hero, or anti-hero: young, frustrated, classless, mildly delinquent, disappointed in love. Though Johnson uses a number of experimental expressive techniques (simultaneous presentation of dialogue and thought in double columns, holes cut in the pages so that the reader can see what is coming), the narrative reads like realistic fiction. Then, at the beginning of the fourth section, comes the shock:

– fuck all this lying look what im really trying to write about is writing not all this stuff about architecture trying to say something about writing about my writing im my hero though what a useless appellation, my first character then im trying to say something about me through him albert an architect when whats the point in covering up covering up covering over pretending pretending i can say anything through him that is anything i would be interested in saying . . .

In brief, Johnson goes on to expose and destroy the fictiveness of the narrative he has elaborately created, telling us the 'true' facts behind the story – for instance, the real name of the girl and the fact that while in the novel the girl jilted Albert, in actuality Johnson jilted her. Of course, one has to take the author's word that he *is* telling the truth in this section; but even if one doubts this, the story of Albert has been drastically stripped of what Henry James called 'authority'. It is an extreme strategy for achieving an effect of sincerity and authenticity, though coming so late in the work it is more of a gesture than an achievement. Having blown up his fictional bridges behind him, the author stands at the end of the book defiant and vulnerable on the bare ground of fact. And there in his subsequent books, *Trawl* (1967) and *The Unfortunates* (1969) he has remained, taking the fundamentalist Platonic position that 'telling stories is telling lies', but at the same time experimenting with form to bring writing into closer proximity with living.

The Unfortunates, for instance, consists of twenty-seven unbound sections, in a box. The first and last sections are marked as such, but the rest are in random order, and the reader is invited to shuffle them further if he so wishes. According to the blurb, this unconventional format is designed to 'represent the random workings of the mind without the forced consecutiveness of a book', but this is not in fact the case. The random flow of sensation and association in the narrator's mind is imitated by the movement of the words, clauses and sentences *within each section* – a stream-of-consciousness technique in the manner of Joyce. The randomness only affects the narrative presentation of this consciousness in time. It makes explicit the almost infinite choice a writer has in representing a particular sequence of events by refusing to commit itself to any one choice. Such is the nature of the human mind, however, that, working with the key of the marked first section, we mentally arrange the events of the book in their chronological order as we read; and the puzzle or game element thus introduced into the reading experience has the effect (ironically, in view of the author's declared intentions, but also advantageously in my opinion) of putting the painful, personal, 'real' experience of the book at an aesthetic distance, making it read more like fiction than autobiography.

For Johnson, one may gather readily from his books, the effort required to throw off the burden of the great tradition of the realistic novel has been considerable. For Frank Conroy, a young American writer whose first book *Stop-time* (1967) attracted considerable attention, it was evidently no effort at all. Where the young writer of an earlier generation would have worked his experience of growing up into a *Bildungsroman*, he simply wrote his autobiography (a form traditionally thought to be the privilege of maturity, if not fame) – but an autobiography with, in the words of Norman Mailer's significant tribute, 'the intimate and unprotected candour of a novel'. Here is a specimen – the author's memories of his father:

> I try to think of him as sane, and yet it must be admitted he did some odd things. Forced to attend a rest-home dance for its therapeutic value, he combed his hair with urine and otherwise played it out like the Southern gentleman he was. He had a tendency to take off his trousers and throw them out the window. (I harbour some secret admiration for this.) At a moment's notice he could blow a thousand dollars at Abercrombie and Fitch and disappear into the Northwest to become an outdoorsman. He spent an anxious few weeks convinced that I was fated to become a homosexual. I was six months old. And I remember visiting him at one of the rest-homes when I was eight. We walked across a sloping lawn and he told me a story, which even then I recognized as a lie, about a man who sat down on the open blade of a penknife embedded in a park bench. (Why, for God's sake would he tell a story like that to his eight-year-old son?)

'The history of the realistic novel,' Harry Levin has observed in his book on Joyce, 'shows that fiction tends towards autobiography. The increasing demands for social and psychological detail that are made upon the novelist can only be satisfied out of his own experience. The forces which make him an outsider focus his observation upon himself.' Johnson and Conroy (and one might mention Henry Miller here as a precursor of this form of the non-fiction novel) take this principle to its logical conclusion. If the fictional reworking of personal experience inevitably falsifies it, and if the writer no longer feels the need or obligation to protect his own and others' privacy, the auto-biographical *novel* is, in this perspective, redundant.

Scholes and Kellogg seem to endorse this point of view in *The Nature of Narrative*:

> If any distinction can be said to exist between the auto-biography and the autobiographical novel it resides not in their respective fidelity to facts but rather in their respective originality in perceiving and telling the facts. It is in the knowing and the telling, and not in the facts,

that the art is to be found (p. 156).

The last sentence is obviously true, but it obscures the point that the autobiographical novelist is free to alter, rearrange and add to 'the facts'; and that this freedom is exercised not merely to protect his privacy, but in the interest of literary values such as representative significance and formal coherence. In practice the reader is rarely in a position to judge with any confidence the 'fidelity to facts' of either the autobiography or the autobiographical novel, but he makes a different 'contract' with each kind of book, and brings different expectations to the reading experience. Works like *The Unfortunates* and *Stop-time* complicate and delay this process by combining the properties of both forms; but sooner or later one decides, I think, to read the former as a novel and the latter as an autobiography.

One can detect in B. S. Johnson's work the influence of Samuel Beckett and of some younger French practitioners of the *nouveau roman*. In French experiments with the nonfiction novel, however, the fiction that is purged from the novel is not so much a matter of invented characters and actions as a philosophical 'fiction', or fallacy, which the traditional novel encourages – namely, that the universe is susceptible of human interpretation. The purest statement of this point of view is to be found in the theoretical writings of Alain Robbe-Grillet. Essentially his argument is that traditional realism has distorted reality by imposing human meanings upon it. That is, in describing the world of things, we are not willing to admit that they are *just* things, with their own existence, indifferent to ours. We make things reassuring by attributing human meanings or 'significations' to them. In this way we create a false sense of solidarity between man and things.

In the realm of literature this solidarity is expressed mainly through the systematic search for analogies or for analogical relationships . . . Metaphor is never an innocent figure of speech . . . the choice of an analogical vocabulary, however simple, always goes beyond giving an account of purely physical data . . . setting up a constant rapport between the universe and the human being who inhabits it . . . It is the whole literary language

T.N.T. – D

that has to change . . . the visual or descriptive adjective
– the word that contents itself with measuring, locating,
limiting, defining – indicates a difficult but most likely
direction for the novel of the future.

Now, the language of analogy to which Robbe-Grillet objects
is exploited much more elaborately in non-realistic narrative (such as allegory) than in the novel, which can claim
to have honoured the world of discrete 'things' more than
any other previous form of literature, by virtue of what
Henry James called its 'solidity of specification'. But Robbe-
Grillet is right to see that the use of descriptive particularity
in realistic fiction assumes a meaningful connection between
the individual and the common phenomenal world; and
from his point of view the way in which traditional realism
conceals this connection while simultaneously exploiting it
– smuggling metaphorical significance into apparently innocent factual descriptions of furniture, dress, weather, etc. –
makes it all the more subversive.

Of Robbe-Grillet's attempt to disinfect his own narratives
of analogical implication, Scholes says in *The Fabulators*:

> This cannot solve the problem, because all language is a
> human product and thus must humanize everything it
> touches. The writer must either acknowledge this and
> accept it as one of the terms of his work or turn to a
> wordless art like cinema – as M. Robbe-Grillet has so
> brilliantly done on occasion.

With the first part of this statement I entirely agree; but it
is precisely for this reason that I cannot accept Mr Scholes's
contention (quoted earlier) that literary realism 'subordinates
words . . . to things'. Being a verbal medium it cannot do
so – it is constantly making 'things' over into 'words'. It
may indeed create the *illusion* of subordinating words to
things, and this may involve a certain restraint in exploiting
the literary resources of language. But the extreme exercise
of such restraint in Robbe-Grillet or (much more poignantly
and meaningfully) in Beckett is not the norm of realistic
fiction, which has, historically, given many great writers
quite as much freedom as they needed to develop the
expressive possibilities of their medium. It is difficult to

think of Jane Austen or George Eliot or Flaubert or Henry James as being less creative users of words because of their commitment to realism.

I am not convinced, either, that the camera is, in human hands, any more neutral than language, or that it renders literary realism redundant. It is true that Robbe-Grillet himself invokes the film to define the 'new realism' he wants to impart to the novel; and other novelists have invoked the film medium in a similar spirit. The narrator of J. D. Salinger's *Zooey* describes the story as a 'sort of prose home-movie'. The main character of Doris Lessing's *The Golden Notebook* – that anguished account of a writer's effort to fix, identify and express reality – finds herself constantly alluding to the cinema to indicate the completely truthful, mimetic quality she is seeking in her writing; and her final, most satisfactory insight into her own experience comes in the form of a hallucination in which she seems to see her life as a film which she has directed herself. There are, however, rhetorical strategies – the visual medium is invoked to reinforce a verbal communication. For this purpose the film is made to stand for a highly mimetic art. Indeed, it is; but it is a commonplace that there is a language of the film which is as much a 'human product' as verbal language. It has its own rules, conventions and possibilities of choice, which have to be learned by both artist and audience, and which make possible an infinite variety of effects, none of them entirely neutral and objective. The contemporary cinema, in fact, exhibits as wide a spectrum of styles as the contemporary novel, all the way from 'non-fiction' underground movies of the Empire State Building or people's bottoms to 'fabulations' like Stanley Kubrick's *2001*, Godard's *Weekend* or *Yellow Submarine*.

Much the same situation obtains in the contemporary theatre, where the 'well-made play' of scrupulously realistic illusion (the dramatic equivalent of the realistic novel and, in many ways, a by-product of the cultural dominance of the novel form) has been to a large extent displaced by experiments corresponding roughly to fabulation and the non-fiction novel in narrative. On the one hand we have drama that exploits the artificiality of theatrical presentation, inventing and often fantasizing freely (e.g. Brecht,

Ionesco, N. F. Simpson), and on the other the 'theatre of fact' (Hochhuth, Weiss) or efforts like those of the American Living Theatre Company, who seek to break down the formal conventions that separate audience from performers and to physically involve both in an uncontrolled and unpredictable 'happening'.

We seem, indeed, to be living through a period of unprecedented cultural pluralism which allows, in all the arts, an astonishing variety of styles to flourish simultaneously. Though they are in many cases radically opposed on aesthetic and epistemological grounds, no one style has managed to become dominant. In this situation, the critic has to be very fast on his feet. He is not, of course, obliged to like all the styles equally, but he must avoid the cardinal error of judging one style by criteria appropriate to another. He needs what Mr Scholes calls 'a highly discriminated sense of genre'. For the practising artist, however, the existence of a bewildering plurality of styles presents problems not so easily solved; and we should not be surprised that many contemporary writers manifest symptoms of extreme insecurity, nervous self-consciousness and even at times a kind of schizophrenia.

The situation of the novelist today may be compared to a man standing at a crossroads. The road on which he stands (I am thinking primarily of the English novelist) is the realistic novel, the compromise between fictional and empirical modes. In the fifties there was a strong feeling that this was the main road, the central tradition, of the English novel, coming down through the Victorians and Edwardians, temporarily diverted by modernist experimentalism, but subsequently restored (by Orwell, Isherwood, Greene, Waugh, Powell, Angus Wilson, C. P. Snow, Amis, Sillitoe, Wain, etc., etc.) to its true course. That wave of enthusiasm for the realistic novel in the fifties has, however, considerably abated. For one thing, the novelty of the social experience the fiction of that decade fed on – the break-up of a bourgeois-dominated class society – has faded. More important, the literary theorizing behind the 'Movement' was fatally thin. For example, C. P. Snow:

Looking back, we can see what an odd affair the 'experimental' novel was. To begin with, the 'experiment' stayed remarkably constant for thirty years. Miss Dorothy Richardson was a great pioneer, so were Virginia Woolf and Joyce: but between *Pointed Roofs* in 1915 and its successors, largely American, in 1945, there was no significant development. In fact there could not be; because this method, the essence of which was to represent brute experience through the moments of sensation, effectively cut out precisely those aspects of the novel where a living tradition can be handed on. Reflection had to be sacrificed; so did moral awareness; so did the investigatory intelligence. That was altogether too big a price to pay and hence the 'experimental novel' . . . died from starvation, because its intake of human stuff was so low.

Or Kingsley Amis:

The idea about experiment being the life-blood of the English novel is one that dies hard. 'Experiment', in this context, boils down pretty regularly to 'obtruded oddity', whether in construction – multiple viewpoints and such – or in style; it is not felt that adventurousness in subject matter or attitude or tone really counts. Shift from one scene to the next in mid-sentence, cut down on verbs or definite articles, and you are putting yourself right up in the forefront, at any rate in the eyes of those who were reared on Joyce and Virginia Woolf and take a jaundiced view of more recent developments.

Simply as literary history, Snow's comment does not survive the most cursory examination (no development between *A Portrait of the Artist* and *Finnegans Wake?* Between *Pointed Roofs* and *The Sound and the Fury?*). Amis's has a certain satiric force and cogency, and is aimed at a more vulnerable target, but that kind of 'cultivated Philistinism', refreshing in its time, could not be maintained indefinitely, even by Amis, let alone anyone else.

Realistic novels continue to be written – it is easy to forget that most novels published in England still fall within this category – but the pressure of scepticism on the aesthetic and epistemological premises of literary realism is now so intense that many novelists, instead of marching confidently straight ahead, are at least considering the two routes that branch off in opposite directions from the cross-roads. One of these routes leads to the non-fiction novel, and the other to what Mr Scholes calls 'fabulation'.

To fill out the latter category we may add to the examples discussed in *The Fabulators*: Günter Grass, William Burroughs, Thomas Pynchon, Leonard Cohen (*Beautiful Losers*), Susan Sontag (*Death Kit*), some of the novels of Anthony Burgess, and individual works by novelists who have remained generally faithful to realism, such as Bellow's *Henderson the Rain King*, Updike's *The Centaur*, Malamud's *The Natural*, Angus Wilson's *The Old Men at the Zoo*, and Andrew Sinclair's *Gog*. Such narratives suspend realistic illusion in some significant degree in the interests of a freedom in plotting characteristic of romance or in the interest of an explicitly allegorical manipulation of meaning, or both. They also tend to draw inspiration from certain popular forms of literature, or subliterature, in which the arousal and gratification of very basic fictional appetites (such as wonder, wish fulfilment, suspense) are only loosely controlled by the disciplines of realism: especially science fiction, pornography and the thriller.

Of these three, science fiction has the most respectable pedigree, going back to Utopian speculation, apocalyptic prophecy, and satirical fantasy like *Gulliver's Travels*, *Candide*, *Alice in Wonderland*, and *Erewhon*. It was this tradition that kept fabulation alive through the period of the realistic novel's dominance, and it continues to offer the most obvious vehicle for the novelist who wants to experiment with a more 'fictional' kind of narrative. Pornography and the thriller, being more debased forms, are approached more gingerly, but the fascination they hold for the contemporary literary imagination cannot be missed in such phenomena as the cult of James Bond (which was a highbrow cult before it was a mass cult). Kingsley Amis seems a representative figure here. His absorption with Fleming (see *The James Bond Dossier*), like his enthusiasm for science fiction (see *New Maps of Hell*), is difficult to reconcile with the stance he adopted in the fifties, both as novelist and critic, as a defender of a traditional kind of literary realism, except as a lust for fabulation, repressed by his literary 'censor', seeking outlet in certain licensed areas where traditional literary values are not expected to obtain. His publication of a James Bond novel, *Colonel Sun* (1968), under the pen-name Robert Markham, is surely a case of the realistic novelist taking a holiday from realism, finding a way to enjoy the forbidden fruit of romance without fully committing himself to the enterprise. (It is, I hope, unnecessary to labour the point that the James Bond novels are essentially romances, and that their superficial realism of presentation – the descriptive set-pieces, the brand-name dropping, the ostentatious display of technical knowledge of various kinds – does not convert the romantic stereotypes into anything individually realized, but merely gives them a gloss of contemporary sophistication and facilitates the reader's willing suspension of disbelief.) In fact *Colonel Sun* is considerably more realistic than most of the Fleming novels (Amis's Bond, for instance, survives by virtue of his wits and good luck rather than the gadgetry which, like the magical weapons of medieval romance, preserves Fleming's hero) and also duller. This is not surprising since the whole enterprise, undertaken, apparently, in a spirit of pious imitation, required Amis to keep in check his natural talent for parody and deflating comic realism. Anthony Burgess's *Tremor of Intent* (1966) is a much more entertaining highbrow contribution to the genre partly because of its parodic exaggerations of Bondian themes and motifs. This is a work of extraordinary virtuosity, in which Burgess sets himself to cap every effect exploited by Fleming and succeeds triumphantly: the sex is sexier, the violence more visceral, the high-living more extravagant, the intrigues and reversals of the plot more stunning, and the style, naturally, infinitely more vivid and evocative. Yet in its overall effect the book wobbles uncertainly between parodying Bond by extravagant exaggeration and reaching after something genuinely felt and realized. Thus at one point in the story a precocious teenage boy has to shoot a man to save the hero and is violently sick immediately after: 'He went and stood, like a naughty boy, in the corner. His shoulders heaved as he tried to throw up the modern world.' This striking image sounds a note too serious for the narrative to bear, and only serves to remind us that it is not the modern world which this character is throwing up but a grotesque comic-strip version of it.

There is, I think, a similar ambiguity of motive, an insecurity of stance, an impression that regressive or perverse fantasies are being indulged under cover of pretensions to satirical caricature or displays of stylistic virtuosity, in so-called 'parodies' or 'spoofs' of pornography, such as *Candy* (1958), or Stephen Schneck's *The Nightclerk* (1965), or Gore Vidal's *Myra Breckinridge* (1968). Of these three novels, Vidal's is easily the most complex and accomplished, parodying and commenting acutely upon not only pornography but also the non-fiction novel of the French variety:

> Nothing is *like* anything else. Things are themselves entirely and do not need interpretation, only a minimal respect for their precise integrity. The mark on the wall is two feet three inches wide and four feet eight and a fraction inches high. Already I have failed to be completely accurate. I must write 'fraction' because I can't read the little numbers on the ruler without my glasses which I never wear.

— and the kind of argument advanced by Mr Scholes, that the cinema has superseded the mimetic possibilities of literature:

> Tyler's close scrutiny of the films of the Forties makes him our age's central thinker, if only because *in the decade between 1935 and 1945 no irrelevant film was made in the United States*. During those years, the entire range of human (which is to say, American) legend was put on film, and any profound study of these extraordinary works is bound to make clear the human condition. For instance, to take an example at random, Johnny Weismuller, the zahftic Tarzan, still provides the last word on the subject of soft man's relationship to hard environment . . . that glistening overweight body set against a limestone cliff at noon says the whole thing. Auden once wrote an entire poem praising limestone, unaware that any one of a thousand frames from *Tarzan and the Amazons* had not only anticipated him but made irrelevant his efforts.

Myra Breckinridge is a brilliant, but somehow sterile and despairing work: as if Vidal, deeply contemptuous of the contemporary *avant garde* and the cultural climate, 'post-Gutenberg, pre-Apocalypse', that fosters it, has abandoned hope of positively resisting either, and cynically set himself to match their wildest excesses.

There are indeed good reasons for anticipating with something less than enthusiasm the disappearance of the novel and its replacement by the non-fiction novel or fabulation. Especially to anyone whose imagination has been nourished by the great realistic novelists of the past, both these side roads will seem to lead all too easily into desert or bog – self-defeating banality or self-indulgent excess. Yet, as I have already suggested, there are formidable discouragements to continuing serenely along the road of fictional realism. The novelist who has any kind of self-awareness must at least hesitate at the crossroads; and the solution many novelists have chosen in their dilemma is to *build their hesitation into the novel itself*. To the novel, the non-fiction novel, and the fabulation, we must add a fourth category : the novel which exploits more than one of these modes without fully committing itself to any, the novel-about-itself, the trick-novel, the game-novel, the puzzle-novel, the novel that leads the reader (who wishes, naïvely, only to be told what to believe) through a fairground of illusions and deceptions, distorting mirrors and trap-doors that open disconcertingly under his feet, leaving him ultimately not with any simple or reassuring message or meaning but with a paradox about the relation of art to life.

This kind of novel, which I shall call the 'problematic novel', clearly has affinities with both the non-fiction novel and fabulation, but it remains distinct precisely because it brings both into play. Mr Scholes's fabulators, for instance, play tricks on their readers, expose their fictive machinery, dally with aesthetic paradoxes, in order to shed the restricting conventions of realism, to give themselves freedom to invent and manipulate. In the kind of novel I am thinking of, however, the reality principle is never allowed to lapse entirely – indeed, it is often invoked, in the spirit of the non-fiction novel, to expose the artificiality of conventional realistic illusion. Whereas the fabulator is impatient with 'reality', and the non-fiction novelist is impatient with fiction, the kind of novelist I am talking about retains a loyalty to both, but lacks the orthodox novelist's confidence in the possibility of reconciling them. He makes the difficulty of his task, in a sense, his subject.

The father and mother of this kind of novel is *Tristram Shandy* – to say which is to concede that we are not dealing with a totally new phenomenon. But it is significant that, while it is difficult to think of anything (apart from feeble imitations) comparable to *Tristram Shandy* in the eighteenth and nineteenth centuries, when the realistic novel developed into maturity, it is not hard to think of parallels in modern literature. Take, for example, J. D. Salinger's Glass stories. When one puts them mentally beside *Tristram Shandy* the essential similarity of each writer's undertaking is striking: the loving, minutely circumstantial evocation and celebration of a richly eccentric family, observed mainly in domestic life, with extraordinary attention to detail of speech, mannerism and gesture, recorded by a narrator who is himself a member of the family (though with certain very pointed, teasing resemblances to the actual, historic author), who is partly dependent on the other members for his information, who addresses the reader directly in a whimsical, garrulous, digressive flow of complex reminiscence and reconstruction, commenting freely on the difficulty of his undertaking, and incorporating into the narrative an account of his personal circumstances at the time of composition. Salinger's stories, it seems to me, have been received with increasing disfavour because they have been taken too much at their face value as disingenuous gospels of a new religion, to the neglect of their literary experimentation. This feature, though less obvious than in *Tristram Shandy*, is clear enough when one reads the stories through in the order of their composition. Then, one cannot fail to notice how, as the record of the Glass family comes more and more to follow the shapelessness and randomness of actuality, as the tone of the narrator (Buddy Glass) becomes more and more personal, idiosyncratic, non-literary – as, in short, the narrator begins to appeal to our interest more and more at the level of anecdote about 'real' people, so a subtly growing amount of highly unusual, objectively improbable and in fact irrational information is conveyed. Thus, in *Raise High the Roofbeam, Carpenters*, Franny Glass is said to remember her brother Seymour (the family *guru*) reading to her when she was ten months old, and Seymour records in his diary the experience of stigmata from touching certain things. In *Seymour; an Introduction* Buddy tells us how he eased the pain of pleurisy by placing 'a perfectly innocent-looking Blake lyric in my shirt pocket', and claims that from early childhood till he was thirty he seldom read fewer than 200,000 words a day, and often 400,000. In other words, as the manner of the saga inclines more and more to that of non-fictional narrative, the matter becomes more and more 'fictive'. There is a similar tension between the bizarre obsessions and eccentricities of the Shandy family and the minutely faithful, realistically particular rendering of them by Tristram. In both cases the normal conventions of narrative fiction are exposed and undermined by the narrator himself, and the stability of the reader's stance towards the experience of the book is always threatened.

It is in fact the transference of the writer's own sense (which may be humorous or deadly serious) of the problematic nature of his undertaking – making the reader *participate* in the aesthetic and philosophical problems the writing of fiction presents, by embodying them directly in the narrative – that characterizes the 'problematic novel'. I would want to make this a large enough category to include such works as Gide's *The Counterfeiters*, Flann O'Brien's *At Swim Two-birds*, Nabokov's *Pale Fire*, Sartre's *La Nausée*, the labyrinthine fables of Jorge Luis Borges, Waugh's *The Ordeal of Gilbert Pinfold*, Amis's *I Like It Here*, Muriel Spark's *The Comforters*, and Doris Lessing's *The Golden Notebook*. No doubt the reader can think of other examples, if not of the fully developed problematic novel, at least of novels that incorporate to some degree its characteristic note of self-consciousness. As Elizabeth Hardwick has written recently:

Many good novels show a degree of panic about the form. Where to start and where to end, how much must be believed and how much a joke, a puzzle; how to combine the episodic and the carefully designed and consequential . . . the mood of the writer is to admit manipulation and design, to exploit the very act of authorship in the midst of the imagined scene.

[A passage discussing Julian Mitchell's *The Undiscovered Country* (1968) has been cut here. (Ed.)]

This brings me to my conclusion, which is a modest affirmation of faith in the future of realistic fiction. In part this is a rationalization of a personal preference. I like realistic novels, and I tend to write realistic fiction myself. The elaborate code of literary decorum that governs the composition of realistic fiction – consistency with history, solidity of specification, and so on – which to many of the writers discussed above seems inhibiting, or evasive, or redundant – is to my mind a valuable discipline and source of strength – or at least can be. Like metrical or stanzaic form in verse, which prevents the poet from saying what he wants to say in the way that comes most readily to his mind, involving him in a laborious struggle with sounds and meanings that, if he is resourceful enough, yields results superior to spontaneous expression, so the conventions of realistic fiction prevent the narrative writer from telling the first story that comes into his head – which is likely to be either autobiography or fantasy – and compel him to a kind of concentration on the possibilities of his *donnée* that may lead him to new and quite unpredictable discoveries of what he has to tell. In the novel personal experience must be explored and transmuted until it acquires an authenticity and persuasiveness independent of its actual origins; while the fictive imagination through which this exploration and transmutation is achieved is itself subject to an empirical standard of accuracy and plausibility. The problem of reconciling these two opposite imperatives is essentially rhetorical and (contrary to Mr Scholes) requires great linguistic resourcefulness and skill for its successful solution. (I am not of course denying that fabulation or autobiography or the non-fiction novel have their own internal disciplines and challenges, but merely trying to define those of the realistic novel.)

If the case for realism has any ideological content it is that of liberalism. The aesthetics of compromise go naturally with the ideology of compromise, and it is no coincidence that both are under pressure at the present time. The non-fiction novel and fabulation are *radical* forms which take their impetus from an extreme reaction to the world we live in – *The Armies of the Night* and *Giles Goat-boy* are equally products of the apocalyptic imagination. The assumption behind such experiments is that our 'reality' is so extraordinary, horrific or absurd that the methods of conventional realistic imitation are no longer adequate. There is no point in carefully creating fiction that gives an illusion of life when life itself seems illusory. (This argument, interestingly, was used by the Marquis de Sade, writing at the time of the French Revolution, to explain the Gothic novel and, by implication, his own pornographic contributions to the genre.) Art can no longer compete with life on equal terms, showing the universal in the particular. The alternatives are either to cleave to the particular – to 'tell it like it is' – or to abandon history altogether and construct pure fictions which reflect in an emotional or metaphorical way the discords of contemporary experience.

The realist – and liberal – answer to this case must be that while many aspects of contemporary experience encourage an extreme, apocalyptic response, most of us continue to live most of our lives on the assumption that the reality which realism imitates actually exists. History may be, in a philosophical sense, a fiction, but it does not feel like that when we miss a train or somebody starts a war. We are conscious of ourselves as unique, historic individuals, living together in societies by virtue of certain common assumptions and methods of communication; we are conscious that our sense of identity, of happiness and unhappiness, is defined by small things as well as large; we seek to adjust our lives, individually and communally, to some order or system of values which, however, we know is always at the mercy of chance and contingency. It is this sense of reality which realism imitates; and it seems likely that the latter will survive as long as the former.

Writing in 1939, at the beginning of the Second World War, George Orwell voiced many of the doubts about the future of the novel reviewed in this essay. The novel, he said in 'Inside the Whale', was inextricably tied up with liberal individualism and could not survive the era of totalitarian dictatorships he saw ahead. In his appreciation of Henry Miller's *Tropic of Cancer* he seems to endorse the confessional non-fiction novel as the only viable alternative ('Get inside the whale . . . Give yourself over to the world process, stop fighting against it or pretending you control it, simply accept it, endure it, record it. That seems to be the formula that any sensitive novelist is likely to adopt.')

Orwell's prophecy was, however, incorrect. Shortly after the War there was a significant revival of the realistic novel in England, inspired partly by Orwell's own fiction of the thirties; and although none of this fiction is of the very first rank, it is not an inconsiderable body of work. Many of the most talented post-war American novelists – John Updike, Saul Bellow, Bernard Malamud and Philip Roth, for example – have worked, for the most part, within the conventions of realistic fiction. Obsequies over the novel may be as premature today as they were in 1939.

FRANK KERMODE

The House of Fiction
Interviews with Seven Novelists

(reprinted with permission from *Partisan Review*,
Vol. xxx, no. 1, Spring 1963)

These conversations are abridged from longer talks; they
were entirely free and unprepared. In cutting them I have
naturally preferred to leave out whatever seemed most
remote from the centre represented by the title. If this
seems a somewhat abstract topic, I can only say that it
proved reasonably easy to keep the mind of the contributors
fixed upon it. Clearly it is a relationship that they all think
about in a more or less abstract way, as well as handling it
daily in terms of technique.

I planned to ask each of the novelists about this abstract
issue, and then to get them on to the subject of their own
books. Sometimes this method didn't work, and the two
questions got involved with each other, beneficially I think.
Though there were no striking divergencies of opinion, there
were considerable and interesting differences of emphasis.
But if I had to decide what this selection of good living
English novelists had most obviously in common I should
say it was a kind of modesty. Not only do they emphasize
their own limitations; for the most part they're happy to
ignore all the larger claims that can be made for their craft.
Obviously none of them subscribes to apocalyptic views
such as Lawrence's: 'Being a novelist, I consider myself
superior to the saint, the scientist, the philosopher and the
poet. The novel is the one bright book of life.' There is
probably no living English novelist who even wants to
believe that. Again, though none of them would accept the
old criterion of naturalism unrevised, none on the other
hand throws it out with the arrogance of Gide: 'Please
understand, I should like to put everything into my novel.'
The old realism will not do, nor the old formalism, for none
of these writers sees himself as making a universe. Each
looks out, as if from one of the windows of James's house

of fiction – 'a number of possible windows not to be reckoned,' as he said – and senses not merely that reality has the limited shape of his window, but also that he has a deep obligation to things as they are – or a not too extraordinary view of them.

For this modesty has a philosophical aspect, too. You might expect that English writers would partake of the national character, at any rate to the extent of dodging discussion of the metaphysics of their form. In fact they were all willing to talk about such matters. But they did so in a peculiarly modest way. Just as they avoid the idea of the novel as an image of all reality, so they don't seem to think of their imaginative powers as a component of or even as a complement to reality. Indeed their concern with this problem seems on the whole strongly ethical rather than epistemological, as we see for instance in Mrs Spark's discriminations between truth and absolute truth, between one kind of lie and another which you render harmless by calling it a story. Not for the English novelists the sophisticated epistemology of the new French writers (of whom few of our subjects were willing, by the way, to speak). Not for them the banner of the antinovel. A French author – M. Butor for instance – might have said that a novel contributes substantially to reality and that a new writer's task might always be seen to be the correction of obsolete versions of reality imposed by earlier novels (hence any good novel is an antinovel). But for the most part our authors see the whole problem of the relation between fiction and reality in terms of their own struggle to be faithful to themselves as perceivers and to fact, as perceived by the eye of informed commonsense. Some of them have performed extraordinary feats of construction – I think here especially of Mr Greene – yet it will be observed that the names of Conrad and Ford Madox Ford are not so much as mentioned. There already exist learned articles with such titles as 'The Epistemology of the Good Soldier', and there is no reason why someone should not write similarly about *The End of the Affair*; but for Mr Greene this is an inconceivable activity, and though what he says about himself has strong roots in Turgeniev and James, he thinks of the problem as largely his own, and in the first place technical rather than as a matter for philosophic enquiry.

I

It seemed to me that a recent article by Miss Iris Murdoch expressed most of the issues we wanted discussed in a clear, usable way. Most of the contributors did in fact find her terminology convenient, so we began with what she said about it. The antithesis of 'crystalline' and 'journalistic', plot and myth, will in fact echo through the conversations.

I first asked Miss Murdoch to enlarge on one of her points, this distinction between 'crystalline' and 'journalistic' modes:

MURDOCH: It's one of these epigrammatic distinctions which are probably themselves rather inexact. This distinction was suggested to me in a way by worrying about my own work and about what was wrong with it. There is a tendency, I think, on the one hand, and especially now, to produce a closely-coiled, carefully-constructed object wherein the story rather than the people is the important thing, and wherein the story perhaps suggests a particular, fairly clear moral. On the other hand, there is and always has been in fiction a desire to describe the world around one in a fairly loose and cheerful way. And it seemed to me at present in the novel that there was a flying apart of these two different aims. Some ideal state of affairs would combine the merits of both.

KERMODE: You spoke of the consolation of form in your article as being a deceptive presentation of reality. Is this a certain kind of form? It doesn't apply to the sort which combines crystalline and journalistic, but only to the crystalline sort?

MURDOCH: This is a delicate question. It's absurd to say that form in art is in any sense a menace, because form is the absolute essence of art. But there can be a tendency too readily to pull a form or a structure out of something one's thinking about and to rest upon that. The satisfaction of the form is such that it can stop one from going more deeply into the contradictions or paradoxes or more painful aspects of the subject matter.

KERMODE: You didn't want myth to the degree that it interferes with the representation of character in a rather old-fashioned sense?

MURDOCH: Yes, this is perhaps my main thought in that article you referred to. I think that it would be coming back to character in the old-fashioned sense which would save one from being too readily consoled.

KERMODE: You also say that writers write what they can and not what they should. May I ask you whether in work that you perhaps have in hand there's any attempt to carry out this programme?

MURDOCH: I always attempt to carry it out but I find it very difficult to do so.

KERMODE: Because of the strength of the myth?

MURDOCH: This sounds pretentious, as if one were thinking of one's work in a rather grandiose way, but yes, I suppose it is. Another way of putting it would be just that one isn't good enough at creating character. One starts off – at least I start off – hoping every time that this is going to happen and that a lot of people who are not me are going to come into existence in some wonderful way. Yet often it turns out in the end that something about the structure of the work itself, the myth as it were of the work, has drawn all these people into a sort of spiral, or into a kind of form which ultimately is the form of one's own mind.

KERMODE: Yes. And in so far as they are absorbed into that, they lose identity.

MURDOCH: I think this tends to happen.

KERMODE: So that the myth is a sort of safety net under the tightrope?

MURDOCH: Well, yes, if you put it so, it's a form of safety. I don't take a low view of it. I think it can be important and beautiful; but I think it comes more easily to writers now than the other thing.

KERMODE: Yes. And although myth is in itself, as you say, a high matter, if it is ultimately something that distorts reality, then it is the enemy, however dignified, of the kind of novel that you feel ought to be written.

MURDOCH: Well, not altogether the enemy. It should be present also. It's perhaps the thing which at the moment one should guard against giving in to.

KERMODE: One of the more sensible definitions of myth in this connection would be one which allowed it to look after itself, wouldn't it?

MURDOCH: Yes.

KERMODE: May I now bring the discussion a little closer to

your own books? Would you feel free to say that in your books since *Under the Net* there has been any movement towards the kind of fiction that you say ought to be written?

MURDOCH: It's very hard to say. Leaving aside the question of whether they're better or worse or anything – well, I don't know that you can leave this question aside quite, but trying to leave it aside – I think they oscillate rather between attempts to portray a lot of people and giving in to a powerful plot or story. I think the last one, *A Severed Head*, probably represents a giving in to the myth; and the previous one, *The Bell*, has more people in it; and the one I've just written now I think again has more people in it. But it's always rather a problem. Given that one hasn't achieved the kind of synthesis which I think is desirable and which would make one's stuff of some use, there is a tendency to oscillate between achieving a kind of intensity through having a very powerful story and sacrificing character, and having the characters and losing the intensity.

KERMODE: It might seem, perhaps, using myth in too crude a sense, that there was more of it, or that it was more openly to be met with in *The Bell* and *The Severed Head* than in *Under the Net*, for example.

MURDOCH: *Under the Net* has in fact got its own myth, but I think it probably just hasn't emerged very clearly in the story.

KERMODE: It's a philosopher's novel?

MURDOCH: In a very simple sense. It plays with a philosophical idea. The problem which is mentioned in the title is the problem of how far conceptualizing and theorizing, which from one point of view are absolutely essential, in fact, divide you from the thing that is the object of theoretical attention. And Hugo is a sort of non-philosophical metaphysician who is supposed to be paralysed in a way by this problem.

KERMODE: And you set this novel quite deliberately in places which are given a good deal of actuality, in London and Paris, for example, as I remember it rendered in some detail.

MURDOCH: That was just self-indulgence. It hadn't any particular significance.

KERMODE: The technical excursions which we all like so much in your novels, how a car turns over, or how you get a bell out of a lake and so on, are they also self-indulgence under this very strict definition?

MURDOCH: Yes. That is just a kind of fascination with completely theoretical amateur mechanics.

KERMODE: Well, someone will come along and call them a myth all the same.

MURDOCH: Of course, the bell itself has significance, and is quite explicitly used as a symbol by the characters. But I think the majority of my 'technical excursions' are pure play.

II

Miss Murdoch, then, finds it clear that the trouble nowadays lies in an over-willingness to depend upon 'myth', and that this premature dependence is falsely consoling; that it takes the bitter flavour out of reality, reduces the identity of characters, and, morally speaking, is a self-indulgence on the part of the writer. Graham Greene uses the term 'myth' differently, and accordingly sees the whole problem in another light. In fact he almost echoes Turgeniev, who said, 'I would, I think, rather have too little architecture than too much – when there's a danger of its interfering with my measure of the truth.'

KERMODE: Mr Greene, in the book in which you describe the genesis of your last novel, *The Burnt Out Case*, you make this remark: 'Am I beginning to plot, to succumb to that abiding temptation to tell a good story?' I'd like to ask you, if I may, in what sense the abiding temptation to tell a good story is to be regarded as inimical, as it presumably is, to the production of a good novel?

GREENE: I'm not sure that one can generalize on that; I feel it's inimical to *my* producing a good novel. My own wish always is to produce a central figure who represents some idea of reasonable simplicity – a mythical figure if you like. And the simplicity often gets damaged by plot making. For instance, if I can just illustrate a point from a book I don't like much called *The Heart of the Matter*, there one wanted to draw a fairly simple portrait of a man who was corrupted by his sense of pity. But in the course of that book, perhaps because one was rusty, not having written for some years during the war, one began to over-load the plot, and I felt the effect of the character was whittled away.

KERMODE: This is a curious comment on the terms plot and myth, because we have had Iris Murdoch telling us that she regarded myth as the great temptation to self-indulgence, when what one ought to be concerned with was the texture of reality. And you are really saying something which is not quite the opposite, but quite close to the opposite, aren't you?

GREENE: Yes, very nearly the opposite.

KERMODE: And it's interesting in that connection that Miss Murdoch's stories do, as she would put it herself, descend into myth-making from time to time, whereas you are a plot-builder, are you not?

GREENE: And I would like to ascend into myth, but find my boots so often muddy with plot. My own feeling is that the nearest I came to hitting the mythical element was in *The Power and the Glory*, where I feel the plot was sufficiently simple for the main purpose of this story to remain clear throughout.

KERMODE: May I mention a novel of yours, which I especially admire, and which I dare say would incur your own criticism that it's too heavily plotted in a slightly different way? That's *The End of the Affair*. What do you feel about that?

GREENE: I like a lot of the book, but I made an appalling mistake, I think, in the last third of the book, which has always spoilt – though I don't read my books – any retrospective enjoyment I might have.

KERMODE: It would be very interesting to know what you thought that mistake was.

GREENE: The introduction of something which had not got a natural explanation. I had intended a much longer last part of the book after the woman had died, where there was to be a succession of coincidences, until the lover became maddened by the coincidences which would not cease. I found it very difficult to continue the book with the loss of the principal figure, and I foreshortened badly by introducing something which was not easily accountable for in natural terms.

KERMODE: This encourages me to believe that I am right in

my own view of the book, which is that it is in a way
a novel about plot-making, isn't it – not only about a
novelist making a plot, but about God making a plot?

GREENE: Yes.

KERMODE: And if you had put in these additional coincidences, you would have strengthened that element?

GREENE: Yes.

KERMODE: Of course, I think in *The End of the Affair* God
the novelist is quite a strong figure in the myth, as it
were.

GREENE: Yes.

KERMODE: In *A Burnt Out Case*, for example, you didn't
feel that your plot had that kind of function as a kind
of mirror image of providence?

GREENE: No.

KERMODE: So this is a different case, in that the element of
plot in it tends to be destructive rather than to augment
the myth?

GREENE: Yes, in a curious way it was more simple plotting,
wasn't it, than, say, *The Heart of the Matter* – less details,
less events, less action. And yet what little action there
was seemed to take too strong a part. Perhaps it would
have seemed less plotted if there had been more plot.

KERMODE: I had intended to ask you whether you feel that
there is a point beyond which you can't dispense with
plot. I mean there obviously is such a point, but where
does this point lie? On what you said at the beginning
of our conversation, it would seem that the less plot a
novel had, the better it was likely to be, broadly speaking.

GREENE: Yes, in a way I agree – but that's my feeling often
when I'm trying to write a novel which conflicts with
passionate liking for melodrama. And a reaction, when
I was a young man, I suppose a reaction from the books
of Virginia Woolf, where narrative was very subordinated
to mood. And I still have a liking for action in the novel.

KERMODE: But on the whole you think that the representation of reality, of the real truth about the world, in a
novel is primarily the burden of what we have agreed to
call myth?

GREENE: Yes.

KERMODE: And that plot on the whole is in opposition, at
any rate, has to be controlled.

GREENE: Yes, it must be controlled. Because after all in *Tom Jones* there is a tremendous amount of plot, but it's subordinated the whole time to the main character, isn't it?

KERMODE: I suppose it's a good case of a novel in which you have a strong myth of a rather ethical cast, and also an extremely complex plot, well timed, and thoroughly worked out and so on.

GREENE: Yes.

KERMODE: Without any sense that the things collide; in fact when they do seem to collide, as in the case of Sophia's muff on the bed, for example, they have a very strong ethical flavour.

GREENE: Yes.

KERMODE: And this is the direction in which you would like to . . .

GREENE: I would like to be able to write.

KERMODE: So in fact there is no real argument against having very complex plots?

GREENE: No, as long as it does not damage the mythical centre.

III

Mr Greene is very actively torn between his ethical myth, a matter largely of character, of 'showing my people', as Turgeniev said; but unlike Turgeniev, who was short on 'story', he regards plot as his self-indulgence, much as myth is Miss Murdoch's. When I asked Angus Wilson about the relation between myth and the significant rendering of 'real life', he said this:

WILSON: That is an essential problem for me. It seems to me that all the novelists that I value have projected a real world which is nevertheless entirely their own vision. How far this will coincide with a myth which they may also discover in life I'm not quite so sure. One shouldn't be too careful about bringing this myth out, because I think it will come through, so long as you are absolutely true to your own vision of life. Of course you must shore yourself up with little bits of facts about real life. The myth element has grown stronger with me as I've written. It was there very strongly in *Hemlock* but I didn't try to bring it out, although the title after all does so. It was there in *Anglo-Saxon Attitudes*, and now I have really tried to deal with the myth in a very much more allegorical way in my last novel.

KERMODE: So on the whole, apart from the last novel, you would say that the deliberate distortion of reality is not one of your aims?

WILSON: No. I'm immensely interested, as you know from my novels, in the shaping of the total novel, but not to reduce life to some sort of formal pattern. I think what I want to do is quite other. It is to amass various reactions to life, strong reactions, to amass various distortions and caricatures, scenes, pictures, and to bombard my readers with these things, having previously, I hope, put them into as strict a formal pattern in the sense of a designed novel as I possibly can. That is why I think people are mistaken when they ask what my novel is telling them. I don't believe, as Snow does, for example, in the didactic novel.

KERMODE: I sometimes have felt, although I wouldn't argue very strongly for this in your novels, that there is a degree of reality, of actuality in the representation of certain kinds of society which diminishes as one moves down the social scale.

WILSON: I think that might be true. The only plea for myself I would put in there is that even though this may be the case, it seems to me that I have a wider range than most novelists writing now. I do want to say something about the total society, and I can't refuse to do that simply because I'm not quite sure whether in working-class homes today you still find those ladies with borzois on the ends of leads. I could go and find this out, probably, but that is not the way I would set about it. I would take a chance on it.

KERMODE: I don't think anybody would think that mattered, provided that the persons involved didn't seem to lose a certain degree of moral reality, if I can use that phrase. But on this question of middle-class, or, as I suspect many people would want to call them, upper middle-class characters in your books, there is a general idea, which one can understand, I think, that all Wilson's characters turn out nasty.

WILSON: I would have said that not all but a good number

of the characters in my books are highly self-conscious. I'm interested in very self-conscious, self-aware people, and on the whole, like Miss Compton-Burnett's characters, they make their own judgement about themselves, almost before I can do so. But it's true that I do make some. Meg Eliot was for me a very heroic character and, if you like, she was a bit drawn from myself, much more so than any other character I've written about. She was the one who could face collapse most easily, but on the other hand she had this same kind of capacity for almost being stultified, as her brother even more so, by self-observation. I regard this as a disease, but a necessary disease, of civilized people. I agree that my characters may not often be entirely virtuous, or even entirely likeable, but they don't try to make themselves into God very much, or if they do, they are very much aware of it.

KERMODE: Yes, well this is a very George Eliot-like way to write books. (Laughter) I don't know if this strengthens the link between you and Mrs Eliot at all.

WILSON: Well, I really don't know why one shouldn't try to write like George Eliot but I –

KERMODE: Not at all – except that when she wants characters to be nasty, even in a complicated way like Rosamund Vincey, she is nasty in a way recognizable by a great many people.

WILSON: Yes, yes.

KERMODE: Your notion of reality is more alien, perhaps, to that of many people than George Eliot's was.

WILSON: I suppose it is. I think that I'm a kinder person really than George Eliot: that is to say that my nasty characters get through better, but perhaps my good characters don't get through so well. I reduce people to a greyer level than she does probably.

KERMODE: You would say that the difference is really a kind of difference in reality rather than difference in your approach, that you have the same kind of approach to fiction, but what you are talking about is a different thing now.

WILSON: Well, I don't know that I would have the right to say that. I would say that there is a great deal of what you call the George Eliot approach. But above all that, and mixed with it, and perhaps swirling it round and distorting it and so on, is a great lump of a kind of Dickensianism, and this is the thing which distinguishes me from that sort of George Eliot writing: that I have got this – how can I say it? – this grand guignol side. I am sure that I have in my character strong sadistic impulses which do come out in my books, and I try to choke that down when I see it in the books, but nevertheless that again is difficult because the modern world is a world in which sadistic impulses have run very rife. Therefore how am I to know whether they are mine, or those of the world in which I live?

IV

At the start of Mr Wilson's remarks we have the already familiar notion, that myths should be left to look after themselves; of course, the difficulty of this in our time is obvious. And he ends by suggesting that his own myth or fantasy may overthrow the whole antithesis on which I was basing the questions by representing not only a 'sadistic impulse' in himself, but a pattern in contemporary reality: this amounts to a theory which it would be difficult to defend in so far as it would make universally valid, for instance, a schizophrenic's account of the world; but of course Mr Wilson is also strongly and self-consciously concerned with the technical and moral problems of justly representing the facts.

It is a good notion, therefore, to turn now to a novelist whose myth might, at first blush, seem to flourish in rarefied isolation from the facts of contemporary existence, indeed its habits of speech and living. Miss Compton-Burnett, however, questions this: of all our contributors she is the most empirically minded; of course there has to be form, of course form doesn't distort reality. Neither does her dialogue.

COMPTON-BURNETT: A novel must have a form and has to be adapted in that way. I don't think that there is any way out of that.

KERMODE: I gather then that you would say that the mere act of devising a plot involves a degree of distortion of reality.

COMPTON-BURNETT: No, not distortion, but I think that it makes a frame to put reality in. I think the reality and the plot have to be adapted a little to each other, not distorted, I think. I don't see why it should.

KERMODE: Well, may I just take another aspect of your work which obviously comes to people's minds when they are thinking about this question, namely the nature of your dialogue, and the relative uniformity of dialect, shall we say. Among people of all classes, parents, children and so on.

COMPTON-BURNETT: It never seems to me that they talk alike, that the servants talk like the children, or that the children or the servants talk like the other people. Some people think they do, and some people think they don't. And I of course think they don't.

KERMODE: Well, I would say as a reader of your novels that they clearly are not talking exactly alike, but that they are all talking the same language.

COMPTON-BURNETT: We all do that, don't we?

KERMODE: Er – yes. Let me return to the word dialect then. They are all talking the same upper-class dialect.

COMPTON-BURNETT: I shouldn't have thought they did. You see, the servants echoed the other people. But I think – I think their talk has, or should have, quite a different – quite a different tone, you know. But of course if people miss it, it may be my fault. Some people miss it, and some people don't. Miss it is perhaps my own word, you see.

KERMODE: Yes, in other words you would explain the similarity – as it falsely appears to me to be . . .

COMPTON-BURNETT: Yes, you put it rather unkindly from your point of view.

KERMODE: Well, let's be unkind to me. The similarity is really a symptom of a sociological situation.

COMPTON-BURNETT: Yes, I think it is, and I should have thought that the children talk quite differently. But children, you know, do really talk rather formally if you listen to them. Colloquialism comes later. It is what people pick up.

KERMODE: May I ask one thing again, with an attempt to save my position, and establish a certain degree of conventionality about the dialect that your people speak. I notice in a good many of your novels a tendency to use what in a play would be called an 'aside', and not to observe the dramatic convention that the aside is never overheard; asides are always overheard in your dialogues.

COMPTON-BURNETT: Yes, I think they are. I put them in to have them overheard. I don't see how you can help it if you write a book that's – in my case – something rather between a novel and a play.

KERMODE: In one of your recent books, one of the characters says: 'None of it is fit to be uttered aloud.' Do you remember that remark? Do you think that that is true of most of your conversation?

COMPTON-BURNETT: Well – not most of it – some of it, I dare say. But I think if you write in dialogue, things must be uttered aloud, otherwise there is no book.

KERMODE: Now, just as you limit the text of your novel to dialogue largely, so you limit the scene of it, as everyone knows, to a particular kind of house, to a particular kind of family, at a time which most people would regard as being about sixty years ago, I suppose.

COMPTON-BURNETT: Yes. Well, I think that when that kind of time comes to an end, you know the time, you understand the time and know the life. But I think there is a lot of that life still left, you know – perhaps more in the country than in London – and I think that people will gradually join it, you know. I think that there is an ambition in a great many people to join that sort of life, and I think human relationships – although they may be more easy to depict and portray in a more or less narrow scene – I think in narrow scenes, in broad scenes, in any scenes, they must be the same.

KERMODE: You regard this kind of family history as archetypal?

COMPTON-BURNETT: No, I don't think I do. I think it must get modified as the years go by. But I think history will repeat itself – and it is beginning to repeat itself a little, and has never really stopped going on in the same way.

KERMODE: You're speaking now of the social conditions, and I'm speaking more of the relationship between parents and children.

COMPTON-BURNETT: I'm speaking of both.

KERMODE: But if one takes that pattern, it's interesting, for example, that the kind of society that you describe would possibly be rather similar to the kind of family life upon which Freud based his observations, so that there is this sense . . .

COMPTON-BURNETT: I think family life will always have its own essence you know. *If* people have family life. They tell me – of course, I don't know if it is true – that some parents leave their children entirely to the state, and there isn't so much family life; but of course I shouldn't meet those people, you see. I think really family life goes on.

KERMODE: Oh, yes. Some of the incidents that occur in the families in your novels aren't of the sort that occur in ordinary families perhaps.

COMPTON-BURNETT: They might occur – I think they did occur more than people know.

KERMODE: So that you would want to say, would you, that for example in the book *A Heritage and its History*, the seduction of the old man's wife by his son, and the consequent embroilment in another generation, that is the kind of thing that you would regard as a not too improbable aspect of family . . . ?

COMPTON-BURNETT: I think it might happen.

KERMODE: What we see is the normal tension that exists in families, in a very pure state.

COMPTON-BURNETT: Yes – er – yes, in a way. Perhaps it is rather keyed up, and a plot has to be imposed if you like because a book must have a form, you see.

KERMODE: Of course, and the similarity between your plots and certain ancient plots which has sometimes been pointed out is because families are always alike.

COMPTON-BURNETT: I think so. But it is true that I was classically educated, and it is possible that I was influenced without knowing it. It isn't conscious. It is true that I read Greek plays when I was young.

KERMODE: So, on the whole, you wouldn't want to say, as some novelists do, that there is an element of myth construction in your plots?

COMPTON-BURNETT: No, I don't think I should.

V

If life isn't like her novels, Miss Compton-Burnett suggests, it was and it will be again and she cannot be bothered to discuss the conventions which distinguish her manner, since to imagine them away is to imagine away the books. Similarly, she will have no nonsense about myth. Yet her characters themselves have been known to pause and consider how absurd it is for them to have got into such primitive situations; and the truth as one sees it in her books seems to be that Miss Compton-Burnett is endlessly aware of the remarkable artifice of her plots and the implications, moral and aesthetic, of her procedures.

For another view of the myth-fact relation we turn to C. P. Snow, who alone of all the contributors does in a sense write the antinovel, in that he is continuously in reaction from the formalist myth-makers of the twenties and thirties. He starts by trying out Miss Murdoch's terms 'journalistic' and 'crystalline' on Tolstoy.

SNOW: Now Tolstoy, for instance, if he comes into either of these categories, certainly must come into the journalistic. That makes me suspicious of the entire dichotomy.

KERMODE: Yes. Miss Murdoch doesn't indeed want novels to be either of these things. She is just as opposed to the crystalline, as I understand her, as she is to the other kind.

SNOW: Yes. Then absence of formal restriction is a thing I find slightly bewildering. You can't invent mystery, it seems to me.

KERMODE: Now, Sir Charles, if this distinction were workable, I suppose we should want to place your novels a little nearer, allowing for the pejorative sound of the word, to the journalistic rather than the crystalline. Would this be fair?

SNOW: Oh, certainly.

KERMODE: Does this mean that you have some kind of mistrust of formal patterning and the suggestions of myth and so on in novels?

SNOW: I'll have to distinguish between those two. I have no objection to formal patterning, and indeed I think it can give great strength to a novel, and a great many novels which would come under the journalistic side of this division would have deep formal patterning. Myth I'm much more suspicious of – unless it comes quite naturally and innately. I don't believe you can put in the myths any more than you can put in the symbols.

KERMODE: On the whole you would certainly at any rate reject the idea of a discontinuity between the real world

—in the terms which we are using in this discussion—
and the reality of the novel. They must be continuous?

SNOW: Yes, yes, quite certainly. Here of course we are
begging terms in using the word 'real' like that, but I
think we both know what we mean.

KERMODE: May we pass on to the idea of novels considered
as social history — novels as related very closely and
continuously to fact. Would you say that your novels
have some kind of meaning in these terms?

SNOW: I should think they have some meaning. That is, I
believe that persons live in their time, and they are tagged
down by their time, and if you try to loosen their feet
from that particular earth, then you get them wrong.
But a novel is never really social history in the exact
sense. Even the novels which seem deeply documentary,
like Balzac's, really are much farther away from real
social history than many of us think, and I believe that's
also true of mine.

KERMODE: To what degree would you say that your being
a scientist has conditioned the view of reality that you
propose in your books?

SNOW: Quite a bit. How much, it is harder for me to say
than it would be for you. But certainly part of my training would make me suspicious of a lot of the categories
which certain writers think in, and also would give me,
I think, a rather simpler view of the kind of truth which
I should like to aim at.

I believe there are certain things you can say about
people in their society which are—slightly begging the
terms but not too much—which are objectively true. That
is, people are like that in those places at that time. Their
temperaments are like that, and their reaction on their
environment, and their environment's reaction on them,
can be with some kind of accuracy stated. Now I believe
a realistic novelist ought to do that, often does do it.
And that seems to me not grossly dissimilar from the
scientific process, or a part of the scientific process. At
least, the spirit behind it is not grossly different.

KERMODE: So that the degree to which you impose, have to
impose, formal patterns on reality when you make fiction
of any sort, does not seem to you to distort that reality,
any more than a scientific experiment would do?

SNOW: To an extent more, but not grossly more. I mean the sort of formal patterns of narrative which are very important in a novel, to an extent, of course, are slightly neater than anything you get in a slice of documentary life, but I don't think it need affect the particular persons, or even the particular scenes, which are really the bread and butter and the heart of the novel.

KERMODE: So that one can't draw any analogy between what you do as a novelist and the degree of distortion that I believe is involved in some kinds of physical experiment. It is the different kind of change that the mind induces in the facts.

SNOW: Yes, I think that is actually a very deep question, because the degree of abstraction, of course, at which physical experiments have to be thought of and constructed is so very far away from the immediate world of reality that the same conditions don't apply. But I think a certain amount of the same spirit can and probably does apply. I would have thought what Tolstoy was trying to do in *War and Peace*, and to an extent what George Eliot tried to do in *Middlemarch*, is very deeply near the spirit of certain scientific processes. Tolstoy wanted to tell a lot of truths, and none of them imagined truths, and none of them things which he was drawing from myth, or drawing from a particular shaping of his own interior experience. He wanted to say that this and this happened, this person behaved so; how they were moved by the mysterious forces of history was deeply occupying him. But this was all going to be expressed, or this was at least the intention, in terms of particular persons in particular situations. And this seemed to me to have the degree of objectivity which you don't get in, say, physical science, I think, so much as, say, in the more observational sciences, like some parts of biology.

KERMODE: I gather from what you say that you don't feel with, say, the new novelists in France that the novel itself has imposed a kind of conventionalized reality upon us, and that this has become evidently obsolete and a new way of looking is required.

SNOW: Well, you know as well as I do, this was being said with the utmost vigour about 1917, by our Bloomsbury forebears. It was exactly the same doctrine which was propounded by Dorothy Richardson, by Virginia Woolf and what not, and it made the novel totally meaningless in a very short time. And some of my colleagues and I have to spend quite a lot of time – unnecessary time – getting rid of that particular legacy and finding a different way of doing things. And I think that in fact it's a curious example of French provincialism that they should think that this is new.

VI

Sir Charles, of course, robustly opposes the notion that there is anything special about the problem of reality in novels, and even the notion that the novel to any serious extent translates fact into its own conventional notations. His own books, most people would say, have their myth or mystique; but he believes that this is to be inferred from an honest account of people behaving, rather than 'put in' by the author. This 'neo-realist' view evidently exercises a powerful appeal at the moment. A much younger writer, with a strong interest in Arnold Bennett, is John Wain; and he certainly does not believe that myth has a free hand with reality; indeed, reality is for him something you stand firmly outside of, that you select from.

WAIN: I don't believe that there is one fixed reality. I think that there is the huge flux of raw experience, experiences of every kind – personal experience, political experience, philosophical, physical, emotional experience. It is all there as a raw welter. All you can do is to select the bit you feel you can handle at the moment, and devise some means of handling it, and make a complete start. So many writers, even quite good ones, write the same book over and over again. And the great danger is that if they keep on doing it year after year, they will begin to feel that the kind of reality they are presenting is something genuinely fixed. I don't really believe it is fixed.

KERMODE: Now, you write other kinds of books besides novels. But just because you think the novel imposes a certain fixed view, fixed within very wide limits of reality, and that this doesn't always please you, you want to do other things?

WAIN: There are certain kinds of experience, and certain

T.N.T. – E

kinds of perception, which are very well suited to be handled with certain kinds of form. For instance, Virginia Woolf's criticism of Arnold Bennett resolved itself into the point that the realistic novel will take care of certain kinds of experience, and other kinds simply can't be caught in that particular scoop, and she wanted to propose another kind of scoop, which I don't think is a valid point at all. The only thing is a complete freedom of attitude, where you are ready to pick up any form once you've taken the trouble to train yourself in any form, whether it be the realistic novel, the romantic or surrealist novel, the play, the ballet, the circus – I don't care what it is as long as you are ready to pick up the form that will take the piece of reality that you have in mind.

KERMODE : Now, may we talk for a moment or two about your novels? A lot of the other people have suggested that there's something they tend to call myth, which is a kind of pattern that their own mind imposes, and which occasionally falsifies the truth, as they sometimes see afterwards. Do you feel that in your novels you've ever indulged yourself in myth in this way, and have you found it a problem?

WAIN : Not all my novels come equally close to being more or less readable and successful, and in one particular case, which is a very bad book, I did impose a certain interpretation upon the events I was going to write about before I wrote about it, and my perception of the way characters actually work and exist, and the way things really work out, was tied from the beginning to an intellectual concept.

KERMODE : What about the odd exception, or apparent exception, as in William Golding, for example, where a series of events clearly suggests a myth, and a myth suggests a series of events which don't in their extent go very much beyond the scope of that myth – at least that would seem to be the way he works?

WAIN : William Golding, a writer I admire enormously, is not a novelist as far as I can see. He is an allegorist. He has certain perceptions about the human condition which he, I should imagine at a guess, goes ahead and creates an allegory to represent.

KERMODE: But you were saying how loose the novel and how undefined a thing it is; is there no reason why this kind shouldn't be included presumably as well as the kind you've been describing?

WAIN: You go a long way before you reach a frontier in the novel, but you do finally reach one; and at the point where you ultimately come up against a frontier, Mr Golding's work is still beyond it, I think.

KERMODE: And what about the frontier on the other side – the frontier where Arnold Bennett is on the novel side of it? What would you place on the far side of it?

WAIN: The newspaper.

KERMODE: Ah, but something that's as near to being a novel, as William Golding's books are?

WAIN: No, because the realistic novel as understood by French writers who invented it, and by writers like Bennett who took it over, is in fact right on the very edge of the newspaper report. It's simply the newspaper report which did not actually take place and which is done at enormous length and with complete fullness of detail.

KERMODE: Finally, holding the views that you've expressed as I understand them, it is not one of your problems to worry about whether you are distorting reality by the mere act of imposing a form upon it?

WAIN: Distorting it, no. Scooping it out with a specially shaped scoop, yes. I feel like a mouse biting into some gigantic cheese. There is the cheese – mile upon mile of it – at least as big in relation to me as Mount Everest is physically, and I am doing all right if I can take a piece of this cheese and shape it into anything; because the whole object of writing is to tell the truth and if you can tell any portion of the truth, and continue to make it truthful, although you are putting it into literary form, then goodness me, that is enough.

VII

The mouse and the cheese is a homely allegory of fiction-writing on the borders of fact, as far as possible from the crystalline or mythic pole. Our last contributor, though, upsets these categories by saying, very reasonably, that myth *is* plot, myth is what you make up about reality.

What seems to concern Muriel Spark more than the myth-fact antithesis is a much purer and much more ancient issue, which lies behind all these conversations, and is, simply, are novelists liars? If not, what kind of truth are they telling?

SPARK: To me the plot is the basic myth. I don't know much about myths, you see. If I think of a plot, I take it for granted that that's a myth. I don't bother about myths apart from that, but I hope that a plot's got something universal in it.

KERMODE: May I bring into the conversation a particular book of yours, *The Comforters*, because here we have something which is very handy to the whole discussion, including what other people have said. This is a book in which you've got your myth, but you've deliberately made it in a sense a game about novels, haven't you? There you are – the novelist herself is mixed up in the story, keeps on breaking in. Is this because you've got a kind of interest in the form of fiction, which some people rather morally think extrudes reality from the whole thing? It becomes a game instead of a transcript?

SPARK: No, I don't think so. It really depends on the fact that this book *The Comforters* was my first novel. I was asked to write a novel, and I didn't think much of novels – I thought it was an inferior way of writing. So I wrote a novel to work out the technique first, to sort of make it all right with myself to write a novel at all – a novel about writing a novel, about writing a novel sort of thing, you see. I think that the set-up of my writing is probably just a justification of the time I wasted doing something else. And it is an attempt to redeem the time, you see.

KERMODE: You use the word 'wasted' advisedly, do you?

SPARK: It wouldn't be wasted if I had my way. It won't be wasted – it won't be known to be wasted until I'm dead.

KERMODE: The novels that you've written since *The Comforters* have not had quite this wantonness, as I called it, about the form which you are employing, though they've had some.

SPARK: Yes. Well, because I observed a kind of wantonness, as you call it, I decided the best thing to do was to stick to a plot, and stick to a formal outline and say what I wanted to say in that limit. And then I decided that I was writing minor novels deliberately, and not major novels. An awful lot of people are telling me to write big long novels – Mrs Tolstoy, you know – and I decided it is no good filling a little glass with a pint of beer.

KERMODE: You tend to pick not a Tolstoyan society, but a rather limited society of very old people, for example. Is this because the other things are on too big a scale for what you want to do?

SPARK: Well, partly because of my own temperament, and my own constitution. When I become interested in a subject, say old age, then the world is peopled for me – just peopled with them. And it is a narrow little small world, but it's full of old people, full of whatever I'm studying. They're the centre of the world, and everyone else is on the periphery. It is an obsession until I've finished writing about them. And that's how I see things. I wrote a book about bachelors and it seemed to me that everyone was a bachelor. It is true, just strangely enough, those people come my way while I am writing – I don't take a long time, so it is not difficult.

KERMODE: And you don't feel that it is necessary to explain the difference between this temporary world and the permanent one in terms of saying that you are a writer of fantasy, that you might as well make the world full of insects, or of very large or very small men?

SPARK: I don't claim that my novels are truth – I claim that they are fiction, out of which a kind of truth emerges. And I keep in my mind specifically that what I am writing is fiction because I am interested in truth – absolute truth – and I don't pretend that what I'm writing is more than an imaginative extension of the truth – something inventive. I don't say that such and such a person lived and such and such a person crossed the road, simply because I write it – in a court of law it wouldn't carry any weight, and it's not true, what I write is not true – it is a pack of lies. There is metaphorical truth and moral truth, and what they call anagogical, you know, the different sorts of truth; and there is absolute truth, in which I believe things which are difficult to believe, but I believe them because they are absolute. And this is one aspect of truth, perhaps. But in fact if we are going to live in the world as reasonable beings, we must call it lies.

But simply because one puts it out as a work of fiction, then one is not a liar. I do think that this ought to be recognized by people. People get very annoyed if you say, look here, Goldilocks and the three bears is a pack of lies.

KERMODE: One of the many senses in which the word myth has been used in these discussions is to cover this unconscious element in any story and any plot – and a lot of people seem to think that the quicker you get down to this level the better the book is going to be, and some others, like Iris Murdoch, think that the minute that you lapse into it, you've started writing badly, self indulgently.

SPARK: Perhaps she is right. I think the best thing is to be conscious of everything that one writes, and let the unconscious take care of itself, if it exists, which we don't know. If we knew it, it wouldn't be the unconscious. I think you should be as conscious as possible of what you are doing, and never give in to the temptation – it comes upon most writers – of 'Oh, I did that wonderfully – now I must go on doing that unconsciously'. It is terribly wrong. The unconscious is completely limitless. The best thing is to know what you are doing, I think.

KERMODE: It's an old charge that poets are liars, and we include novelists among poets; and the old defence is that he nothing affirmeth and therefore never lieth. Is this very much what you have been saying in this conversation?

SPARK: Yes, I think so. I think that the novelist is out just to say what happened. I express it in the past tense, but in the actual process, as far as I am concerned, it happens in the present tense. Things just happen and one records what has happened a few seconds later. I don't mean, of course, that one is that recording instrument that Blake thought of himself, just a kind of medium between the angels and the creatures, but I do know events occur in my mind, and I record them. Whether it fits in with this theory, that theory, this myth, that myth, has nothing to do with me.

For Mrs Spark the novel is true because it happens in the author's mind as he writes; in this sense it is a completely accurate transcript of events, and as an account of character not to be faulted. It may be a corollary of this that the outside world becomes, momentarily for such a novelist, a world populated by a limited class of persons behaving in unusual ways; but the novelist is not affirming this, and in any case distinguishes between absolute truth (revealed religion) and other less important kinds of truth, of which the novel might produce one.

This is a question which will look different according as you believe or do not believe in absolute truth. Yet to the agnostic Wilson and the Catholic Spark the 'myth' is something best left to take care of itself; whereas to Miss Murdoch it is a temptation to abandon uncompleted the great task of exploring personality; and I have an idea that Miss Murdoch would include Mrs Spark's 'absolute truths' among the myths because they too 'break bitter furies of complexity'. On the other hand, to Mr Greene it is precisely those furies of complexity that damage the important thing, the central static myth.

The house of fiction has many windows, but at any given period they may all be designed as variations on a few basic shapes. What you see from them varies more considerably within these limits: irreducibly complex personalities, a sadistic landscape, a gaunt country house full of secrets that cannot survive the preternatural explicitness of the inhabitants, a mountain of cheese. And for the most part the people at present standing at these windows are content to say 'My window is shaped thus and thus,' rather than 'all windows should be myth-shaped or fact-shaped' – there may be above all a God-shaped window giving perfect all-round visibility, but theirs is in no case held to resemble it.

JOHN FOWLES

Notes on an Unfinished Novel

(reprinted with permission from *Afterwords*,
ed. by Thomas McCormack, Harper and Row, 1969)

The novel I am writing at the moment (provisionally entitled
The French Lieutenant's Woman) is set about a hundred
years back. I don't think of it as a historical novel, a genre
in which I have very little interest. It started four or five
months ago as a visual image. A woman stands at the end
of a deserted quay and stares out to sea. That was all. This
image rose in my mind one morning when I was still in bed
half asleep. It corresponded to no actual incident in my life
(or in art) that I can recall, though I have for many years
collected obscure books and forgotten prints, all sorts of
flotsam and jetsam from the last two or three centuries,
relics of past lives – and I suppose this leaves me with a sort
of dense hinterland from which such images percolate down
to the coast of consciousness.

These mythopoeic 'stills' (they seem almost always static)
float into my mind very often. I ignore them, since that is
the best way of finding whether they really are the door
into a new world.

So I ignored this image; but it recurred. Imperceptibly it
stopped coming to me. I began deliberately to recall it and
to try to analyse and hypothesize why it held some sort of
imminent power. It was obviously mysterious. It was
vaguely romantic. It also seemed, perhaps because of the
latter quality, not to belong to today. The woman obstinately refused to stare out of the window of an airport
lounge; it had to be this ancient quay – as I happen to live
near one, so near that I can see it from the bottom of my
garden, it soon became a specific ancient quay. The woman
had no face, no particular degree of sexuality. But she was
Victorian; and since I always saw her in the same static
long shot, with her back turned, she represented a reproach
on the Victorian Age. An outcast. I didn't know her crime,
but I wished to protect her. That is, I began to fall in love
with her. Or with her stance. I didn't know which.

This – not literally – pregnant female image came at a time (the autumn of 1966) when I was already half-way through another novel and had, still have, three or four others planned to follow it. It was an interference, but of such power that it soon came to make the previously planned work seem the intrusive element in my life. This accidentality of inspiration has to be allowed for in writing; both in the work one is on (unplanned development of character, unintended incidents, and so on) and in one's works as a whole. Follow the accident, fear the fixed plan – that is the rule.

Narcissism, or pygmalionism, is the essential vice a writer must have. Characters (and even situations) are like children or lovers, they need constant caressing, concern, listening to, watching, admiring. All these occupations become tiring for the active partner – the writer – and only something akin to love can provide the energy. I've heard people say, 'I want to write a book.' But wanting to write a book, however ardently, is not enough. Even to say, 'I want to be possessed by my own creations,' is not enough; all natural or born writers are possessed, and in the old magical sense, by their own imaginations long before they even begin to think of writing.

This fluke genesis must break all the rules of creative writing; must sound at best childlike, at worst childish. I suppose the orthodox method is to work out what one wants to say and what one has experience of, and then to correlate the two. I have tried that method and started out with an analytically arrived-at theme and a set of characters all neatly standing for something; but the manuscripts have all petered out miserably. *The Magus* (written before *The Collector*, which also originated in a single image) sprang from a very trivial visit to a villa on a Greek island; nothing in the least unusual happened. But in my unconscious I kept arriving at the place again and again; something wanted to happen there, something that had not happened to me at the time. Why it should have been at *that* villa, *that* one visit, among so many thousands of other possible launching-pads, I do not know. Only a month ago someone showed me some recent photographs of the villa, which is now deserted; and it was just a deserted villa. Its mysterious significance to me fifteen years ago remains mysterious.

Once the seed germinates, reason and knowledge, culture and all the rest have to start to grow it. You cannot create a world by hot instinct; but only by cold experience. That is one good reason why so many novelists produce nothing until, or do all their best work after, the age of forty.

I find it very difficult to write if I don't know I shall have several days absolutely clear. All visits, all intrusions, all daily duties become irksome. This is during the first draft. I wrote the first draft of *The Collector* in under a month; sometimes ten thousand words a day. Of course a lot of it was poorly written and had to be endlessly amended and revised. First-draft and revision writing are so different they hardly seem to belong to the same activity. I never do any 'research' until the first draft is finished; all that matters to begin with is the flow, the story, the narrating. Research material then is like swimming in a straitjacket.

During the revision period I try to keep some sort of discipline. I make myself revise whether I feel like it or not; in some ways, the more disinclined and dyspeptic one feels, the better – one is harsher with oneself. All the best cutting is done when one is sick of the writing.

But all this advice from senior writers to establish a discipline always, to get down a thousand words a day whatever one's mood, I find an absurdly puritanical and impractical approach. Writing is like eating or making love; a natural process, not an artificial one. Write, if you must, because you feel like writing; never because you feel you ought to write.

I write memoranda to myself about the book I'm on. On this one: *You are not trying to write something one of the Victorian novelists forgot to write; but perhaps something one of them failed to write.* And: *Remember the etymology of the word. A novel is something new. It must have relevance to the writer's now – so don't ever pretend you live in 1867; or make sure the reader knows it's a pretence.*

In the matter of clothes, social manners, historical background, and the rest, writing about 1867 is merely a question of research. But I soon get into trouble over dialogue, because the genuine dialogue of 1867 (in so far as it can be heard in books of the time) is far too close to our own to sound convincingly old. It very often fails to agree with our psychological picture of the Victorians – it is not stiff enough, not euphemistic enough, and so on; and here at once I have to start cheating and pick out the more formal and archaic (even for 1867) elements of spoken speech. It is this kind of 'cheating', which is intrinsic to the novel, that takes the time.

Even in modern-novel dialogue the most real is not the most conformable to actual current speech. One has only to read a transcribed tape of actual conversation to realize that it is, in the literary context, not very real. Novel dialogue is a form of shorthand, an *impression* of what people actually say; and besides that it has to perform other functions – to keep the narrative moving (which real conversation rarely does), to reveal character (real conversation often hides it) and so on.

This is the greatest technical problem I have; it is hard enough with modern characters, and doubly so with historical ones.

Memorandum: *If you want to be true to life, start lying about the reality of it.*

And: *One cannot describe reality; only give metaphors that indicate it. All human modes of description (photographic, mathematical and the rest, as well as literary) are metaphorical. Even the most precise scientific description of an object or movement is a tissue of metaphors.*

Alain Robbe-Grillet's polemical essay *Pour un nouveau roman* (1963) is indispensable reading for the profession, even where it produces no more than total disagreement. His key question: *Why bother to write in a form whose great masters cannot be surpassed?* The fallacy of one of his conclusions – we must discover a new form to write in if the novel is to survive – is obvious. It reduces the purpose of the novel to the discovery of new forms: whereas its other purposes – to entertain, to satirize, to describe new sensibilities, to record life, to improve life, and so on – are

clearly just as viable and important. But his obsessive plead-
ing for new form places a kind of stress on every passage
one writes today. To what extent am I being a coward by
writing inside the old tradition? To what extent am I being
panicked into avant-gardism? Writing about 1867 doesn't
lessen the stress; it increases it, since so much of the
subject matter must of its historical nature be 'traditional'.
There are apparent parallels in other arts: Stravinsky's
eighteenth-century rehandlings, Picasso's and Francis Bacon's
use of Velasquez. But in this context words are not nearly
so tractable as musical notes or brush-strokes. One can
parody a rococo musical ornament, a baroque face. Very
early on I tried, in a test chapter, to put modern dialogue
into Victorian mouths. But the effect was absurd, since the
real historical nature of the characters is hopelessly distorted; the only people to get away with this (Julius Caesar
speaking with a Brooklyn accent, and so on) are the professional funny men. One is led inevitably, by such a
technique, into a comic novel.

My two previous novels were both based on more or less
disguised existentialist premises. I want this one to be no
exception; and so I am trying to show an existentialist
awareness before it was chronologically possible. Kierkegaard was, of course, totally unknown to the British and
American Victorians; but it has always seemed to me that
the Victorian Age, especially from 1850 on, was highly
existentialist in many of its personal dilemmas. One can
almost invert the reality and say that Camus and Sartre
have been trying to lead us, in their fashion, to a Victorian
seriousness of purpose and moral sensitivity.

Nor is this the only similarity between the 1960s and
1860s. The great nightmare of the respectable Victorian
mind was the only too real one created by the geologist
Lyell and the biologist Darwin. Until then man had lived
like a child in a small room. They gave him – and never
was a present less welcome – infinite space and time, and
a hideously mechanistic explanation of human reality into
the bargain. Just as we 'live with the bomb' the Victorians
lived with the theory of evolution. They were hurled into
space. They felt themselves infinitely isolated. By the 1860s
the great iron structures of their philosophies, religions,

and social stratifications were already beginning to look dangerously corroded to the more perspicacious.

Just such a man, an existentialist before his time, walks down the quay and sees that mysterious back, feminine, silent, also existentialist, turned to the horizon.

Magnificent though the Victorian novelists were, they almost all (an exception, of course, is the later Hardy) failed miserably in one aspect; nowhere in 'respectable' Victorian literature (and most of the pornography was based on the brothel – or eighteenth-century accounts) does one see a man and a woman described together in bed. We do not know how they made love, what they said to each other in their most intimate moments, what they felt then.

Writing as I have been today – about two Victorians making love – with no guides except my imagination and vague deductions from the spirit of the age and so on – is really science fiction. A journey is a journey, backwards or forwards.

The most difficult task for a writer is to get the right 'voice' for his material; by voice I mean the overall impression one has of the creator behind what he creates. Now I've always liked the ironic voice that the line of great nineteenth-century novelists, from Austen through to Conrad, all used so naturally. We tend today to remember the failures of that tone – the satirical overkill in Dickens, the facetiousness of Thackeray, the strained sarcasm of Mark Twain, the priggishness in George Eliot – rather than its virtues. The reason is clear enough; irony needs the assumption of superiority in the ironist. Such an assumption must be anathema to a democratic, egalitarian century like our own. We suspect people who pretend to be omniscient; and that is why so many of us twentieth-century novelists feel driven into first-person narration.

I have heard writers claim that this first-person technique is a last bastion of the novel against the cinema, a form where the camera dictates an inevitable third-person point of view of what happens, however much we may identify with one character. But the matter of whether a contemporary novelist uses 'he' or 'I' is largely irrelevant. The great majority of modern third-person narration is 'I' narration very thinly disguised. The real 'I' of the Victorian writers – the writer himself – is as rigorously repressed there (out of fear of seeming pretentious, etc.) as it is, for obvious semantic and grammatical reasons, when the narration is in literal first-person form.

But in this new book, I shall try to resurrect this technique. It seems in any case natural to look back at the England of a hundred years ago with a somewhat ironical eye – and 'I' – although it is my strong belief that history is horizontal in terms of the ratio between understanding and *available* knowledge and (far more important) horizontal in terms of the happiness the individual gets from being alive. In short, there is a danger in being ironic about the apparent follies and miseries of any past age. So I have written myself another memorandum : *You are not the 'I' who breaks into the illusion, but the 'I' who is a part of it.*

In other words, the 'I' who will make first-person commentaries here and there in my story, and who will finally even enter it, will not be my real 'I' in 1967; but much more just another character, though in a different category from the purely fictional ones.

An illustration. Here is the beginning of a minor novel (*Lovel the Widower*, 1861) by Thackeray :

> Who shall be the hero of this tale? Not I who write it. I am but the Chorus of the Play. I make remarks on the conduct of the characters : I narrate their simple story.

Today I think we should assume (not knowing who the writer was) that the 'I' here is the writer's 'I'. For three or four pages more we might still just believe this; but then suddenly Thackeray introduces his eponymous hero as 'my friend Lovel' and we see we've been misled. 'I' is simply another character. But then a few pages on the 'I' cuts in again in the description of a character.

> She never could speak. Her voice was as hoarse as a fishwoman's. Can that immense stout old box-keeper at the —— theatre . . . be the once brilliant Emily Montanville? I am told there are *no* lady box-keepers in the English theatres. This, I submit, is a proof of my consummate

care and artifice in rescuing from a prurient curiosity the individual personages from whom the characters of the present story are taken. Montanville is *not* a box-opener. She *may*, under another name, keep a trinket-shop in the Burlington Arcade, for what you know : but this secret no torture shall induce me to divulge. Life has its rises and downfalls, and you have had yours, you hobbling old creature. Montanville, indeed! Go thy ways! Here is a shilling for thee. (Thank you, sir.) Take away that confounded footstool, and never let us see thee more!

We can just still suppose that the 'I' is another character here; but the strong suspicion is that it is Thackeray himself. There is the characteristic teasing of the reader, the shock new angle of the present tense, the compensatory self-mocking in the already revealed 'secret no torture shall induce me to divulge'. But clearly he doesn't mean us to be sure; it is not the whole Thackeray.

Lovel rates poorly by Thackeray's own standards elsewhere; it is nevertheless a brilliant technical exercise in the use of 'voice'. I cannot believe that it is a dead technique. Nothing can get us off the charge of omniscience – and certainly not the *nouveau roman* theory. Even that theory's most brilliant practical demonstrations – say Robbe-Grillet's own *La Jalousie* – fail to answer the accusation. Robbe-Grillet may have removed the writer Robbe-Grillet totally from the text; but he has never denied he wrote it. If the writer really believes in the statement 'I know nothing about my characters except what can be tape-recorded and photographed (and then "mixed" and "cut"),' the logical step is to take up tape-recording and photography – not writing. But if he still writes, and writes well, as Robbe-Grillet does, then he is self-betrayed : he belongs to Cosa Nostra, and is transparently far more deeply implicated than he will admit.

September 2, 1967. Now I am about two-thirds of the way through. Always a bad stage, when one begins to doubt major things like basic motivations, dramatic design, the whole bloody enterprise; in the beginning one tends to get dazzled by each page, by one's fertility, those nice Muses always at one's shoulder . . . but then the inherent faults in the plot and characters begin to emerge. One starts to doubt the wisdom of the way the latter make things go; at the stage in an *affaire*, when one begins to thank God that marriage never raised its ugly head. But here one is condemned to a marriage of sorts – I have the woman on the quay (whose name is Sarah) for better or for worse, so to speak; and all seems worse.

I have to break off for a fortnight to go down to Majorca, where they're filming *The Magus*. I have written the script, but like most scripts it's really a team effort. The two producers have had their say, and the director; and a number of non-human factors, such as the budget, the nature of the locations, and the casting of the main roles, have had theirs. Most of the time I feel like a skeleton at the feast; this isn't what I had imagined, either in the book or in the script.

Yet it is interesting to watch, on a big film production, how buttressed each key man is by the other key men; to see how often one will turn to the other and say, 'Will it work?' I compare this with the loneliness of the long-distance writer; and I come back with a sort of relief, a re-affirmation in my faith in the novel. For all its faults, it is a statement by one person. In my novels I am the producer, director, and all the actors; I photograph it. This may seem a megalomania beside which the more celebrated cases from Hollywood pale to nothingness. There *is* a vanity about it, a wish to play the godgame, which all the random and author-removing devices of avant-garde technique cannot hide. But there must be a virtue, in an age that is out to exterminate both the individual and the enduring, in the individual's attempt to endure by his own efforts alone.

The truth is, the novel is a free form. Unlike the play or the filmscript, it has no limits other than those of the language. It is like a poem; it can be what it wants. This is its downfall and its glory; and explains why both forms have been so often used to establish freedom in other fields, social and political.

A charge all of us who sell film rights have to answer is that we wrote our books with this end in view. What has to be distinguished here is the legitimate and the illegitimate influence of the cinema on the novel. I saw my first film when I was six; I suppose I've seen on average – and dis- counting television – a film a week ever since; let's say some two and a half thousand films up to now. How can so frequently repeated an experience not have indelibly stamped itself on the *mode* of imagination? At one time I analysed my dreams in detail; again and again I recalled purely cinematic effects . . . panning shots, close shots, tracking, jump cuts, and the rest. In short, this mode of imagining is far too deep in me to eradicate – not only in me, in all my generation.

This doesn't mean we have surrendered to the cinema. I don't share the general pessimism about the so-called decline of the novel and its present status as a minority cult. Except for a brief period in the nineteenth century, when a literate majority and a lack of other means of entertain- ment coincided, it has always been a minority cult.

One has in fact only to do a filmscript to realize how inalienably in possession of a still vast domain the novel is; how countless the forms of human experience only to be described in and by it. There is too an essential difference in the quality of image evoked by the two media. The cinematic visual image is virtually the same for all who see it; it stamps out personal imagination, the response from individual *visual* memory. A sentence or paragraph in a novel will evoke a different image in each reader. This necessary co-operation between writer and reader, the one to suggest, the other to make concrete, is a privilege of *verbal* form; and the cinema can never usurp it.

Nor is that all. Here (the opening four paragraphs of a novel) is a flagrant bit of writing for the cinema. The man has obviously spent too much time on filmscripts, and can now think only of his movie sale.

The temperature is in the 90's and the boulevard is absolutely empty.

Lower down, the inky water of a canal reaches in a straight line. Midway between two locks is a barge full of timber. On the bank, two rows of barrels.

Beyond the canal, between houses separated by work- yards, a huge cloudless tropical sky. Under the throbbing sun white façades, slate roofs and granite quays hurt the eyes. An obscure distant murmur rises in the hot air. All seems drugged by the Sunday peace and the sadness of summer days.

Two men appear.

It first appeared on March 25, 1881. The writer's name is Flaubert. All I have done is to transpose his past historic into the present.

I woke in the small hours, and the book tormented me. All its failings rose up in the darkness. I saw the novel I dropped in order to write *The French Lieutenant's Woman* was much better. This one was not my sort of book; but an aberration, a folly, a delusion. Sentences from vitriolic reviews floated through my mind . . . 'a clumsy pastiche of Hardy', 'pretentious imitation of an inimitable genre', 'pointless exploration of an already over-explored age . . .', and so on and so on.

Now it is day, I am back on it again, and it denies what I felt in the night. But the horror of such realizations is that someone, some reader or reviewer, *will* realize them. The nightmare of the writer is that all his worst private fears and self-criticisms will be made public.

The shadow of Thomas Hardy, the heart of whose 'country' I can see in the distance from my workroom window, I cannot avoid. Since he and Peacock are my two favourite male novelists of the nineteenth century I don't mind the shadow. It seems best to use it; and by a curious coincidence, which I didn't realize when I placed my own story in that year, 1867 was the crucial year in Hardy's own mysterious personal life. It is somehow encouraging that while my fictitious characters weave their own story in their 1867, only thirty miles away in the real 1867 the pale young architect was entering his own fatal life-incident.

My female characters tend to dominate the male. I see man as a kind of artifice, and woman as a kind of reality. The one is cold idea, the other is warm fact. Daedalus faces Venus, and Venus must win. If the technical problems hadn't been so great, I should have liked to make Conchis in *The Magus* a woman. The character of Mrs de Seitas at the end of the book was simply an aspect of his character; as was Lily. Now Sarah exerts this power. She doesn't realize how. Nor do I yet.

I was stuck this morning to find a good answer from Sarah at the climax of a scene. Characters sometimes reject all the possibilities one offers. They say in effect: *I would never say or do a thing like that*. But they don't say what they would say; and one has to proceed negatively, by a very tedious coaxing kind of trial and error. After an hour over this one wretched sentence, I realized that she had in fact been telling me what to do: silence from her was better than any line she might have said.

By the time I left Oxford I found myself much more at home in French than in English literature. There seems to me to be a vital distinction between the French and Anglo-Saxon cultures in this field. Since 1650 French writers have assumed an international audience; and the Anglo-Saxons a national one. This may be no more than a general tendency; the literatures of the two cultures offer hundreds of exceptions, even among the best-known books. Nevertheless I have always found this French assumption that the proper audience of a book is one without frontiers more attractive than the extreme opposite view, which is still widely held in both Britain and America, that the proper job of a writer is to write of and for his own country and countrymen.

I am aware of this when I write, and especially when I revise. English references that will mean nothing to a foreigner I usually cut out, or avoid in the first place. In the present book I have the ubiquity in the West of the Victorian ethos: that helps greatly.

Various things have long made me feel an exile in England. Some years ago I came across a sentence in an obscure French novel: *Ideas are the only motherland*. Ever since I have kept it as the most succinct summary I know of what I believe. Perhaps 'believe' is the wrong verb – if you are without national feeling, if you find many of your fellow countrymen and most of their beliefs and their institutions foolish and antiquated, you can hardly *believe* in anything, but only accept the loneliness that results.

So I live completely away from other English writers and the literary life of London. What I have to think of as my 'public' self is willy-nilly absorbed into or rejected by (mostly the latter, in my case) the national literary 'world'. Even to me it seems, that public self, very remote and often distastefully alien and spurious; just one more thing that I feel my real self in exile from.

My real self is here and now, writing. Whenever I think of this (the writing, not the written) experience, images to do with exploring, singlehanded voyages, lone mountain ascents always spring unwanted to my mind. They sound romantic, but they're not meant to. It's the damned solitude, the fear of failure (by which I do *not* mean bad reviews), the tedium of the novel form, the often nauseating feeling that one is prey to an unhealthy obsession . . .

When I go out and meet other people, become mixed in their lives and social routines, my own solitude, routinelessness, and freedom (which is a subtle imprisonment) from economic 'worries' often make me feel like a visitor from outer space. I like earthmen, but I'm not quite sure what they're at. I mean we regulate things better at home. But there it is – I've been posted here. And there's no transport back.

Something like this lies behind all I write.

This total difference between the written and the writing world is what non-writers never realize about us. They see us as we were; we live with what we are. It is not subjects that matter to writers; but the experience of handling them. In those romantic terms, a difficult pitch scaled, a storm survived, the untrodden moon beneath one's feet. Such pleasures are unholy; and the world in general does right to regard us with malice and suspicion.

I loathe the day a manuscript is sent to the publisher, because on that day the people one has loved die; they become what they are – petrified, fossil organisms for others to study and collect. I get asked what I meant by this and by that. But what I wrote is what I meant. If it wasn't clear in the book, it shouldn't be clear now.

I find Americans, especially the kind people who write and

ask questions, have a strangely pragmatic view of what books are. Perhaps because of the miserable heresy that creative writing can be taught ('creative' is here a euphemism for 'imitative') they seem to believe that a writer always knows exactly what he's doing. Obscure books, for them, are a kind of crossword puzzle. Somewhere, they feel, in some number of a paper they missed, all the answers have been given to all the clues.

They believe, in short, that a book is like a machine; that if you have the knack, you can take it to bits.

Ordinary readers can hardly be blamed for thinking like this. Both academic criticism and weekly reviewing have in the last forty years grown dangerously scientific, or pseudo-scientific, in their general tenor. Analysis and categorization are indispensable scientific tools *in the scientific field*; but the novel, like the poem, is only partly a scientific field. No one wants a return to the kind of bellelettrist and onanistic accounts of new books that were fashionable in the early years of the century; but we could do with something better than what we have got.

I am an interested party? I confess it. Ever since I began writing *The French Lieutenant's Woman* I've been reading obituaries of the novel; a particularly gloomy one came from Gore Vidal in the December 1967 issue of *Encounter*. And I have been watching novel-reviewing in England become this last year increasingly impatient and dismissive. Any moment now I expect one of our fashionable news-papers to decide to drop their *New Novels* column for good and give the released space over to television or pop music. Of course I am interested – but, like Mr Vidal, I can hardly be personally resentful. If the novel is dead, the corpse still remains oddly fertile. We are told no one reads novels any more; so the authors of *Julian* and *The Collector* must be grateful to the two million ghosts or more who have bought copies of their respective books. But I don't want to be sarcastic. More is at issue here than self-interest.

One has the choice of two views: either that the novel, along with printed-word culture in general, is moribund, or that there is something sadly shallow and blinded in our age. I know which view I hold; and the people who astound me are the ones who are sure that the first view is true.

If you want omniscience, you have it there, and it ought to worry you, you the reader who is neither critic nor writer, that this omniscient contempt for print is found so widely among people who make a living out of literary dissection. Surgery is what we want, not dissection. It is not only the extirpation of the mind that kills the body; the heart will do the trick just as well.

October 27, 1967. I finished the first draft, which was begun on January 25. It is about 140,000 words long, and exactly as I imagined it: perfect, flawless, a lovely novel. But that, alas, is indeed only how I imagine it. When I re-read it I see 140,000 things need to be changed; then it will, perhaps, be less imperfect. But I haven't the energy; the dreaded research now, the interminable sentence-picking. I want to get on with another book. I had a strange image last night . . .

B. S. JOHNSON

Introduction to *Aren't You Rather Young to be Writing Your Memoirs?*

(reprinted with permission from *Aren't You Rather Young to be Writing Your Memoirs?*, Hutchinson, 1973)

It is a fact of crucial significance in the history of the novel this century that James Joyce opened the first cinema in Dublin in 1909. Joyce saw very early on that film must usurp some of the prerogatives which until then had belonged almost exclusively to the novelist. Film could tell a story more directly, in less time and with more concrete detail than a novel; certain aspects of character could be more easily delineated and kept constantly before the audience (for example, physical characteristics like a limp, a scar, particular ugliness or beauty); no novelist's description of a battle squadron at sea in a gale could really hope to compete with that in a well-shot film; and why should anyone who simply wanted to be told a story spend all his spare time for a week or weeks reading a book when he could experience the same thing in a version in some ways superior at his local cinema in only one evening?

It was not the first time that storytelling had passed from one medium to another. Originally it had been the chief concern of poetry, and long narrative poems were best-sellers right up to the works of Walter Scott and Byron. The latter supplanted the former in the favours of the public, and Scott adroitly turned from narrative poems to narrative novels and continued to be a bestseller. You will agree it would be perversely anachronistic to write a long narrative poem today? People still do, of course; but such works are rarely published, and, if they are, the writer is thought of as a literary flat-earther. But poetry did not die when storytelling moved on. It concentrated on the things it was still best able to do: the short, economical lyric, the intense emotional statement, depth rather than scale, the exploitation of rhythms which made their optimum impact at short lengths but which would have become monotonous and unreadable if maintained longer than a few pages. In the same way, the novel may not only survive but evolve to greater achievements by concentrating on those things it can still do best : the precise use of language, exploitation of the technological fact of the book, the explication of thought. Film is an excellent medium for showing things, but it is very poor at taking an audience inside characters' minds, at telling it what people are thinking. Again, Joyce saw this at once, and developed the technique of interior monologue within a few years of the appearance of the cinema. In some ways the history of the novel in the twentieth century has seen large areas of the old territory of the novelist increasingly taken over by other media, until the only thing the novelist can with any certainty call exclusively his own is the inside of his own skull : and that is what he should be exploring, rather than anachronistically fighting a battle he is bound to lose.

Joyce is the Einstein of the novel. His subject-matter in *Ulysses* was available to anyone, the events of one day in one place; but by means of form, style and technique in language he made it into something very much more, a novel, not a story about anything. What happens is nothing like as important as how it is written, as the medium of the words and form through which it is made to happen to the reader. And for style alone *Ulysses* would have been a revolution. Or, rather, styles. For Joyce saw that such a huge range of subject-matter could not be conveyed in one style, and accordingly used many. Just in this one innovation (and there are many others) lie a great advance and freedom offered to subsequent generations of writers.

But how many have seen it, have followed him? Very few. It is not a question of influence, of writing like Joyce. It is a matter of realizing that the novel is an evolving form, not a static one, of accepting that for practical purposes where Joyce left off should ever since have been regarded as the starting point. As Sterne said a long time ago :

Shall we for ever make new books, as apothecaries make new mixtures, by pouring only out of one vessel into another? Are we for ever to be twisting, and untwisting the same rope? For ever in the same track – for ever at the same pace?

The last thirty years have seen the storytelling function pass on yet again. Now anyone who wants simply to be told a story has the need satisfied by television; serials like *Coronation Street* and so on do very little more than answer the question 'What happens next?' All other writing possibilities are subjugated to narrative. If a writer's chief interest is in telling stories (even remembering that telling stories is a euphemism for telling lies; and I shall come to that) then the best place to do it now is in television, which is technically better equipped and will reach more people than a novel can today. And the most aware film-makers have realized this, and directors such as Godard, Resnais, and Antonioni no longer make the chief point of their films a story; their work concentrates on those things film can do solely and those things it can do best.

Literary forms do become exhausted, clapped out, as well. Look what had happened to five-act blank-verse drama by the beginning of the nineteenth century. Keats, Shelley, Wordsworth and Tennyson all wrote blank-verse, quasi-Elizabethan plays; and all of them, without exception, are resounding failures. They are so not because the men who wrote them were inferior poets, but because the form was finished, worn out, exhausted, and everything that could be done with it had been done too many times already.

That is what seems to have happened to the nineteenth-century narrative novel, too, by the outbreak of the First World War. No matter how good the writers are who now attempt it, it cannot be made to work for our time, and the writing of it is anachronistic, invalid, irrelevant, and perverse.

Life does not tell stories. Life is chaotic, fluid, random; it leaves myriads of ends untied, untidily. Writers can extract a story from life only by strict, close selection, and this must mean falsification. Telling stories really is telling lies. Philip Pacey took me up on this to express it thus:

Telling stories is telling lies   is telling

lies about people   is creating or
hardening prejudices   is providing an
alternative to real communication not a stimulus
to communication and/or communication itself
          is an escape from the challenge of coming
to terms with real people

I am not interested in telling lies in my own novels. A useful distinction between literature and other writing for me is that the former teaches one something true about life: and how can you convey truth in a vehicle of fiction? The two terms, *truth* and *fiction*, are opposites, and it must logically be impossible.

The two terms *novel* and *fiction* are not, incidentally, synonymous, as many seem to suppose in the way they use them interchangeably. The publisher of *Trawl* wished to classify it as autobiography, not as a novel. It is a novel, I insisted and could prove; what it is not is fiction. The novel is a form in the same sense that the sonnet is a form; within that form, one may write truth or fiction. I choose to write truth in the form of a novel.

In any case, surely it must be a confession of failure on the part of any novelist to rely on that primitive, vulgar and idle curiosity of the reader to know 'what happens next' (however banal or hackneyed it may be) to hold his interest? Can he not face the fact that it is his choice of words, his style, which ought to keep the reader reading? Have such novelists no pride? The drunk who tells you the story of his troubles in a pub relies on the same curiosity.

And when they consider the other arts, are they not ashamed? Imagine the reception of someone producing a nineteenth-century symphony or a Pre-Raphaelite painting today! The avant-garde of even ten years ago is now accepted in music and painting, is the establishment in these arts in some cases. But today the neo-Dickensian novel not only receives great praise, review space and sales but also acts as a qualification to elevate its authors to chairs at universities. On reflection, perhaps the latter is not so surprising; let the dead live with the dead.

All I have said about the history of the novel so far seems to me logical, and to have been available and obvious to anyone starting seriously to write in the form today.

Why then do so many novelists still write as though the revolution that was *Ulysses* had never happened, still rely on the crutch of storytelling? Why, more damningly for my case you might think, do hundreds of thousands of readers still gorge the stuff to surfeit?

I do not know. I can only assume that just as there seem to be so many writers imitating the act of being nineteenth-century novelists, so there must be large numbers imitating the act of being nineteenth-century readers, too. But it does not affect the logic of my case, nor the practice of my own work in the novel form. It may simply be a matter of education, or of communication; when I proposed this book to my publisher and outlined its thesis, he said it would be necessary for me to speak very clearly and very loudly. Perhaps the din of the market-place vendors in pap and propaganda is so high that even doing that will not be enough.

The architects can teach us something: their aesthetic problems are combined with functional ones in a way that dramatizes the crucial nature of their final actions. *Form follows function* said Louis Sullivan, mentor of Frank Lloyd Wright, and just listen to Mies van der Rohe:

> To create form out of the nature of our tasks with the methods of our time – this is our task.

> We must make clear, step by step, what things are possible, necessary, and significant.

> Only an architecture honestly arrived at by the explicit use of available building materials can be justified in moral terms.

Subject-matter is everywhere, general, is brick, concrete, plastic; the ways of putting it together are particular, are crucial. But I recognize that there are not simply problems of form, but problems of writing. Form is not the aim, but the result. If form were the aim then one would have formalism; and I reject formalism.

The novelist cannot legitimately or successfully embody

present-day reality in exhausted forms. If he is serious, he will be making a statement which attempts to change society towards a condition he conceives to be better, and he will be making at least implicitly a statement of faith in the evolution of the form in which he is working. Both these aspects of making are radical; this is inescapable unless he chooses escapism. Present-day reality is changing rapidly; it always has done, but for each generation it appears to be speeding up. Novelists must evolve (by inventing, borrowing, stealing or cobbling from other media) forms which will more or less satisfactorily contain an ever-changing reality, their own reality and not Dickens's reality or Hardy's reality or even James Joyce's reality.

Present-day reality is markedly different from, say, nineteenth-century reality. Then it was possible to believe in pattern and eternity, but today what characterizes our reality is the probability that chaos is the most likely explanation; while at the same time recognizing that even to seek an explanation represents a denial of chaos. Samuel Beckett, who of all living is the man I believe most worth reading and listening to, is reported thus:

> What I am saying does not mean that there will henceforth be no form in art. It only means that there will be new form, and that this form will be of such a type that it admits the chaos, and does not try to say that the chaos is really something else. The forms and the chaos remain separate . . . to find a form that accommodates the mess, that is the task of the artist now.

Whether or not it can be demonstrated that all is chaos, certainly all is change: the very process of life itself is growth and decay at an enormous variety of rates. Change is a condition of life. Rather than deplore this, or hunt the chimæræ of stability or reversal, one should perhaps embrace change as all there is. Or might be. For change is never for the better or for the worse; change simply *is*. No sooner is a style or technique established than the reasons for its adoption have vanished or become irrelevant. We have to make allowances and imaginative, lying leaps for Shakespeare, for even Noël Coward, to try to understand how they must have seemed to their contemporaries. I feel myself fortunate sometimes that I can laugh at the joke that just as I was beginning to think I knew something about how to write a novel it is no longer of any use to me in attempting the next one. Even in this introduction I am trying to make patterns, to impose patterns on the chaos, in the doubtful interest of helping you (and myself) to understand what I am saying. When lecturing on the same material I ought to drop my notes, refer to them in any chaotic order. *Order* and *chaos* are opposites, too.

This (and other things I have said) must appear paradoxical. But why should novelists be expected to avoid paradox any more than philosophers?

While I believe (as far as I believe anything) that there may be (how can I know?) chaos underlying it all, another paradox is that I still go on behaving as though pattern could exist, as though day will follow night will follow breakfast. Or whatever the order should be.

I do not really know why I write. Sometimes I think it is simply because I can do nothing better. Certainly there is no single reason, but many. I can, and will, enumerate some of them; but in general I prefer not to think about them.

I think I write because I have something to say that I fail to say satisfactorily in conversation, in person. Then there are things like conceit, stubbornness, a desire to retaliate on those who have hurt me paralleled by a desire to repay those who have helped me, a need to try to create something which may live after me (which I take to be the detritus of the religious feeling), the sheer technical joy of forcing almost intractable words into patterns of meaning and form that are uniquely (for the moment at least) mine, a need to make people laugh with me in case they laugh at me, a desire to codify experience, to come to terms with things that have happened to me, and to try to tell the truth (to discover what is the truth) about them. And I write especially to exorcise, to remove from myself, from my mind, the burden of having to bear some pain, the hurt of some experience: in order that it may be over there, in a book, and not in here in my mind.

The following tries to grope towards it, in another way:

I have a (vision) of something that (happened) to me
  something which (affected) me
  something which meant (something) to me

and I (wrote) (filmed) it
because
I wanted it to be fixed
  so that I could refer to it
  so that I could build on it
  so that I would not have to repeat it

Such a hostage to fortune!

What I have been trying to do in the novel form has been too much refracted through the conservativeness of reviewers and others; the reason why I have written in the ways that I have done have become lost, have never reached as many people, nor in anything like a definitive form. 'Experimental' to most reviewers is almost always a synonym for 'unsuccessful'. I object to the word *experimental* being applied to my own work. Certainly I make experiments, but the unsuccessful ones are quietly hidden away and what I choose to publish is in my terms successful: that is, it has been the best way I could find of solving particular writing problems. Where I depart from convention, it is because the convention has failed, is inadequate for conveying what I have to say. The relevant questions are surely whether each device works or not, whether it achieves what it set out to achieve, and how less good were the alternatives. So for every device I have used there is a literary rationale and a technical justification; anyone who cannot accept this has simply not understood the problem which had to be solved.

I do not propose to go through the reasons for all the devices, not least because the novels should speak for themselves; and they are clear enough to a reader who will think about them, let alone be open and sympathetic towards them. But I will mention some of them, and deal in detail with *The Unfortunates*, since its form seems perhaps the most extreme.

Travelling People (published 1963) had an explanatory

prelude which summed up much of my thinking on the novel at that point, as follows:

Seated comfortably in a wood and wickerwork chair of eighteenth-century Chinese manufacture, I began seriously to meditate upon the form of my allegedly full-time literary sublimations. Rapidly, I recalled the conclusions reached in previous meditations on the same subject: my rejection of stage-drama as having too many limitations, of verse as being unacceptable at the present time on the scale I wished to attempt, and of radio and television as requiring too many entrepreneurs between the writer and the audience; and my resultant choice of the novel as the form possessing fewest limitations, and closest contact with the greatest audience.

But, now, what kind of novel? After comparatively little consideration, I decided that one style for one novel was a convention that I resented most strongly: it was perhaps comparable to eating a meal in which each course had been cooked in the same manner. The style of each chapter should spring naturally from its subject-matter. Furthermore, I meditated, at ease in far eastern luxury, Dr Johnson's remarks about each member of an audience always being aware that he is in a theatre could with complete relevance be applied also to the novel reader, who surely knows that he is reading a book and not, for instance, taking part in a punitive raid on the curiously-shaped inhabitants of another planet. From this I concluded that it was not only permissible to expose the mechanism of a novel, but by so doing I should come nearer to reality and truth: adapting to refute, in fact, the ancients:

Artis est monstrare artem

Pursuing this thought, I realized that it would be desirable to have interludes between my chapters in which I could stand back, so to speak, from my novel, and talk about it with the reader, or with those parts of myself which might hold differing opinions, if necessary; and in which technical questions could be considered, and quotations from other writers included, where relevant, without any question of destroying the reader's suspension of disbelief, since such suspension was not to be attempted.

I should be determined not to lead my reader into believing that he was doing anything but reading a novel, having noted with abhorrence the shabby chicanery practised on their readers by many novelists, particularly of the popular class. This applied especially to digression, where the reader is led, wilfully and wantonly, astray; my novel would have clear notice, one way or another, of digressions, so that the reader might have complete freedom of choice in whether or not he would read them. Thus, having decided in a general way upon the construction of my novel I thought about actually rising to commence its composition; but persuaded by oriental comfort that I was nearer the Good Life engaged in meditation, I turned my mind to the deep consideration of such other matters as I deemed worthy of my attention, and, after a short while thus engaged, fell asleep.

Travelling People employed eight separate styles or conventions for nine chapters; the first and last chapters sharing one style in order to give the book cyclical unity within the motif announced by its title and epigraph. These styles included interior monologue, a letter, extracts from a journal, and a film script. This latter illustrates the method of the novel typically. The subject-matter was a gala evening at a country club, with a large number of characters involved both individually and in small groups. A film technique, cutting quickly from group to group and incidentally counterpointing the stagey artificiality of the occasion, seemed natural and apt. It is not, of course, a film; but the way it is written is intended to evoke what the reader knows as film technique.

The passage quoted above was deliberately a pastiche of eighteenth-century English, for I had found that it was necessary to return to the very beginnings of the novel in England in order to try to re-think it and re-justify it for myself. Most obvious of my debts was to the black pages of *Tristram Shandy*, but I extended the device beyond Sterne's simple use of it to indicate a character's death. The section concerned is the interior monologue of an old man prone to heart attacks; when he becomes unconscious he obviously cannot indicate this in words representing thought, but a modified form of Sterne's black pages solves the problem. First I used random-pattern grey to indicate unconsciousness after a heart attack, then a regular-pattern grey to indicate sleep or recuperative unconsciousness; and subsequently black when he dies.

Since *Travelling People* is part truth and part fiction it now embarrasses me and I will not allow it to be reprinted; though I am still pleased that its devices work. And I learnt a certain amount through it; not least that there was a lot of the writing I could do in my head without having to amass a pile of paper three feet high to see if something worked.

But I really discovered what I should be doing with *Albert Angelo* (1964) where I broke through the English disease of the objective correlative to speak truth directly if solipsistically in the novel form, and heard my own small voice. And again there were devices used to solve problems which I felt could not be dealt with in other ways. Thus a specially-designed type-character draws attention to physical descriptions which I believe tend to be skipped, do not usually penetrate. To convey what a particular lesson is like, the thoughts of a teacher are given on the right-hand side of a page in italic, with his and his pupils' speech on the left in roman, so that, though the reader obviously cannot read both at once, when he has read both he will have seen that they are simultaneous and have enacted such simultaneity for himself. When Albert finds a fortune-teller's card in the street it is further from the truth to describe it than simply to reproduce it. And when a future event must be revealed, I could (and can; can you?) think of no way nearer to the truth and more effective than to cut a section through those pages intervening so that the event may be read in its place but before the reader reaches that place.

Trawl (1966) is all interior monologue, a representation of the inside of my mind but at one stage removed; the closest one can come in writing. The only real technical problem was the representation of breaks in the mind's workings; I finally decided on a stylized scheme of 3 em, 6 em and 9 em spaces. In order not to have a break which ran-on at the end of a line looking like a paragraph, these spaces were punctuated by dots at decimal point level. I now doubt whether these dots were necessary. To make up for the absence of those paragraph breaks which give the reader's eye rest and location on the page, the line length was deliberately shortened; this gave the book a long, narrow format.

The rhythms of the language of *Trawl* attempted to parallel those of the sea, while much use was made of the trawl itself as a metaphor for the way the subconscious mind may appear to work.

With each of my novels there has always been a certain point when what has been until then just a mass of subject-matter, the material of living, of my life, comes to have a shape, a form that I recognize as a novel. This crucial interaction between the material and myself has always been reduced to a single point in time: obviously a very exciting moment for me, and a moment of great relief, too, that I am able to write another novel.

The moment at which *The Unfortunates* (1969) occurred was on the main railway station at Nottingham. I had been sent there to report a soccer match for the *Observer*, a quite routine League match, nothing special. I had hardly thought about where I was going, specifically: when you are going away to report soccer in a different city each Saturday you get the mechanics of travelling to and finding your way about in a strange place to an almost automatic state. But when I came up the stairs from the platform into the entrance hall, it hit me: I knew this city. I knew it very well. It was the city in which a very great friend of mine, one who had helped me with my work when no one else was interested, had lived until his tragic early death from cancer some two years before.

It was the first time I had been back since his death, and all the afternoon I was there the things we had done together kept coming back to me as I was going about this routine job of reporting a soccer match: the dead past and the living present interacted and transposed themselves in my mind. I realized that afternoon that I had to write a novel about this man, Tony, and his tragic and pointless death and its effect on me and the other people who knew him and whom he had left behind. The following passage from *The Unfortunates* explains his importance to me:

> To Tony, the criticism of literature was a study, a pursuit, a discipline of the highest kind in itself: to me, I told him, the only use of criticism was if it helped people to write better books. This he took as a challenge, this he accepted. Or perhaps I made the challenge, said that I would show him the novel as I wrote it, the novel I had in mind or was writing: and that he would therefore have a chance of influencing, of making better, a piece of what set out to be literature, for the sake of argument, rather than expend himself on dead men's work.

The main technical problem with *The Unfortunates* was the randomness of the material. That is, the memories of Tony and the routine football reporting, the past and the present, interwove in a completely random manner, without chronology. This is the way the mind works, my mind anyway, and for reasons given the novel was to be as nearly as possible a re-created transcript of how my mind worked during eight hours on this particular Saturday.

This randomness was directly in conflict with the technological fact of the bound book: for the bound book imposes an order, a fixed page order, on the material. I think I went some way towards solving this problem by writing the book in sections and having those sections not bound together but loose in a box. The sections are of different lengths, of course: some are only a third of a page long, others are as long as twelve pages. The longer ones were bound in themselves as sections, or signatures, as printers call them.

The point of this device was that, apart from the first and last sections which were marked as such, the other sections arrived in the reader's hands in a random order: he could read them in any order he liked. And if he imagined the printer, or some previous reader, had selected a special order, then he could shuffle them about and achieve his own random order. In this way the whole novel reflected the randomness of the material: it was itself a physical tangible metaphor for randomness and the nature of cancer.

Now I did not think then, and do not think now, that this

solved the problem completely. The lengths of the sections were really arbitrary again; even separate sentences or separate words would be arbitrary in the same sense. But I continue to believe that my solution was nearer; and even if it was only marginally nearer, then it was still a better solution to the problem of conveying the mind's randomness than the imposed order of a bound book.

What matters most to me about *The Unfortunates* is that I have on recall as accurately as possible what happened, that I do not have to carry it around in my mind any more, that I have done Tony as much justice as I could at the time; that the need to communicate with myself then, and with such older selves as I might be allowed, on something about which I cared and care deeply may also mean that the novel will communicate that experience to readers, too.

I shall return shortly to readers and communicating with them. But first there are two other novels, and they represent a change (again!) of direction, an elbow joint in the arm, still part of the same but perhaps going another way. Perhaps I shall come to the body, sooner or later. The ideas for both *House Mother Normal* (1971) and *Christie Malry's Own Double-Entry* (1973) came to me whilst writing *Travelling People* (indeed, I discussed them with Tony) but the subsequent three personal novels interposed themselves, demanded to be written first. I also balked at *House Mother Normal* since it seemed technically so difficult. What I wanted to do was to take an evening in an old people's home, and see a single set of events through the eyes of not less than eight old people. Due to the various deformities and deficiencies of the inmates, these events would seem to be progressively 'abnormal' to the reader. At the end, there would be the viewpoint of the House Mother, an apparently 'normal' person, and the events themselves would then be seen to be so bizarre that everything that had come before would seem 'normal' by comparison. The idea was to say something about the things we call 'normal' and 'abnormal' and the technical difficulty was to make the same thing interesting nine times over since that was the number of times the events would have to be described. By 1970 I thought that if I did not attempt the idea soon then I never would; and so sat down to it. I was relieved to find that the novel did work, on

its own terms, while not asking it to do anything it clearly
should not be trying to do. Each of the old people was
alloted a space of twenty-one pages, and each line on each
page represented the same moment in each of the other
accounts; this meant an unjustified right-hand margin and
led more than one reviewer to imagine the book was in
verse. House Mother's account has an extra page in which
she is shown to be

> the puppet or concoction of a writer (you
> always knew there was a writer behind it all?
> Ah, there's no fooling you readers!)

Nor should there be.

The reader is made very much aware that he is reading
a book and being addressed by the author in *Christie
Malry's Own Double-Entry*, too. The idea was that a young
man who had learned the double-entry system of book-
keeping started applying his knowledge to society and life;
when society did him down, he did society down in order
to balance the books. Form following function, the book
is divided into five parts each ended by a page of accounts
in which Christie attempts to draw a balance with life.

I do not really relish any more description of my work; it
is there to be read, and in writing so much about technique
and form I am diverting you from what the novels are
about, what they are trying to say, and things like the
nature of the language used, and the fact that all of them
have something comic in them and three are intended to be
very funny indeed. When I depart from what may mistakenly be extracted from the above as rigid principles it is
invariably for the sake of the comic, for I find Sterne's
reasons all-persuasive:

> . . . 'tis wrote, an' please your worships, against the
> spleen! in order, by a more frequent and a more convul-
> sive elevation and depression of the diaphragm, and the
> succussations of the inter-costal and abdominal muscles
> in laughter, to drive the *gall* and other *bitter juices* from
> the gall-bladder, liver, and sweet-bread of his majesty's
> subjects, with all the inimicitious passions which belong

to them, down into their duodenums.

For readers it is often said that they will go on reading the novel because it enables them, unlike film or television, to exercise their imaginations, that that is one of its chief attractions for them, that they may imagine the characters and so on for themselves. Not with my novels; it follows from what I have said earlier that I want my ideas to be expressed so precisely that the very minimum of room for interpretation is left. Indeed I would go further and say that to the extent that a reader can impose his own imagination on my words, then that piece of writing is a failure. I want him to see my (vision), not something conjured out of his own imagination. How is he supposed to grow unless he will admit others' ideas? If he wants to impose his imagination, let him write his own books. That may be thought to be anti-reader; but think a little further, and what I am really doing is challenging the reader to prove his own existence as palpably as I am proving mine by the act of writing.

Language, admittedly, is an imprecise tool with which to try to achieve precision; the same word will have slightly different meanings for every person. But that is outside me; I cannot control it. I can only use words to mean something to me, and there is simply the hope (not even the expectation) that they will mean the same thing to anyone else.

Which brings us to the question of for whom I write. I am always sceptical about writers who claim to be writing for an identifiable public. How many letters and phone calls do they receive from this public that they can know it so well as to write for it? Precious few, in my experience, when I have questioned them about it. I think I (after publishing some dozen books) have personally had about five letters from 'ordinary readers', people I did not know already that is; and three of those upbraided me viciously because I had just published the book that they were going to have written.

No, apart from the disaster of *Travelling People*, I write perforce for myself, and the satisfaction has to be almost all for myself; and I can only hope there are some few people like me who will see what I am doing, and understand what I am saying, and use it for their own devious purposes.

Yet it should not have to be so. I think I do have a right to expect that most readers should be open to new work, that there should be an audience in this country willing to try to understand and be sympathetic to what those few writers not shackled by tradition are trying to do and are doing. Only when one has some contact with a continental European tradition of the avant-garde does one realize just how stultifyingly philistine is the general book culture of this country. Compared with the writers of romances, thrillers, and the bent but so-called straight novel, there are not many who are writing as though it mattered, as though they meant it, as though they meant it to matter.

Perhaps I should nod here to Samuel Beckett (of course), John Berger, Christine Brooke-Rose, Brigid Brophy, Anthony Burgess, Alan Burns, Angela Carter, Eva Figes, Giles Gordon, Wilson Harris, Rayner Heppenstall, even hasty, muddled Robert Nye, Ann Quin, Penelope Shuttle, Alan Sillitoe (for his last book only, Raw Material indeed), Stefan Themerson, and (coming) John Wheway; (stand by): and if only Heathcote Williams would write a novel . . .

Anyone who imagines himself or herself slighted by not being included above can fill in his or her name here:

....

It would be a courtesy, however, to let me know his or her qualifications for so imagining.

Are we concerned with courtesy?

Nathalie Sarraute once described literature as a relay race, the baton of innovation passing from one generation to another. The vast majority of British novelists has dropped the baton, stood still, turned back, or not even realized that there is a race.

Most of what I have said has been said before, of course; none of it is new, except possibly in context and combination. What I do not understand is why British writers have not accepted it and acted upon it.

The pieces of prose (you will understand my avoidance of

the term *short story*) which follow were written in the interstices of novels and poems and other work between 1960 and 1973; the dates given in the Contents are those of the year of completion. None of them seem to me like each other, though some have links and cross-references; neither can I really see either progression or retrogression. The order is that which seemed least bad late on one particular May evening; perhaps I shall regret it as soon as I see it fixed.

Make of them what you will. I offer them to you despite my experience that the incomprehension and weight of prejudice which faces anyone trying to do anything new in writing is enormous, sometimes disquieting, occasionally laughable. A national daily newspaper (admittedly one known for its reactionary opinions) returned a review copy of *Travelling People* with the complaint that it must be a faulty copy for some of the pages were black; the Australian Customs seized *Albert Angelo* (which had holes justifiably cut in some pages, you will remember) and would not release it until they had been shown the obscenities which (they were convinced) had been excised; and in one of our biggest booksellers *Trawl* was found in the Angling section . . .

DORIS LESSING

Preface to *The Golden Notebook*

(reprinted with permission from *The Golden Notebook*,
Simon & Schuster, 1972; Michael Joseph, new edition, 1972;
Panther Books, 1973)

The shape of this novel is as follows:

There is a skeleton, or frame, called *Free Women*, which
is a conventional short novel, about 60,000 words long, and
which could stand by itself. But it is divided into five sections and separated by stages of the four Notebooks, Black,
Red, Yellow and Blue. The Notebooks are kept by Anna
Wulf, a central character of *Free Women*. She keeps four,
and not one, because, as she recognizes, she has to separate
things off from each other, out of fear of chaos, of formlessness – of breakdown. Pressures, inner and outer, end the
Notebooks; a heavy black line is drawn across the page of
one after another. But now that they are finished, from their
fragments can come something new, *The Golden Notebook*.

Throughout the Notebooks people have discussed, theo-
rized, dogmatized, labelled, compartmented – sometimes in
voices so general and representative of the time that they
are anonymous, you could put names to them like those in
the old Morality Plays, Mr Dogma and Mr I-am-Free-Because-
I-Belong-Nowhere, Miss I-Must-Have-Love-and-Happiness and
Mrs I-Have-to-be-Good-At-Everything-I-do, Mr Where-is-a-
Real-Woman? and Miss Where-is-a-Real-Man?, Mr I'm-Mad-
Because-They-Say-I-Am, and Miss Life-Through-Experiencing-
Everything, Mr I-Make-Revolution-and-Therefore-I-Am, and
Mr and Mrs If-We-Deal-Very-Well-With-This-Small-Problem-
Then - Perhaps - We - Can - Forget - We - Daren't - Look - at-
The-Big-Ones. But they have also reflected each other, been
aspects of each other, given birth to each other's thoughts
and behaviour – *are* each other, form wholes. In the inner
Golden Notebook, things have come together, the divisions
have broken down, there is formlessness with the end of
fragmentation – the triumph of the second theme, which is
that of unity. Anna and Saul Green the American 'break
down'. They are crazy, lunatic, mad – what you will. They

'break down' into each other, into other people, break through the false patterns they have made of their pasts, the patterns and formulas they have made to shore up themselves and each other, dissolve. They hear each other's thoughts, recognize each other in themselves. Saul Green, the man who has been envious and destructive of Anna, now supports her, advises her, gives her the theme for her next book, *Free Women* – an ironical title, which begins: 'The two women were alone in the London flat.' And Anna, who has been jealous of Saul to the point of insanity, possessive and demanding, gives Saul the pretty new notebook, *The Golden Notebook*, which she has previously refused to do, gives him the theme for his next book, writing in it the first sentence: 'On a dry hillside in Algeria a soldier watched the moonlight glinting on his rifle.' In the inner Golden Notebook, which is written by both of them, you can no longer distinguish between what is Saul and what is Anna, and between them and the other people in the book.

This theme of 'breakdown', that sometimes when people 'crack up' it is a way of self-healing, of the inner self's dismissing false dichotomies and divisions, has of course been written about by other people, as well as by me, since then. But this is where, apart from the odd short story, I first wrote about it. Here it is rougher, more close to experience, before experience has shaped itself into thought and pattern – more valuable perhaps because it is rawer material.

But nobody so much as noticed this central theme, because the book was instantly belittled, by friendly reviewers as well as by hostile ones, as being about the sex war, or was claimed by women as a useful weapon in the sex war.

I have been in a false position ever since, for the last thing I have wanted to do was to refuse to support women.

To get the subject of Women's Liberation over with – I support it, of course, because women are second-class citizens, as they are saying energetically and competently in many countries. It can be said that they are succeeding, if only to the extent they are being seriously listened to. All kinds of people previously hostile or indifferent say: 'I support their aims but I don't like their shrill voices and their nasty ill-mannered ways.' This is an inevitable and easily recognizable stage in every revolutionary movement: reformers must expect to be disowned by those who are only too happy to enjoy what has been won for them. I don't think that Women's Liberation will change much though – not because there is anything wrong with their aims, but because it is already clear that the whole world is being shaken into a new pattern by the cataclysms we are living through: probably by the time we are through, if we do get through at all, the aims of Women's Liberation will look very small and quaint.

But this novel was not a trumpet for Women's Liberation. It described many female emotions of aggression, hostility, resentment. It put them into print. Apparently what many women were thinking, feeling, experiencing, came as a great surprise. Instantly a lot of very ancient weapons were unleashed, the main ones, as usual, being on the theme of 'She is unfeminine', 'She is a man-hater'. This particular reflex seems indestructible. Men – and many women – said that the suffragettes were defeminized, masculine, brutalized. There is no record I have read of any society anywhere when women demanded more than nature offers them that does not also describe this reaction from men – and some women. A lot of women were angry about *The Golden Notebook*. What women will say to other women, grumbling in their kitchens and complaining and gossiping or what they make clear in their masochism, is often the last thing they will say aloud – a man may overhear. Women are the cowards they are because they have been semi-slaves for so long. The number of women prepared to stand up for what they really think, feel, experience with a man they are in love with is still small. Most women will still run like little dogs with stones thrown at them when a man says: You are unfeminine, aggressive, you are unmanning me. It is my belief that any woman who marries, or takes seriously in any way at all, a man who uses this threat, deserves everything she gets. For such a man is a bully, does not know anything about the world he lives in, or about its history – men and women have taken infinite numbers of roles in the past, and do now, in different societies. So he is ignorant, or fearful about being out of step – a coward . . . I write all these remarks with exactly the same feeling as if I were writing a letter to post into the distant past: I am so sure that everything we now take for granted is going to be utterly swept away in the next decade.

(So why write novels? Indeed, why! I suppose we have to go on living *as if* . . .)

Some books are not read in the right way because they have skipped a stage of opinion, assume a crystallization of information in society which has not yet taken place. This book was written as if the attitudes that have been created by the Women's Liberation movements already existed. It came out first ten years ago, in 1962. If it were coming out now for the first time it might be read, and not merely reacted to: things have changed very fast. Certain hypocrisies have gone. For instance, ten, or even five, years ago – it has been a sexually contumacious time – novels and plays were being plentifully written by men furiously critical of women – particularly from the States but also in this country – portrayed as bullies and betrayers, but particularly as underminers and sappers. But these attitudes in male writers were taken for granted, accepted as sound philosophical bases, as quite normal, certainly not as woman-hating, aggressive or neurotic. It still goes on, of course – but things are better, there is no doubt of it.

I was so immersed in writing this book, that I didn't think about how it might be received. I was involved not merely because it was hard to write – keeping the plan of it in my head I wrote it from start to end, consecutively, and it was difficult – but because of what I was learning as I wrote. Perhaps giving oneself a tight structure, making limitations for oneself, squeezes out new substance where you least expect it. All sorts of ideas and experiences I didn't recognize as mine emerged when writing. The actual time of writing, then, and not only the experiences that had gone into the writing, was really traumatic: it changed me. Emerging from this crystallizing process, handing the manuscript to publisher and friends, I learned that I had written a tract about the sex war, and fast discovered that nothing I said then could change that diagnosis.

Yet the essence of the book, the organization of it, everything in it, says implicitly and explicitly, that we must not divide things off, must not compartmentalize.

'Bound. Free. Good. Bad. Yes. No. Capitalism. Socialism.

Sex. Love . . .' says Anna, in *Free Women*, stating a theme –
shouting it, announcing a motif with drums and fanfares
. . . or so I imagined. Just as I believed that in a book called
The Golden Notebook the inner section called the Golden
Notebook might be presumed to be a central point, to carry
the weight of the thing, to make a statement.

But no.

Other themes went into the making of this book, which
was a crucial time for me: thoughts and themes I had been
holding in my mind for years came together.

One was that it was not possible to find a novel which
described the intellectual and moral climate of a hundred
years ago, in the middle of the last century, in Britain, in
the way Tolstoy did it for Russia, Stendhal for France. (At
this point it is necessary to make the obligatory disclaimers.)
To read *The Red and the Black* and *Lucien Leuwen* is to
know that France as if one were living there, to read *Anna
Karenina* is to know that Russia. But a very useful Victorian
novel never got itself written. Hardy tells us what it was
like to be poor, to have an imagination larger than the
possibilities of a very narrow time, to be a victim. George
Eliot is good as far as she goes. But I think the penalty she
paid for being a Victorian woman was that she had to be
shown to be a good woman even when she wasn't according
to the hypocrisies of the time – there is a great deal she
does not understand because she is moral. Meredith, that
astonishingly underrated writer, is perhaps nearest. Trollope
tried the subject but lacked the scope. There isn't one novel
that has the vigour and conflict of ideas in action that is in
a good biography of William Morris.

Of course this attempt on my part assumed that that filter
which is a woman's way of looking at life has the same
validity as the filter which is a man's way . . . Setting that
problem aside, or rather, not even considering it, I decided
that to give the ideological 'feel' of our mid-century, it
would have to be set among socialists and marxists, because
it has been inside the various chapters of socialism that the
great debates of our time have gone on; the movements, the
wars, the revolutions, have been seen by their participants
as movements of various kinds of socialism, or Marxism, in
advance, containment, or retreat. (I think we should at least
concede the possibility that people looking back on our time

may see it not at all as we do – just as we, looking back on
the English, the French, or even the Russian Revolutions see
them differently from the people living then.) But 'Marxism',
and its various offshoots, has fermented ideas everywhere,
and so fast and energetically that, once 'way out', it has
already been absorbed, has become part of ordinary thinking. Ideas that were confined to the far left thirty or forty
years ago had pervaded the left generally twenty years
ago, and have provided the commonplaces of conventional
social thought from right to left for the last ten years.
Something so thoroughly absorbed is finished as a force –
but it was dominant, and in a novel of the sort I was trying
to do, had to be central.

Another thought that I had played with for a long time
was that a main character should be some sort of an artist,
but with a 'block'. This was because the theme of the artist
has been dominant in art for some time – the painter, writer,
musician, as exemplar. Every major writer has used it, and
most minor ones. Those archetypes, the artist and his
mirror-image the businessman, have straddled our culture,
one shown as a boorish insensitive, the other as a creator,
all excesses of sensibility and suffering and a towering
egotism which has to be forgiven because of his products –
in exactly the same way, of course, as the businessman has
to be forgiven for the sake of his. We get used to what
we have, and forget that the artist-as-exemplar is a new
theme. Heroes a hundred years ago weren't often artists.
They were soldiers and empire builders and explorers and
clergymen and politicians – too bad about women who had
scarcely succeeded in becoming Florence Nightingale yet.
Only oddballs and eccentrics wanted to be artists, and had
to fight for it. But to use this theme of our time, 'the artist',
'the writer', I decided it would have to be developed by
giving the creature a block and discussing the reasons for
the block. These would have to be linked with the disparity
between the overwhelming problems of war, famine,
poverty, and the tiny individual who was trying to mirror
them. But what was intolerable, what really could not be
borne any longer, was this monstrously isolated, monstrously narcissistic, pedestalled paragon. It seems that in
their own way the young have seen this and changed it,
creating a culture of their own in which hundreds and

thousands of people make films, assist in making films, make newspapers of all sorts, make music, paint pictures, write books, take photographs. They have abolished that isolated, creative, sensitive figure – by copying him in hundreds of thousands. A trend has reached an extreme, its conclusion, and so there will be a reaction of some sort, as always happens.

The theme of 'the artist' had to relate to another subjectivity. When I began writing there was pressure on writers not to be 'subjective'. This pressure began inside communist movements, as a development of the social literary criticism developed in Russia in the nineteenth century, by a group of remarkable talents, of whom Belinsky was the best known, using the arts and particularly literature in the battle against Czarism and oppression. It spread fast everywhere, finding an echo as late as the fifties, in this country, with the theme of 'commitment'. It is still potent in communist countries. 'Bothering about your stupid personal concerns when Rome is burning' is how it tends to get itself expressed, on the level of ordinary life – and was hard to withstand, coming from one's nearest and dearest, and from people doing everything one respected most : like, for instance, trying to fight colour prejudice in Southern Africa. Yet all the time novels, stories, art of every sort, became more and more personal. In the Blue Notebook, Anna writes of lectures she has been giving : ' "Art during the Middle Ages was communal, unindividual; it came out of a group consciousness. It was without the driving painful individuality of the art of the bourgeois era. And one day we will leave behind the driving egotism of individual art. We will return to an art which will express not man's self-divisions and separateness from his fellows but his responsibility for his fellows and his brotherhood. Art from the West becomes more and more a shriek of torment recording pain. Pain is becoming our deepest reality . . ." I have been saying something like this. About three months ago, in the middle of this lecture, I began to stammer and couldn't finish . . .'

Anna's stammer was because she was evading something. Once a pressure or a current has started, there is no way of avoiding it : there was no way of *not* being intensely subjective : it was, if you like, the writer's task for that time. You couldn't ignore it : you couldn't write a book

about the building of a bridge or a dam and not develop
the mind and feelings of the people who built it. (You think
this is a caricature? – Not at all. This *either/or* is at the
heart of literary criticism in communist countries at this
moment.) At last I understood that the way over, or through
this dilemma, the unease at writing about 'petty personal
problems', was to recognize that nothing is personal, in the
sense that it is uniquely one's own. Writing about oneself,
one is writing about others, since your problems, pains,
pleasures, emotions – and your extraordinary and remarkable ideas – can't be yours alone. The way to deal with the
problem of 'subjectivity', that shocking business of being
preoccupied with the tiny individual who is at the same
time caught up in such an explosion of terrible and marvellous possibilities, is to see him as a microcosm and in this
way to break through the personal, the subjective, making
the personal general, as indeed life always does, transforming a private experience – or so you think of it when still
a child, '*I* am falling in love', '*I* am feeling this or that
emotion, or thinking that or the other thought' – into something much larger : growing up is after all only the understanding that one's unique and incredible experience is what
everyone shares.

Another idea was that if the book were shaped in the
right way it would make its own comment about the conventional novel : the debate about the novel has been going
on since the novel was born, and is not, as one would
imagine from reading contemporary academics, something
recent. To put the short novel *Free Women* as a summary
and condensation of all that mass of material, was to say
something about the conventional novel, another way of
describing the dissatisfaction of a writer when something is
finished : 'How little I have managed to say of the truth,
how little I have caught of all that complexity; how can
this small neat thing be true when what I experienced was
so rough and apparently formless and unshaped.'

But my major aim was to shape a book which would
make its own comment, a wordless statement : to talk
through the way it was shaped.

As I have said, this was not noticed.

One reason for this is that the book is more in the European tradition than the English tradition of the novel. Or

rather, in the English tradition as viewed at the moment. The English novel after all does include *Clarissa* and *Tristram Shandy*, *The Tragic Comedians* – and Joseph Conrad.

But there is no doubt that to attempt a novel of ideas is to give oneself a handicap: the parochialism of our culture is intense. For instance, decade after decade bright young men and women emerge from their universities able to say proudly: 'Of course I know nothing about German literature.' It is the mode. The Victorians knew everything about German literature, but were able with a clear conscience not to know much about the French.

As for the rest – well, it is no accident that I got intelligent criticism from people who were, or who had been, marxists. They saw what I was trying to do. This is because Marxism looks at things as a whole and in relation to each other – or tries to, but its limitations are not the point for the moment. A person who has been influenced by Marxism takes it for granted that an event in Siberia will affect one in Botswana. I think it is possible that Marxism was the first attempt, for our time, outside the formal religions, at a worldmind, a world ethic. It went wrong, could not prevent itself from dividing and subdividing, like all the other religions, into smaller and smaller chapels, sects and creeds. But it was an attempt.

This business of seeing what I was trying to do – it brings me to the critics, and the danger of evoking a yawn. This sad bickering between writers and critics, playwrights and critics: the public have got so used to it they think, as of quarrelling children: 'Ah yes, dear little things, they are at it again.' Or: 'You writers get all that praise, or if not praise, at least all that attention – so why are you so perennially wounded?' And the public are quite right. For reasons I won't go into here, early and valuable experiences in my writing life gave me a sense of perspective about critics and reviewers; but over this novel, *The Golden Notebook*, I lost it: I thought that for the most part the criticism was too silly to be true. Recovering balance, I understood the problem. It is that writers are looking in the critics for an *alter ego*, that other self more intelligent than oneself who has seen what one is reaching for, and who judges you only by whether you have matched up to your aim or not. I have never yet met a writer who, faced at last with that rare being, a real critic, doesn't lose all paranoia and becomes gratefully attentive – he has found what he thinks he needs. But what he, the writer, is asking is impossible. Why should he expect this extraordinary being, the perfect critic (who does occasionally exist), why should there be anyone else who comprehends what he is trying to do? After all, there is only one person spinning that particular cocoon, only one person whose business it is to spin it.

It is not possible for reviewers and critics to provide what they purport to provide – and for which writers so ridiculously and childishly yearn.

This is because the critics are not educated for it; their training is in the opposite direction.

It starts when the child is as young as five or six, when he arrives at school. It starts with marks, rewards, 'places', 'streams', stars – and still, in many places, stripes. This horse-race mentality, the victor and loser way of thinking, leads to 'Writer X is, is not, a few paces ahead of Writer Y. Writer Y has fallen behind. In his last book Writer Z has shown himself as better than Writer A.' From the very beginning the child is trained to think in this way : always in terms of comparison, of success, and of failure. It is a weeding-out system : the weaker get discouraged and fall out; a system designed to produce a few winners who are always in competition with each other. It is my belief – though this is not the place to develop this – that the talents every child has, regardless of his official 'I.Q.', could stay with him through life, to enrich him and everybody else, if these talents were not regarded as commodities with a value in the success-stakes.

The other thing taught from the start is to distrust one's own judgement. Children are taught submission to authority, how to search for other people's opinions and decisions, and how to quote and comply.

As in the political sphere, the child is taught that he is free, a democrat, with a free will and a free mind, lives in a free country, makes his own decisions. At the same time he is a prisoner of the assumptions and dogmas of his time, which he does not question, because he has never been told they exist. By the time a young person has reached the age when he has to choose (we still take it for granted that a choice is inevitable) between the arts and the sciences, he often chooses the arts because he feels that here is humanity, freedom, choice. He does not know that he is already moulded by a system: he does not know that the choice itself is the result of a false dichotomy rooted in the heart of our culture. Those who do sense this, and who don't wish to subject themselves to further moulding, tend to leave, in a half-unconscious, instinctive attempt to find work where they won't be divided against themselves. With all our institutions, from the police force to academia, from medicine to politics, we give little attention to the people who leave – that process of elimination that goes on all the time and which excludes, very early, those likely to be original and reforming, leaving those attracted to a thing because that is what they are already like. A young police-man leaves the Force saying he doesn't like what he has to do. A young teacher leaves teaching, her idealism snubbed. This social mechanism goes almost unnoticed – yet it is as powerful as any in keeping our institutions rigid and oppressive.

These children who have spent years inside the training system become critics and reviewers, and cannot give what the author, the artist, so foolishly looks for – imaginative and original judgement. What they can do, and what they do very well, is to tell the writer how the book or play accords with current patterns of feeling and thinking – the climate of opinion. They are like litmus paper. They are wind gauges – invaluable. They are the most sensitive of barometers of public opinion. You can see changes of mood and opinion here sooner than anywhere except in the political field – it is because these are people whose whole education has been just that – to look outside themselves for their opinions, to adapt themselves to authority figures, to 'received opinion' – a marvellously revealing phrase.

It may be that there is no other way of educating people. Possibly, but I don't believe it. In the meantime it would be a help at least to describe things properly, to call things by their right names. Ideally, what should be said to every child, repeatedly, throughout his or her school life is something like this:

You are in the process of being indoctrinated. We have not yet evolved a system of education that is not a system of indoctrination. We are sorry, but it is the best we can do. What you are being taught here is an amalgam of current prejudice and the choices of this particular culture. The slightest look at history will show how impermanent these must be. You are being taught by people who have been able to accommodate themselves to a regime of thought laid down by their predecessors. It is a self-perpetuating system. Those of you who are more robust and individual than others, will be encouraged to leave and find ways of educating yourself – educating your own judgement. Those that stay must remember, always and all the time, that they are being moulded and patterned to fit into the narrow and particular needs of this particular society.

Like every other writer I get letters all the time from young people who are about to write theses and essays about my books in various countries – but particularly in the United States. They all say : 'Please give me a list of the articles about your work, the critics who have written about you, the authorities.' They also ask for a thousand details of total irrelevance, but which they have been taught to consider important, amounting to a dossier, like an immigration department's.

These requests I answer as follows: 'Dear Student. You are mad. Why spend months and years writing thousands of words about one book, or even one writer, when there are hundreds of books waiting to be read? You don't see that you are the victim of a pernicious system. And if you have yourself chosen my work as your subject, and if you do have to write a thesis – and believe me I am very grateful that what I've written is being found useful by you – then why don't you read what I have written and make up your own mind about what you think, testing it against your own life, your own experience. Never mind about Professors White and Black.'

'Dear Writer' – they reply. 'But I have to know what the authorities say, because if I don't quote them, my professor won't give me any marks.'

This is an international system, absolutely identical from the Urals to Yugoslavia, from Minnesota to Manchester.

The point is, we are all so used to it, we no longer

see how bad it is.

I am not used to it, because I left school when I was fourteen. There was a time I was sorry about this, and believed I had missed out on something valuable. Now I am grateful for a lucky escape. After the publication of *The Golden Notebook*, I made it my business to find out something about the literary machinery, to examine the process which made a critic, or a reviewer. I looked at innumerable examination papers – and couldn't believe my eyes; sat in on classes for teaching literature, and couldn't believe my ears.

You might be saying: That is an exaggerated reaction, and you have no right to it, because you say you have never been part of the system. But I think it is not at all exaggerated, and that the reaction of someone from outside is valuable simply because it is fresh and not biased by allegiance to a particular education.

But after this investigation, I had no difficulty in answering my own questions: Why are they so parochial, so personal, so small-minded? Why do they always atomize, and belittle, why are they so fascinated by detail, and uninterested in the whole? Why is their interpretation of the word *critic* always to find fault? Why are they always seeing writers as in conflict with each other, rather than complementing each other . . . simple, this is how they are trained to think. That valuable person who understands what you are doing, what you are aiming for, and can give you advice and real criticism, is nearly always someone right outside the literary machine, even outside the university system; it may be a student just beginning, and still in love with literature, or perhaps it may be a thoughtful person who reads a great deal, following his own instinct.

I say to these students who have to spend a year, two years, writing theses about one book: 'There is only one way to read, which is to browse in libraries and bookshops, picking up books that attract you, reading only those, dropping them when they bore you, skipping the parts that drag – and never, never reading anything because you feel you ought, or because it is part of a trend or a movement. Remember that the book which bores you when you are twenty or thirty will open doors for you when you are forty or fifty – and vice versa. Don't read a book out of its right time for you. Remember that for all the books we have in print, are as many that have never reached print, have never been written down – even now, in this age of compulsive reverence for the written word, history, even social ethic, are taught by means of stories, and the people who have been conditioned into thinking only in terms of what is written – and unfortunately nearly all the products of our educational system can do no more than this – are missing what is before their eyes. For instance, the real history of Africa is still in the custody of black storytellers and wise men, black historians, medicine men: it is a verbal history, still kept safe from the white man and his predations. Everywhere, if you keep your mind open, you will find the truth in words *not* written down. So never let the printed page be your master. Above all, you should know that the fact that you have to spend one year, or two years, on one book, or one author, means that you are badly taught – you should have been taught to read your way from one sympathy to another, you should be learning to follow your own intuitive feeling about what you need: that is what you should have been developing, not the way to quote from other people.'

But unfortunately it is nearly always too late.

It did look for a while as if the recent student rebellions might change things, as if their impatience with the dead stuff they are taught might be strong enough to substitute something more fresh and useful. But it seems as if the rebellion is over. Sad. During the lively time in the States, I had letters with accounts of how classes of students had refused their syllabuses, and were bringing to class their own choice of books, those that they had found relevant to their lives. The classes were emotional, sometimes violent, angry, exciting, sizzling with life. Of course this only happened with teachers who were sympathetic, and prepared to stand with the students against authority – prepared for the consequences. There are teachers who know that the way they have to teach is bad and boring – luckily there are still enough, with a bit of luck, to overthrow what is wrong, even if the students themselves have lost impetus.

Meanwhile there is a country where . . .

Thirty or forty years ago, a critic made a private list of writers and poets which he, personally, considered made up what was valuable in literature, dismissing all others. This list he defended lengthily in print, for The List instantly became a subject for much debate. Millions of words were written for and against – schools and sects, for and against, came into being. The argument, all these years later, still continues . . . no one finds this state of affairs sad or ridiculous . . .

Where there are critical books of immense plexity and and learning, dealing, but often at second- or third-hand, with original work – novels, plays, stories. The people who write these books form a stratum in universities across the world – they are an international phenomenon, the top layer of literary academia. Their lives are spent in criticizing, and in criticizing each other's criticism. They at least regard this activity as more important than the original work. It is possible for literary students to spend more time reading criticism and criticism of criticism than they spend reading poetry, novels, biography, stories. A great many people regard this state of affairs as quite normal, and not sad and ridiculous . . .

Where I recently read an essay about Antony and Cleopatra by a boy shortly to take A levels. It was full of originality and excitement about the play, the feeling that any real teaching about literature aims to produce. The essay was returned by the teacher like this : I cannot mark this essay, you haven't quoted from the authorities. Few teachers would regard this as sad and ridiculous . . .

Where people who consider themselves educated, and indeed as superior to and more refined than ordinary non-reading people, will come up to a writer and congratulate him or her on getting a good review somewhere – but will not consider it necessary to read the book in question, or ever to think that what they are interested in is success . . .

Where when a book comes out on a certain subject, let's say star-gazing, instantly a dozen colleges, societies, television programmes, write to the author asking him to come and speak about star-gazing. The last thing it occurs to them to do is to read the book. This behaviour is considered quite normal, and not ridiculous at all . . .

Where a young man or woman, reviewer or critic, who has not read more of a writer's work than the book in front of him, will write patronizingly, or as if rather bored with the whole business, or as if considering how many marks to give an essay, about the writer in question – who might have written fifteen books, and have been writing for twenty or thirty years – giving the said writer instruction on what to write next, and how. No one thinks this is absurd, certainly not the young person, critic or reviewer, who has been taught to patronize and itemize everyone for years, from Shakespeare downwards.

Where a Professor of Archaeology can write of a South American tribe which has advanced knowledge of plants, and of medicine and of psychological methods: 'The astonishing thing is that these people have no written language . . .' And no one thinks him absurd.

Where, on the occasion of a centenary of Shelley, in the same week and in three different literary periodicals, three young men, of identical education, from our identical universities, can write critical pieces about Shelley, damning him with the faintest possible praise, and in identically the same tone, as if they were doing Shelley a great favour to mention him at all – and no one seems to think that such a thing can indicate that there is something seriously wrong with our literary system.

Finally . . . this novel continues to be, for its author, a most instructive experience. For instance. Ten years after I wrote it, I can get, in one week, three letters about it, from three intelligent, well-informed, concerned people, who have taken the trouble to sit down and write to me. One might be in Johannesburg, one in San Francisco, one in Budapest. And here I sit, in London, reading them, at the same time, or one after another – as always, grateful to the writers, and delighted that what I've written can stimulate, illuminate – or even annoy. But one letter is entirely about the sex war, about man's inhumanity to woman, and woman's inhumanity to man, and the writer has produced pages and pages all about nothing else, for she – but not always a she, can't see anything else in the book.

The second is about politics, probably from an old Red like myself, and he or she writes many pages about politics, and never mentions any other theme.

These two letters used, when the book was, as it were, young, to be the most common.

The third letter, once rare but now catching up on the others, is written by a man or a woman who can see nothing in it but the theme of mental illness.

But it is the same book.

And naturally these incidents bring up again questions of what people see when they read a book, and why one person sees one pattern and nothing at all of another pattern, and how odd it is to have, as author, such a clear picture of a book, that is seen so very differently by its readers.

And from this kind of thought has emerged a new conclusion: which is that it is not only childish of a writer to want readers to see what he sees, to understand the shape and aim of a novel as he sees it – his wanting this means that he has not understood a most fundamental point. Which is that the book is alive and potent and fructifying and able to promote thought and discussion *only* when its plan and shape and intention are not understood, because that moment of seeing the shape and plan and intention is also the moment when there isn't anything more to be got out of it.

And when a book's pattern and the shape of its inner life is as plain to the reader as it is to the author – then perhaps it is time to throw the book aside, as having had its day, and start again on something new.

PHILIP STEVICK

Scheherezade runs out of plots, goes on talking; the King, puzzled, listens: an Essay on New Fiction

(reprinted with permission from *Triquarterly*, 1973)

I

'Endings are elusive, middles are nowhere to be found, but worst of all is to begin, to begin, to begin,' writes Barthelme, sympathizing with Edgar, a character with whom he shares certain problems. We all share Edgar's problems. Is it possible to begin to talk about fiction that strikes us as being in some way new or experimental without making large constructs that try to take stock of the very art of fiction itself? Indeed, of the very vitality and integrity of our time? Let us begin with no assumptions about the life of our time. The world, somebody says, is now so complicated that anything one says about it is true. As for the nature of fiction at the present time, two rather plain assumptions will suffice.

Lionel Trilling, in a recent essay in *Commentary*, has claimed that the very narrative impulse itself is exhausted, that we do not tell stories to each other any more, do not believe in stories, do not choose them as the vehicles for our deepest feelings, simply do not bother with narrative any more. Anthony Burgess, on the other hand, in his book *The Novel Now*, sets out to survey prose fiction since the great figures of the modernist period, and, although he obviously means his book to be inclusive, encyclopaedic, and rather undiscriminating, it is still surprising in the sheer bulk of its subject: some two hundred writers of fiction of sufficient quality to seem to Burgess worth discussing. In fact one comes to realize that anybody with a different background, an extensive but different reading experience, and a different temperament from Burgess could easily add a hundred more writers of fiction, all of considerable seriousness and significance. Trilling's essay seems to me among the

least persuasive pieces he has ever done, a last stage in
Trilling's willed and rationalized withdrawal from the contemporary. That a mind so fine as Trilling's should be so
repelled as he is at the narrative art of the present time and
so ingenious at explaining it away is one of the reasons that
we don't understand contemporary fiction any better than
we do. It is true, all the same, that Trilling's hostility to
the contemporary leads him to a premise that we can adopt
to a different context. Something very basic *has* changed in
the primacy and centrality of the narrative motive and the
narrative appeal in the last ten years. Let Trilling's essay
point us toward our first assumption: that the difference
between Barthelme and Katherine Mansfield, between Pynchon and Hemingway, is not a difference of historical setting, or style, or technique, or subject, or tone, or mode,
although it involves all of these. The difference between
the two goes to the roots of the narrative act itself, is a
difference in what it means to tell. Let Burgess's inclusiveness point us towards our second assumption: that a
perfectly amazing number of writers of considerable skill
and utterly varied convictions about the nature of their art
are flourishing at the present time, that along with some
remarkably innovative fiction there are also some true and
moving books being written with the technical resources of
Balzac and Trollope, and that anything we say about any
segment of the enormous body of contemporary fiction is
bound to look partial and unjustifiably exclusive to anyone
with a modest breadth of response.

The first fiction of Donald Barthelme's *City Life* begins:

An aristocrat was riding down the street in his carriage.
He ran over my father.

    After the ceremony I walked back to the city. I was
trying to think of the reason my father had died. Then
I remembered: he was run over by a carriage.

A short fiction by Richard Brautigan entitled *The World
War I Los Angeles Airplane* begins:

He was found lying dead near the television set on the
front room floor of a small rented house in Los Angeles.
My wife had gone to the store to get some ice cream.

It was an early-in-the-night-just-a-few-blocks-away store. We were in an ice-cream mood. The telephone rang. It was her brother to say that her father had died that afternoon.

Robert Coover begins his fiction *A Pedestrian Accident* in this way:

Paul stepped off the curb and got hit by a truck. He didn't know what it was that hit him at first, but now, here on his back, under the truck, there could be no doubt. Is it me? he wondered. Have I walked the earth and come here?

It is obvious at first that there are certain common characteristics of method, voice, and sensibility in the three beginnings: an extraordinary innocence, either genuine or feigned, even a kind of common prose rhythm deriving from the unwillingness to subordinate and complicate that is an attribute of that innocence, a readiness to confront certain extremities of life, in these cases pain, accident, death, and mourning, but an investing of these extremities with an odd and terribly distant artifice, a playing off of a method of wit, tough, flip, and facile, that is reminiscent of the stand-up comic ('Then I remembered . . .' 'We were in an ice-cream mood.' 'Is it me? he wondered.') against a personal fragility and vulnerability that is very different from the classic toughness, knowingness, and irony of the dominant modernists. It is odd how quickly these qualities of 'voice' can register on us, so that we know, before the structure of the fiction begins to take shape in our minds, that we are being spoken to by an imagination post-Joycean and very much of our time, the theatricality of our three fictions being different in its tone of voice from anything we are accustomed to in Dostoevsky and Gide and Faulkner. Finally what unites the three fictions is the common presentation of the kind of event, death and violent accident, that *must* be led up to, or explained, or prepared for, or set in a context, but is, in these three cases, simply told. It is the chilling, almost pathological directness of beginning in the three fictions that is likely to seem to us most striking, for the fictions do not seem particularly 'experimental', as we might use the word of other arts – their syntax is conventional and the words follow one another on the page. The beginnings seem to be as striking as they are because they are more than simply violations of conventions. They are epistemic dislocations, and the clearest analogue that I can think of is Kafka's great beginning, 'As Gregor Samsa awoke one morning from a troubled dream, he found himself changed in his bed to some monstrous kind of vermin.'

The differences of the three beginnings from each other are as obvious as the similarities. Barthelme exploits his fondness for the absurdities of a bookish past, the camp obliquity that corresponds, in his prose, to his use of old engravings in the texts of his more recent work. Brautigan superimposes a deliberate and affectatious *naïveté* upon the plausable details of California. Coover begins to play back and forth between what one does feel at moments of extreme pain and what one thinks one ought to feel, between speech which is deeply felt yet comes out as cliché and speech which is formulaic yet comes out as existential cry. It is by observing the differences between the fictions that we might assume what I believe to be true, that what we have is not a movement, not a clique, not a group, not a school, not a unified assertion of anything nor a reaction against anything, not a conspiracy. On the other hand, it is by pointing to the similarities between the fictions that we might assume what I also believe to be true, that there are indeed some shared traits among writers of non-traditional fiction, a common sense of what they are not a part of, certain shared enthusiasms, certain common characteristics of voice and technique. Both the similarities and the differences suggest why it is that we have very little critical description worth attending to that would help us make sense out of recent non-traditional fiction.

New directions in the art of the last century and a half have generally been surrounded with the appearance of social agonism (consider Spender's title *The Struggle of the Modern*, the sense at least since Wordsworth and commonplace in our time that one's own art is a counterforce, in combat with the torpor and stupidity of one's own time) and a defensive verbalism, in which the legitimacy of the new art was described in a never-ending 'introduction'. Every generation of poets since Wordsworth has claimed to

be writing the language actually used by men, in contrast
to its lumpish and stilted predecessors. Every generation of
novelists has claimed to be in touch with reality in a way
denied its predecessors. These defensive manœuvres loom
so large that it would not be surprising to find a reader who
recalled 'Tradition and the Individual Talent' as clearly as
The Waste Land, who relished Shaw's introductions rather
more than the plays themselves, and who recalled that there
was one such a thing as 'Vorticism' without being able to
name a single literary work that was in any way related to
it. Of recent non-traditional fiction, however, there is not
much sense of social agonism: writers like Heller, Barth,
and Vonnegut are lionized. As for the manifestoes, the
polemical introductions, the defensive stance-taking so
commonplace in the past, they are all virtually nonexistent.
There has probably not been a comparable body of writing
since the Romantic period in which the writers themselves
have told us so little about what was wrong with their
predecessors, how they hoped to improve upon them, and
why we ought to be reading their works.

In the absence of tactical statements by the writers themselves, we can map out areas of coherence in literary
history in a number of ways. One is by finding a command-
ing, charismatic figure who seems to have dominated the art
of his time, allowing the figure's dominance to provide the
centre of that coherence. The Age of Pope is defined by
defining both the nature of Pope's genius and the nature of
his dominance. American tough-guy fiction is ordinarily
understood by fixing Hemingway at its origins and its
centre. One could guess from the three passages just quoted
that although the three writers might well share some
affinities (for Beckett and Kafka, perhaps for Céline and
Nathaniel West, or among older writers for Sterne and
Rabelais), they are not dominated by anybody. There is no
peak to the pyramid and our search for *that* kind of
coherence is pointless.

Another way of finding coherence is to discover a common ideology. The Oxford Movement is defined by what
its members believed. And our habit of grouping writers
according to decade or generation is based on the assumption that writers grouped in that way can be seen to cohere
by reason of their shared assumptions about the nature of

the world. Of our three initial examples, I am not sure
what ideology means when applied to Barthelme and
Coover; I think that the word may mean something when
applied to Brautigan. But in any case, if we are equipped to
define literary coherence by finding a common ideology, we
do seem to be out of luck here.

Still another way of defining literary coherence is to look
at the aesthetic transaction itself. We have a movement, or
a school, when we can point to a coherent audience or a
specific group of periodicals or publishers especially recep-
tive to a specialized kind of art. The nature of *The Yellow
Book*, its contributors, and its audience all cohere as a unit.
And we naturally seek to understand 'Southern Agrarianism'
or 'The New Criticism' by understanding the journals, such
as the *Sewanee* and *Kenyon Reviews*, in which those aesthetic and intellectual transactions were presented. Among
our three examples, there is, again, no coherence at all.
The audience for Coover does not overlap, so far as one
can tell, with the audience for Brautigan, and the two are
rarely published in the same places. Barthelme's case is the
most peculiar of the three. *City Life* is made up of work
published in *The New Yorker* and *Paris Review*; as a book,
City Life was reviewed as an avant-garde mystification – and
was offered as an alternate to the members of the Book-of-
the-Month Club: I bought my copy from the revolving rack
at a drugstore. In short, almost all of the equipment which
we have for defining a direction in the history of an art,
setting it off from what has gone before and what comes
after, breaks down in the face of those writers whom we
would easily call non-traditional writers of fiction, an
incongruous and highly individual lot.

On the other hand, the correspondences among new
writers of fiction suggest, as much as the differences
between them, why it is that new fiction is so little understood. 'Post-modernist' is an epithet that I, for one, find
annoying and unhelpful. But it is true, all the same, that
recent fiction no longer orients itself according to its own
relations to the modernist masters and that this sense of
discontinuity with the dominant figures of modernism is
one of the few qualities that unite new fiction. (Ihab
Hassan's contention that the great fountainhead of 'postmodernist' fiction is *Finnegans Wake* seems to me perverse,

bizarre, and unsupportable.) Yet most criticism still defines
the art of our own time as being, in the case of fiction,
the art of the twentieth century. A professional interest in
Joyce need not be exclusive of a professional interest in
Coover; but in fact the two almost always are exclusive of
each other, a fact not surprising when one reflects on the
gulf in time between the two, Coover being as far in time
from Joyce as Joyce is from George Eliot. What recent
fiction tells us on every page is that it is of another age
than the modernist masters. And what we are further
obliged to recognize is that our public conceptualizing has
not even acknowledged the transition, much less provided
the organizing devices by means of which we can make
sense of it.

There was a time when the kind of public understanding
that we lack was supplied by the 'man of letters'. But, as
John Gross has magisterially demonstrated, the man of
letters has fallen and figures comparable to Henley, Saints-
bury, and Middleton Murry, or more recently Edmund
Wilson, are not likely to arise in our own time to mediate
between new art and its anxious public in a way that those
older figures did. Even if such figures did exist, they would
find their function difficult to perform, since new fiction
tends to mock, subvert, and pre-empt any traditional
attempts at critical interpretation of itself. And thus recent
narrative art (with the exception of 'new' French fiction,
which has not lacked apologetics for itself) has set about
creating a new set of narrative possibilities in a time when
the public for fiction does not expect or wish for anybody
to seek to form its taste and instruct its response and in a
time when the professional interpreters of contemporary
narrative art tend to be, in fact, interpreters of modernist
art, which is to say the art of the half-century now past.

Finally we understand less than we should about art like
that of Barthelme, Brautigan, and Coover because our modes
of critical understanding are undermined by a family of
metaphors to which we continue to cling with obsessive
tenacity, namely the organic metaphors by which we
describe the 'birth', the 'growth', and the 'death' of fiction.
Certain genres in literary history, especially the more rigid,
stylized, and highly specialized ones, have been invented,
have been extensively used, and have been ultimately aban-

doned; but such formal exhaustion has always been the result of a complex of causes involving audience, ideas, authorial motives, even the economics of publication and presentation. When we apply the organic metaphors to the flourishing and declining of literary genres, however, we pretend that no complex of causes need be found because genres, we seem to say, contain within themselves their own vitality. Furthermore, the organic metaphor is extremely tendentious. If the novel, or the short story, is, as a genre, comparable to a body, then it contains the elements of itself and is threatened by alien elements, those alien elements being, of course, prose fictions that lie eccentric to the unstated norm with which the body of fiction is identified. William Park has described the use of the organic metaphor by early historians of fiction, with all of their talk of forerunners and founders, so that by the time of Ernest Baker's *History of the English Novel* in 1924, 'the growth, evolution, branches, roots, stems, and trunks occur in such profusion that we can only assume that the novel, as botanical garden, had been taken for granted, as indeed it still is by present-day writers, who while concerning themselves with rhetoric and "strategy" continue to use the evolutionary metaphors'. As for the dying of the body of fiction, readers of the novel in the latter third of the eighteenth century, as J. M. S. Tompkins observes, thought the novel dead, its possibilities played out. Which means that, if the novel has been dying for two centuries, there is something wrong not with the novel but with the metaphor. For a long time serious discussion of new fiction has been hindered by the cumbersome, vacuous business of dying forms. The new fiction of the past twenty years is worth attending to on its own terms, not because it is living while something else has died.

I suggest two ways into the new fiction I describe. One is by comparison with the recent past, a piece of good fiction of not very long ago which is, most emphatically, the kind of thing which new fictions are not. The other is by something larger and riskier, an aesthetics of new fiction, set against the classic premises of prose fiction since the beginning of the novel.

I I

Jean Stafford's 'A Country Love Story' begins in this way:

> An antique sleigh stood in the yard, snow after snow
> banked up against its eroded runners. Here and there
> upon the bleached and splintery seat were wisps of horse-
> hair and scraps of the black leather that had once uphol-
> stered it. It bore, with all its jovial curves, an air not so
> much of desuetude as of slowed-down dash, as if weary
> horses, unable to go another step, had at last stopped here.
> The sleigh had come with the house. The former owner,
> a gifted businesswoman from Castine who bought old
> houses and sold them again with all their pitfalls still
> intact, had said when she was showing them the place, 'A
> picturesque detail, I think,' and, waving it away, had
> turned to the well, which, with enthusiasm and at con-
> siderable length, she said had never gone dry. Actually,
> May and Daniel had found the detail more distracting
> than picturesque, so nearly kin was it to outdoor arts and
> crafts . . .

Moving from Barthelme, Brautigan, and Coover to Jean
Stafford represents no particular difference in quality. Questions of qualitative ranking tend to occupy readers and
critics less than they used to; but it is clear enough that all
four writers are in command of their materials and are in
their quite different ways artful and sophisticated. All four
works are short fiction, in which the beginnings I quote set
in motion aesthetic objects which turn out to be of comparable size. The four fictions are not far from each other
in time, less than twenty years. Yet the beginning of Jean
Stafford's story, in comparison with the more recent fictions,
reads like something from the other side of the moon. The
most immediately striking differences lie in what Jean Stafford does, and the more recent writers do not do, with
time and with physical objects.

'An antique sleigh', 'snow after snow', 'eroded runners',
phrases like these from the first sentence begin to present a
durational mode that is little short of obsessive, projecting
us immediately into a world of waiting, expecting, con-

templating, appreciating, hoping, wondering, all of those experiences in which the mind and the sensibility are deployed around the central object of their contemplation, slow change. Both objects and people bear with them the marks of their own past; everything decays and disintegrates; both nature and people present the appearance of cyclic or ritualistically recurring behaviour. In addition, time, in such fiction, always carries with it an implicit valuation. A character shows his age gracefully or clumsily; the process of aging carries with it great dignity or great pathos; an aging object carries with it a sense of decreased value, as a result of its tasteful durability. And so it is that we are unsure, in that first paragraph, whether the sleigh is worn out, and should be discarded, or is an authentic antique, and should be preserved. There is no doubt that the cyclic, ritualistic house-buying and -selling of the 'gifted businesswoman' is specious and faintly repulsive.

It need hardly be said that no one goes through life with his eye so firmly fixed on the clock as this, saying to himself, A is older than B, but B bears its age more gracefully than A. Such an obsession with time is a convention which we never particularly noticed as a convention when a great deal of fiction was written in that way. There is a perverse kind of time sense at work in new fiction, centring especially around a fascination with the junk of our culture, both linguistic and material. But it is in no way comparable to the durational quality of Jean Stafford's story. If we recall the enormous amount of critical attention given to the philosophy of Bergson and the temporal techniques of Proust, Virginia Woolf, and Joyce, and if we then regard the use of time in Jean Stafford's story as a stylized domestication of one of the chief modernist preoccupations, then the atemporality of such fiction as Barthelme's, the indifference to slow change and the lack of interest in the value-conferring process I have described all become highly significant. The high-handed atemporality of new fiction is a remarkable abandonment of a set of conventions and an epistemic orientation that we had grown accustomed to thinking absolutely essential to the fictive act.

Secondly, to return to Jean Stafford's paragraph, a set of relationships is evoked between two different modes of existence, in this case the man-made object and the forces of the natural world, and these relationships are played upon in a symbolistic way. The function of a sleigh is to ride on the snow, not be covered by it. And we know, even from the first sentence, that the presence of the sleigh, immobile and nonfunctional, will be made into a metaphor, charged with a flexible, ironic, noncommittal value, a metaphor for the presence of man in the world. As in the case of time, such a man-nature dichotomy, as a centre for a symbolistic charge of meaning, is a convention, present in a large amount of modernist fiction, extended and refined in the kind of sensibility fiction which Jean Stafford represents. But here again it is a convention of no use to new fiction, in which the made and the born, the authentic and the schlock, the natural and the manufactured are all taken as the given data of a difficult world which simply cannot be divided into two halves.

Thirdly, there is, in Jean Stafford's story, the presence of the thing itself, an object pulled out of the background and conspicuously placed before our attention, described from a double viewpoint, near and far, given a touch of the pathetic fallacy (the sleigh has 'jovial curves'), and above all invested with 'taste'. The sleigh, of course, is a chameleon image and is in good taste or bad according to its human context. And it is a marvellously versatile structural device, which compresses and gathers together a number of attitudes axial to the story that follows. But there is not much doubt that the image of the sleigh is more than a trope or a structural device to Jean Stafford and her readers; it is a thing, with intricacy of contour, complexity of texture, solidity, and the marks of its own past. Whatever its usefulness in the story, it is an image that issues from the imagination of a writer fascinated with the material objects of daily, sensory existence.

Such 'solidity of specification', in James's phrase, is central to the purpose of the classic realistic novel. It survives, abstracted and intensified, in certain works of recent French fiction such as those of Robbe-Grillet. But again, to recall the material texture of the three beginnings, the narrator's father, in Barthelme's tale, is run over by 'a carriage'. The carriage is driven by 'an aristocrat'. Brautigan gives us something more to consider: 'he' is found dead near 'the television set on the front room floor . . .' Paul, in Coover's fiction, does see and feel with painful acuity. But he is in no position to show much interest in the texture of things. Fiction of the Robbe-Grillet model has never really caught on in the United States. But allowing an affectionate interest in things to stand at the very centre of one's fiction is in the Anglo-American tradition. And thus new fiction seems, at least from our sample, to have gone some distance toward disavowing the empirical solidity of classic fiction, especially the value-loaded qualities with which we invest material objects, in favour of a narrative rhythm closer to the fabulist and romantistic traditions, as nearly devoid of materiality as fiction can be and still be plausibly set in a recognizable world.

The points of contrast between Jean Stafford's story and new fiction are almost limitless. Take the phenomenal settings, for a further example, the ways in which the characters' conscious experience is controlled by the spaces in which the authors choose to present it. Jean Stafford's story begins in a front yard, but its energy and attention are directed toward a house. In due course certain exterior events will take place, but the characters' most intense emotional scenes are lived out within rooms. It is not merely a convenience of staging, to place the characters within those spaces in which they most conveniently interact. And it is not merely the realistic result of the fact that the characters, being upper middle class, do spend most of their time in rooms. There is an obsessive, house-bound quality in such fiction, reminiscent of Samuel Richardson, in which doors and windows, corridors and stairs, beds, tables, and chairs all figure heavily. Once again, it occurs to me that there was a time when it seemed to all of us that that was simply the way very much fiction was written, with characters condemned to work out their fates in studies, kitchens, and living-rooms. And once again, new fiction presents a remarkable break with that convention. It is a fairly atypical beginning for Brautigan, in which rooms figure as heavily as they do. More generally, in the fiction I have been trying to describe, the physical space that encloses the consciousness of the action is undefined, nonspecific, in some vaguely hallucinatory way, or extreme, artificially constricted perhaps, or unaccountably open, or visionary, in which the contours of physical space are heavily shaped by the experiencing mind. If the action in new fiction does take place in houses, it is never for purposes of defining the 'usualness' of a cast of domestic characters or for rendering the room-bound effect so useful to Jean Stafford.

Or consider matters of style. In some seemingly indefinable way, Jean Stafford's opening paragraph sounds not only characteristic of her work as a whole. It also sounds like countless other stories of about the same period. The traits of style are not really indefinable, however, are all too obvious, if anything. Take the preciousness of a phrase like 'an air not so much of desuetude as of slowed-down dash'. Why 'desuetude'? Why not 'disuse'? Consider the 'as if' clause that follows. That single sentence contains the effect of two principles, one a movement toward elegance when directness would seem to interfere in the wit and flair of the phrase, second a movement toward embellishment in the interests of demonstrating an imagination expansively and leisurely at work upon its materials, comparing, supposing, qualifying, conjuring alternatives, musing. It goes without saying that the 'as if' clause, as a syntactic strategy, does not exist in new fiction. The 'as if' clause seems to imply that the empirical reality being described is rather bizarre, sufficiently unfamiliar so that some conjectural cause must be supplied to account whimsically for its being so bizarre. The writer of new fiction does not know why empirical reality is as bizarre as it is. He does know that the stylistic patterns which render the introspective, contemplative, domestic imagination of the fiction of the fifties are unavailable to him.

It is probably by its structure that we are best equipped to recognize the difference between fiction that seems to be classic modernist and fiction that seems to be audacious or experimental in some distinctly new way. In Jean Stafford's story, the events consist of tensions made only partly overt, harsh words, misunderstandings. Any sharply exterior events clearly exist to figure forth the moral and psychological dynamics of the characters. Ultimately the story ends with a kind of plateau of understanding toward which the rest of the fiction has worked. Epiphany is too facile and imprecise a word for what happens at the end of the story. It is a moment both of resignation and of awesome frustration in the face of the future, and any word, such as epiphany, which implies sudden insight is misleading. Still, the structure of the story is in the tradition of epiphany fiction, which is to say that it values the private and the domestic over the public and the external, that it demonstrates a belief in the possibility that an intuitive self-knowledge can cut through accumulations of social ritual and self-deception, a belief so firm that it permits the intuitive act to serve as dramatic end point and structural principle, indeed as the very moral justification for the fiction.

It takes only a sentence or two of Barthelme, Brautigan, and Coover to recognize how far they are from epiphanic form. All three tend to find more interest in the public than in the private, in the external than the internal, in the freakish and extreme than the middle range of experience. Nothing in the beginnings of the three fictions points to or seems to create the enabling conditions for the epiphanic illumination. None of the three writers seems to have much interest in such intuitive insights, perhaps not even much belief that they exist. And thus we do not need to read to the ends of the three fictions to know that their structures are antithetical to what is the most conventionalized, imitated, standardized feature of modernist fiction, especially shorter fiction, of the last generation, the epiphanic illumination, or, as in Jean Stafford, the self-generated plateau of understanding which transcends the plane of social conventionality and habitual self-deception which has made the self-understanding both possible and necessary.

As for the three examples, it is hard to say what structural principles underlie their composition. Perhaps the best way to approach the question of structure is to jettison the word structure altogether. Structure, whether we wish it to or not, carries with it connotations of economy, symmetry, accountable proportion, organic form. If pressed, most of us could apply any of those connoted values to any well-known piece of modernist fiction, certainly to Jean Stafford's story, could construct a systematic analysis by means of which every event, every image, every word could be accounted for by aesthetic principles apparently derived from the work itself. I do not think that that habit of mind is appropriate to the three examples and I do not think that that relentlessness of method will carry us very far. 'We like books,' says one of the characters in a well-known passage of Barthelme's *Snow White*, 'that have a lot of *dreck* in them, matter which presents itself as not wholly relevant (or indeed, at all relevant) but which, carefully attended to, can supply a kind of "sense" of what is going on. This "sense" is not to be obtained by reading between the lines (for there is nothing there, in those white spaces) but by reading the lines themselves – looking at them and so arriving at a feeling not of satisfaction exactly, that is too much to expect, but of having read them, of having "completed" them.'

All three of our exemplary new fictions extend themselves in ways that are more additive than dramatic or progressive. In the barest and still the best definition of form, Kenneth Burke writes, '*Form* in literature is an arousing and fulfilment of desires. A work has form in so far as one part of it leads a reader to anticipate another part, to be gratified by the sequence.' Basically such 'desires' in shorter fiction are of three kinds: problematic, psychological, and conventional. We have a problematic desire when we have a secret to be discovered during the course of the fiction, a relationship to be perceived, a motive to be revealed. When the problem is resolved our 'desire' is 'fulfilled'. We have a psychological desire when we expect a mental process within the fiction to run its course, self-ignorance to proceed to self-knowledge, perhaps, or personal hostility to proceed to personal accommodation. When the psychological process is complete, when the character has come to know what we have expected he must know, then our 'desire' is 'fulfilled'. We have a conventional desire when we are led to expect events, devices, and tonal manipulations typical of the genre. Jean Stafford's story is full of such conventional desires and fulfilments, the sophisticated mastery of the characters alternating with their humiliation and ineffectuality, the compassion of the author alternating with her ironic distance, the diminuendo into generalized pathos at the end, all of these being typical of the genre. In our three exemplary fictions there is no problematic desire: each begins with a death but our natural tendency to see a fictional death as a problem, to ask why, where, by whose hand, in what manner, is dissolved by the fact that in Barthelme and Brautigan we are told all that we need to know at once, in so unproblematic a way that no residue of curiosity remains, and in Coover, while the manner of death extends over the duration of the fiction, there is nothing that we might *wish* to know, as a key to understanding the death. In none of the three fictions is there any interplay between the psychological desires which the reader might project into the fiction and the fulfilment of them: the characters are constructs, types, quite deliberately devoid of much inner life. What they know they gather by bits and pieces. If they solve a problem, the solution becomes a new problem and nothing is gained. Needless to say the three fictions do not give us much in the way of conventional form. An alternative to saying that the fictions are formless, which sounds gratuitously pejorative, is to extend the idea of form, beyond the linear progression defined by Burke, towards something more mosaic, or concentric, or circular, an idea of form which is, as I suggested at the beginning of the paragraph, additive, in which the work grows by certain loosely associative principles but not with the covert purpose of arousing and fulfilling our desires at all.

The three fictions are, in different ways, variations around a thematic centre. In literature an analogue is the encyclopaedic passage in Rabelais, several pages of variations on the name and nature of the codpiece, for example. In experience, a loose analogy is the looking up of a word in a dictionary, finding a different word instead, becoming interested in the derivation of the second word, forgetting the word one began to look up, remembering it again, being reminded of a related word. In Brautigan's 'story', each paragraph, after several introductory paragraphs, is numbered. The effect is certainly to add to the illusion of innocence, making the fiction look rather like a schoolboy's composition. But the numbering also creates a peculiar ambiguity around the form of the work. Each paragraph concerns one of the events in the life of the father mentioned in the beginning paragraph. The effect of numbering these unmodulated and disconnected 'deeds' of the father is, at first, to make them seem to be about to come to an especially contrived whole, in the way in which an argument presents three points in its support, then its conclusion, or in the way in which a romance presents three adventures before certifying its hero as truly heroic. But it becomes obvious that those numbered paragraphs add up to less and less as the work proceeds. And by the time one has finished, it seems as if Brautigan's narrator has gathered random recollections, given each a number as it occurred to him, and then put them together according to the number which he had arbitrarily assigned to them. The events do, to be sure, take place in some kind of chronological order. But there is no reason why the father should have been an Idaho banker first and a parking-lot attendant later. Both Coover's and Barthelme's fictions are alike in this respect: both share with Brautigan's a form in which images and events accumulate and sometimes gather great force but do not arrange themselves so as to demonstrate a theme or so as to gradually gratify the expectations and resolve the tensions generated in the beginning of the work.

It is possible, then, to disarrange prose more radically than anything in the new fiction I have been describing, as those experiments in concrete prose indicate. Older explanations of avant-garde art, accounting for the work of the Italian futurists and the Dadaists as an alienated, disencumbered attempt to violate tradition, insult taste, and shock the bourgeoisie, don't have much bearing here. What we do have is a body of fiction perfectly intelligible and not very shocking but strikingly different from the customary fiction of the late modernists.

III

I have kept the discussion up to this point as constricted as I have because it seems to me that some rather narrow things need to be said, about a manageable group of examples. We have now gone far enough to be able to decide what can and cannot be said, in general, theoretical, methodological ways, about recent experimental fiction.

In a finely perceptive essay in a recent *Partisan Review*, Richard Wasson begins by describing the modernist imagination, which he sees as being best characterized by its use of myth without any particular belief, as an organizing structure for literary works and as 'a mode of perception, even of vision, which provides the unstable subjective self with a world order that transcends individuality'. Drawing primarily on Iris Murdoch, Robbe-Grillet, Pynchon, and Barth,

Wasson describes the contrary position, post-modernist if one wishes, which aims its antagonism squarely at the mythic centre of the modernist aesthetic. In Barth's *End of the Road*, that older mythicizing penchant is caricatured in the Mythotherapy of the Remobilization Farm in which Jacob Horner submits to his grotesque therapist. Implicitly the achieved art of Barth within this novel is the opposite of, 'antidote to' says Wasson, the speciousness of myth. 'Such an art,' Wasson writes,

> is aware of its artificiality, its incompleteness, its partial dumbness before reality. Mythotherapy tries to force the whole world into the self and the self into the world, to make everything in the world subordinate to the drama of the self; mythoplastic art turns ironically on itself, works to recognize the separate and mysterious difference between self and other, artifice and reality.

There is nothing procrustean about Wasson's essay. Yet it is finally too narrow either to define for us its object, recent fiction, or to lay out for us a method and a theoretical centre. It is partly not Wasson's fault at all but merely the result of writing about something which is still happening; the volume of fiction in the Barth-Pynchon mode grows year by year and each year looks a little different in its totality. Certain features of Wasson's description apply to anybody who strikes us as non-traditional (his remarks on the diminishing interest in the drama of the self seem to me most durable), but if the import of Barth's *End of the Road* and the aesthetic of the end of myth are really at the centre of recent fiction, it is hard to know how to account for Coover's *The Universal Baseball Association*, which is, in some legitimate sense, quite relentlessly mythic, or Gass's *Omensetter's Luck*, or Gardner's *Grendel*, which are, in ways quite different from each other, also mythic, all three of which are indisputably of the non-traditional mode we are considering. Joyce Carol Oates, in an interview, speaks of her intention to rewrite, in her own terms, a number of classic works of fiction, an enterprise rather Borgesian, very neomodern, and quite mythic. Even Barth himself will not hold still but destroys myth with one book, only to revive it in several of the fictions of *Lost in the Funhouse*.

It is sometimes said, by Philip Roth, for example, in his essay 'Writing American Fiction', that recent fiction has a bizarre, neurotic quality precisely in response to the bizarre quality of American life in the last decade. Locating the cause of the discontinuities and extremities of recent fiction in the extremities of social fact doesn't help us very much, however. Here is Roth on that set of relationships:

> The American writer in the middle of the twentieth century has his hands full in trying to understand, and then describe, and then make *credible* much of the American reality. It stupefies, it sickens, it infuriates, and finally it is even a kind of embarrassment to one's own meagre imagination. The actuality is continually outdoing our talents, and the culture tosses up figures almost daily that are the envy of any novelist. Who, for example, could have invented Charles Van Doren? Roy Cohn and David Schine? Sherman Adams and Bernard Goldfine? Dwight David Eisenhower?

Those names! One realizes as the passage proceeds that the essay was written in the early sixties *about* the dear, dull fifties, and that *that* was the time of our national experience that was so bizarre that it compelled our writers to respond with ever more bizarre books.

Inevitably such arguments, Roth's or anybody else's, go in search of historical cause only to demonstrate a lack of historical perspective of astonishing dimensions. Do those who argue in this way really propose that street life in American cities is more bizarre than street life in Mayhew's Victorian London? or that public figures in Washington are more venal than the clowns who surrounded, say, the Harding administration? or that the 'news' in metropolitan daily newspapers is more hysterical than it was during the lifetime of William Randolph Hearst? New fiction may be more responsive than much previous fiction to the discontinuous and surreal, the bizarre and the aberrant in current society. But it simply cannot be demonstrated that there has been some kind of quantitative increase in lunacy and that that is the cause of the newness of new fiction.

Rather than attempting to explain new fictions by social fact and rather than looking within new fiction for the indications of a new sensibility, as Wasson does, a few critics, Susan Sontag most conspicuously, attempt to define a new sensibility in world culture at large, in which some few works of recent fiction participate. 'The primary feature of the new sensibility,' writes Susan Sontag,

> is that its model product is not the literary work, above all, the novel. A new non-literary culture exists today, of whose very existence, not to mention significance, most literary intellectuals are entirely unaware. This new establishment includes certain painters, sculptors, social planners, film-makers, TV technicians, neurologists, musicians, electronics engineers, dancers, philosophers, and sociologists. (A few poets and prose writers can be included.)

I, for one, find it difficult to take this passage seriously. There is the dipping down into various areas so as to choose, Calvinist fashion, a body of the elect. There is the calculated incongruity of the series. More than an attempt to win assent to her notion that older, compartmentalized versions of culture are now insupportable, the series is an attempt to 'mau-mau', in Tom Wolfe's phrase, the literati, who have enough guilt without worrying whether we are taking with proper seriousness the TV technicians, neurologists, musicians, and electronics engineers. There is the condescension, the offensiveness of the inside-dopesterism. The passage asserts that one finds the characteristic tone of our age in a variety of 'media' and hesitates to locate the dominant tone of our period in our prose fiction with the same confidence that we might once have done; with that position it is hard to quarrel. The notion, however, that prose fiction is a phenomenon on the fringes of a transformation of world consciousness and that we can only comprehend such a transformation by accepting the peripheral position of literature and attending to what the TV technicians and neurologists are trying to tell us, such a notion seems to me finally only a substitution of a very masochistic kind of polemic for the understanding that is so badly needed.

One thing that we can say about new fiction is that the range of fictional options has increased enormously in the last decade. It has occurred to me as I have been writing this essay that I have shifted in my allusions, without any feeling of constraint, between long and short fictional forms. This, in itself, is new, a tendency to be able to take short forms as seriously as one takes the novel, the result of writers like Borges, Landolfi, and a dozen others, and a tendency to be able to speak interchangeably about long and short forms as exhibits in a total range of fictional possibilities rather than stylized, circumscribed, discrete genres. Three forces have coincided to increase the range of fictional possibility in the last decade: the fatigue of the conventional modernist forms (the epiphany story, the reliance upon a heavy symbology, both public and private, to carry the import of the fiction, all of those conventions associated with interiority and the rendering of the sensibility), the influence of several individual figures, and the academic training of most writers of new fiction.

Along with the eroding of the stock of modernist forms, we have seen the vogue of Borges, the success of Gass, the transition from underground to overground of figures like Brautigan, the considerable American interest in the inimitable French *chosistes*, the conspicuousness of Mailer, the work of a considerable group of extraordinary journalists and virtuosi of the tape-recorder extending from Tom Wolfe to Studs Terkel to Oscar Lewis, a collection of models remarkable for the way in which they all stretch the boundaries of fiction. In a recent issue of *Triquarterly* a work appears entitled 'Abandoned Cities' by Jack Anderson, consisting of four entries, descriptions, rather mock descriptions, of four cities. One of them is titled 'Bismarck, North Dakota' and it begins in this way: 'There are no suburbs. The streets stop at the wheatfields, where the iron helmets are set on black sticks to frighten off eagles. Beyond this point, the wind begins, as hard to ignore as stomachache. The townspeople fear two things always: drought and frost.' Before the erosion of the modernist forms and before the interest in a dozen figures had done its work on what we thought fiction ought to be, no periodical would have known what to do with 'Abandoned Cities'. No readers would have known how to respond to it. And its author would not have known it could be written.

It is perhaps the academic training and associations of so many practitioners of new fiction that is most difficult to come to terms with. The old prejudices hang on and we continue to think, despite all the evidence to the contrary, that there is something about the academy that is irreconcilably opposed to the imagination of the writer, something stifling, cloying, deadening. Even those of us who are academics still take a special pleasure in the fading but still vital image of Dylan Thomas telling dirty stories to Bryn Mawr girls. I suppose, reaching into our literary past, there would have been something destructive had Dreiser or Crane or Bierce or any of the Redskins of our literary history picked up a position as a writer in residence. Yet, God knows, the lives of most of our Redskins were tortured enough and who is to say that a tenured position as professor of English and teacher of creative writing would have led them to do worse work than they did. Of our three exemplary figures, Coover has moved in and out of the academy; neither Brautigan nor Barthelme, so far as I know, has had anything to do with academic life since their emergence as writers, although Brautigan is obviously more learned than he contrives to look and Barthelme is one of the most bookish authors ever to have gained prominence in the United States. A large number of writers, among the most audacious and exciting we have, do teach, Barth and Joyce Carol Oates, for example, John Hawkes, William Gass, John Gardner. Sooner or later a writer who teaches and who has a modest respect for his occupation will learn a body of other people's books, many of which are not particularly congenial to him, most of them with a kind of explicator's intensity. He will have to work his way through problems of craft that he may not feel in his own work but that other writers have felt in theirs and that his students will confront him with as genuine curiosities of their own. He will learn that our Anglo-American sense of formal possibilities is terribly limited, that the French, for example, have, for a long time, written a species of prose composition, called the *récit*, which is a most marvellously inclusive category, perfectly legitimized by French culture, in which one can make prose poems, meditations, fables, confessions, introspective interludes, an extraordinary number of things for which we have no generic home. The idea that such an involvement with the teaching of literature is somehow destructive of a writer's art seems to me preposterous. That it has made a difference with writers of new fiction, particularly in enlarging their sense of formal options, seems to me undeniable.

It is a pity that some hard questions need to be asked about the formal possibilities of prose fiction at a time when 'formalism' has an increasingly bad name. It would help if someone were to do for formalism what A. O. Lovejoy once did for romanticism, that is, discriminate the several senses in which the word is used. What we do not need is criticism of new fiction as pure technique, disengaged from its cultural ambiance, 'read', explicated, exhausted, like a metaphysical lyric. What we also do not need is more criticism which uses fiction as an exhibit in a historical design, new fiction being the end of something, or the beginning of something else, or an element in a cyclic movement, or evidence for the triumph of one historical principle or the defeat of another. What we do need is an aesthetic of new fiction. As a step toward that aesthetic, I propose the axioms that follow.

1. *New fiction, although aggressively non-traditional, shows less involvement with the tradition of prose fiction than any fiction since the beginning of the novel.* Nearly all fiction of any real quality reacts against some area of the fiction of its past: Cervantes against romance, Fielding against early Richardson and bad history, Thackeray against the Silver Fork School, Virginia Woolf against the late realists, and so on. There is much in the fiction of the past which writers of new fiction choose not to emulate. But it is extraordinary, for a body of fiction so non-traditional, how little of traditional fiction is struggled with, polemicized against, seriously parodied, denied, inverted, surmounted. New fiction, more than any fiction since Cervantes, chooses self-consciously to depart from tradition without investing that departure with any particular urgency or without making that act of departure the starting point of the fiction at all, in the way that such departure virtually animates the fiction of Cervantes, Fielding, Jane Austen, Flaubert, Hemingway, and a hundred others.

2. *New fiction is the first substantial body of fiction that self-consciously seeks an audience that is less than universal, attempting to establish a community of sensibility that is wilfully limited.* It is the fate of the novel to be a middle-

class form and at the same time to be unaware that it *is* a middle-class form. No classic novelist ever set out to address the members of a particular class, or locality, or historical time. Every novelist's tacit assumption is that his book puts us in touch with 'reality', not the reality of a highly specific class, not reality circumscribed by place and time: in that sense, every classic novelist's work is addressed to everybody, everywhere, to his own time and to posterity. Even those novelists who seem to us especially class-bound, Meredith and James let us say, would never have acknowledged that the truth of their books was specific, partial, local, and parochial. It is only the very minor figures such as Ronald Firbank who aim at a coterie public out of a recognition of their own exotic sensibilities. In the older neo-modern figures such as Borges and Cortázar, Landolfi and Anderson Imbert, one has, precisely, exotic sensibilities going in quest of other exotic sensibilities for their readers. And in American writers like Barth, Heller, Pynchon, and Gass one has an extension of the phenomenon, fiction which is by no means coterie writing, precious and cynical in the manner of Firbank, but which willingly acknowledges the partiality of its truth, the oddity of its vision, and the limits of its audience.

3. *New fiction contains and often intensifies the tendency in most fiction of any period to assimilate and transform the bad art of its own time.* Wellek and Warren articulate such a principle, deriving it from the Russian formalists. They summarize: 'Shklovsky, one of the Russian formalists, holds that new art forms are "simply the canonization of inferior (sub-literary) genres". Dostoevsky's novels are a series of glorified crime novels, *romans à sensation*, "Push-kin's lyrics come from album verses, Blok's from gipsy songs, Mayakovsky's from funny-paper poetry". Bertolt Brecht in German and Auden in English both show the deliberate attempt at this transformation of popular poetry into serious literature. This might be called the view that literature needs constantly to renew itself by "rebarbarization".' We read Joyce, amused and entertained with the assimilation of the popular songs, headlines, religious tracts, and pornographic fiction into the texture of *Ulysses*. We may very well read new fiction, however, with dismay and irritation, because the bad art which is being assimilated

is *our* bad art, what most of us have become accustomed to thinking of as a threat to the very survival of mind. Thus it is that new fiction, while extending a principle common to very much fiction, seems more audacious and abrasive than it really is, because it willingly occupies a place at what William Gass, following Barthelme, calls 'the leading edge of the trash phenomenon'.

4. *New fiction consolidates an attempt rare in fiction before the modern period to present elements of its texture as devoid of value; yet new fiction, in contrast to certain areas of modern fiction, seeks this value-less quality not as an act of subtraction, or dehumanization, or metaphysical mystification, not as a gesture of despair or nihilism, but as a positive act in which the joy of the observer is allowed to prevail as the primary quality of the experience.* In the fiction of Richardson the principle is most fully realized and firmly established, that the data of the fiction, its places, things, and events, are phenomena, rendered by Richardson as perceived by the characters, which means not only perceived but valued. Everything in Richardson, to put it succinctly, is worth something to the person who sees it and reports it to us. So it has been with fiction ever since. To see, in fiction, is to rank, to prefer or to deprecate, the value. One way of attempting to break with such a compulsion to value is to experiment with point of view, as Dos Passos does, for example, in those passages of his fiction that are made to seem unselectively documentary, mechanically recorded as it were. Another way is to arrange the elements of the fiction serially or capriciously so that the mode of presentation undercuts the possibilities of conventional value, a very old technique that serves the exuberance of Rabelais, the irony of Swift, and the associative anarchy of Sterne. Beckett's fiction is the most fully realized and powerfully executed attempt in modernist literature to undercut the value implicit in syntax, conventional arrangement, and in the very act of telling, all in the service of his nihilistic vision.

In new fiction, the nihilism is still there since no structure of values has arisen to move into Beckett's vacuum. What is different is that fiction now has the luxury of taking for granted what the modernists had to demonstrate. A writer of new fiction no more needs now to strain to demonstrate the absurd than a Victorian novelist had to strain to demonstrate a Christian-capitalist ethic. A peculiarly indirect way into the value-less surface I am describing is through the description by John Barth of the substance of Smollett's *Roderick Random*.

Sailors, soldiers, fine gentlemen and ladies, whores, homosexuals, cardsharpers, fortune hunters, tradesmen of all description, clerics, fops, scholars, lunatics, highwaymen, peasants, and poets both male and female – they crowd a stage that extends from Glasgow to Guinea, from Paris to Paraguay, and among themselves perpetrate battles, debaucheries, swindles, shanghais, rescues, pranks, poems, shipwrecks, heroisms, murders, and marriages. They wail and guffaw, curse and sing, make love and foul their breeches : in short they *live*, at a clip and with a brute *joie de vivre* that our modern spirits can scarcely comprehend.

Elsewhere in the same essay, Barth summarizes the import of Smollett's novel :

In short, *Roderick Random* is *par excellence* a novel of nonsignificant surfaces – which is not to say it's a superficial, insignificant novel, any more than the age that produced it, the age that invented the English novel, was superficial or insignificant.

Compare the texture Barth finds in Smollett, the syntax of seriality, the obvious pleasure in amplitude, with a passage from a fiction by Kenneth Gangemi entitled *Olt* :

Robert Olt walked into the department store and went directly to the TV department, where he sniffed the ozone and watched a programme that showed high school kids dancing. In the jewellery department he stood in a crowd of people and watched a silversmith demonstrate the lost-wax process. In the pet department he looked at a cage of saw-whet owls and a cage of baby coatimundis. In the record department he picked up a free Köchel listing and then sat in a soundproof cubicle and listened to a new comedian. In the gourmet department he tasted a free sample of smoked sturgeon.

Once he had sat in on the orientation movie shown to new salesgirls. Once he had spent two hours riding up and down the escalators on the last Saturday before Christmas. That was the Christmas they had fired their Santa Claus when a newspaper disclosed that he had been a communist.

Or compare a passage from Rudolph Wurlitzer's *Nog*:

> I ventured a peek out the door, but she had left the bedroom. I preferred to think she hadn't heard me; that, indeed, she had never heard me. I could still slip out. The terrycloth bathrobe was hanging behind the door. I put it on and turned to investigate the bathroom. It was a beautiful bathroom. There was a huge green tile tub, a new toilet and washbowl. I opened the cabinet over the washbowl. I couldn't stop looking at the objects on the top two shelves: suntan oil, Anacins, cold cream, three pink hair curlers, two yellow toothbrushes, one of which was very dirty. Dramamine pills, Itolsol eye bath, Ban, Kolex cold capsules, Ammens Medicated Powder and a small box of Benzedrine pills. I stared at each object and then went over them again.

Not all of new fiction is so gaily encyclopaedic as these passages, so fascinated with variety and unordered assemblage, so determined not to confer value. But most of new fiction shares, to some degree, the spirit of those passages. It is, incidentally, the aspect of new fiction that is likely to make it most congenial to experienced readers of Joyce.

5. *New fiction presents its texture as devoid as possible of aesthetic and philosophical depth.* In some sense, nearly all writers resist assignments to them of depth. Isherwood's character George, in *A Single Man*, who teaches English, asks his class what a novel by Huxley is 'about'. And the narrator comments: 'Nearly all of them, despite their academic training, deep, deep down still regard this *about* business as a tiresomely sophisticated game. As for the minority who have cultivated the *about* approach until it has become second nature, who dream of writing an *about* book of their own one day, on Faulkner, James, or Conrad, proving definitively that all previous *about* books on that

subject are about nothing – they aren't going to say anything yet awhile.' Novelists and critics as disparate as Saul
Bellow, Harry Levin, and Mary McCarthy have complained
of the tendency of readers to find symbols where no
symbols were intended. Every novelist, out of mere self-
respect, is obliged to resist the conventionalized and
mechanical methods of discovering 'meaning', imputing
system, stating the implicit in his works. Still, no one needs
to be told that modern fiction is relentlessly symbolic,
enthusiastically multi-levelled, that it invites exegesis like
nothing since the *Talmud*. It is the single quality that most
firmly unites such otherwise quite different writers as
Lawrence, Mann, Broch, Silone, Malcolm Lowry, their
intention to use those techniques that permit the greatest
possible resonance and amplitude of signification and that
insist at every point on the existence of unstated levels of
'depth' that the surface of the fiction figures forth.

The contrary principle is expressed by Wylie Sypher. In
scientific observation at the present time, in contrast to
classic patterns of scientific thought, 'the data are the
system; the matter-of-fact concreteness may or may not be
explained by natural law. Accidents happen, and accidents
are real.' Elsewhere, he allows the principle to broaden:

Like the recent scientist, the contemporary novelist or
painter detects that the ordinary, the commonplace, the
superficial, the quotidian is the very mystery most in-
accessible to reason and explanation and method. The
immediate occasion is sufficient unto itself, and this
recognition has led to a new humility, as well as a new
frustration. If the significance is on the surface, then the
need for depth explanation has gone, and the contingent,
the everyday happening, is more authentic than the
ultimate or absolute . . . The old systems of meaning – the
Newtonian solid geometry locating things at appropriate
distances or the theoretic order of Alberti's perspective,
which foreshortened – are suspect. Novelist, painter, and
scientist have given up foreshortening. Plot itself was a
mode of foreshortening. To accept the accidental or
casual is to recognize that irrationality of the obvious, to
dispense with the need for a logic accounting for everything by cause and effect, action and reaction.

Sypher's examples, in the case of fiction, come largely from the *chosistes*. But his discussion applies remarkably to American writers of new fiction, many of whom share next to nothing with the French writers, except a denial of depth. There is no clearer break than this between modernist (and late Victorian) fiction and new fiction – the implicit intention to let the surface be the meaning, let the possibility of a symbolistic level of reference be consistently undercut, let the data be the system, let there be nothing between the lines, as Barthelme puts it, but white space.

6. *New fiction permits itself a degree of latitude from the illusionist tradition greater than in any body of fiction since the beginning of the novel.* Classic fiction, of course, varies in the degree of its fidelity to an illusionist aesthetic, from the dull fidelity of Zola to the involutions and indirections of dozens of others whom we might place at some kind of polar extreme. It is difficult to imagine, however, that any classic work of fiction ever represents the wish that the reader apprehend it mainly as a self-referential literary construct, or mainly allegory, or mainly myth, or mainly private vision. Always, in figures so various as Scott or James, Mme de Lafayette or Tolstoy, we are compelled to say, in Trollope's phrase, yes, that is 'the way we live now' or to say, yes, that is the way it must have been, at Bath or Lyme, Waterloo or Leningrad; that is the way it must have looked and sounded, what people must have said and thought. It is hard to see how fiction, in its classic formulations, could escape this common mimetic centre without ceasing to be prose fiction and becoming something else.

Irving Howe, some years ago in an essay titled 'Mass Society and Post-Modern Fiction', took note of the comparative lack of interest in social fact, in class, in institutions and manners that characterized the fiction that seemed most compelling at that time, the fiction of Salinger, Wright Morris, Herbert Gold, and Saul Bellow. Howe at that time could not have foreseen a disengagement from the mimetic impulse more thorough by far than what was occurring at that time, a progressive lack of interest not only in institutions but in the very 'solidity of specification' that the novel seems to need to survive. It is partly the result of the revival of interest in pre-novelistic forms, the fabulistic, proto-realistic works that echo through much of new fiction, allowing a kind of power to grow out of the invention itself rather than depending upon the solidity with which the figures of the fiction are placed. For whatever reason, it is possible to read for many pages of Cortázar, Landolfi, and Borges, Barth, Barthelme, and Coover, with a constant delight in the craft displayed, with a constant sense of recognition, a feeling that the fiction is, in some oddly tangential way, powerfully pertinent to one's inner life, yet never once saying, yes, that is the way things look and feel, that is the way time passes, that is the way people really speak, that is the way we live now.

7. *New fiction, finally, in common with only a few scattered instances before it, seeks to represent, explicitly or implicitly, the act of writing as an act of play.* In the novels of Fielding or Jane Austen or Dickens or Thackeray, the compositional act is made to seem at once pleasurable and difficult, an act of play and an act of heavy moral responsibility. There is not much doubt, I think, that the play is subordinate to the hard work, that the energies of invention, the joys of making, are always less significant than the difficult work of making a big book into an intelligible aesthetic object, along with a heavy responsibility to the author's audience and to literature as an institution. Had the novel been invented by a Cavalier poet of the seventeenth century, perhaps, or had the example of Petronius or Rabelais really served as the cornerstone of the great tradition, the novel might have escaped its heavy burden of seriousness, both moral and vocational, and, having been conceived as a thing made with self-justifying invention and a large measure of fun, it might have been unnecessary for Flaubert to have worked so hard, to have told us he worked so hard, to have flayed the bourgeoisie so relentlessly, to have felt Emma Bovary's poison in his own vitals, to have sweat over every word.

New fiction, on the other hand, elevates play to the very centre of the complex of apparent motives that animate the work. Barth, in any given work, is doing many things: working very hard, thinking, shaping, hoping, giving up and starting over, planning, expecting, learning, imitating, trying not to imitate. It does not surprise me, how could it surprise anyone, to hear, through some dubious grapevine, that Barth is not writing, that he is in despair, having written himself out. Still, can there be any doubt that writing fiction is very centrally, for Barth, an act of play? One can differ with the particulars of Robert Scholes's *The Fabulators*; but I would not choose to differ with its donnée. New fiction can be differentiated from old on the basis of its fabulation, its willingness to allow the compositional act a self-conscious prominence and to invest that act with love, a sense of game, invention for its own sake, joy.

GERALD GRAFF

The Myth of the
Postmodernist Breakthrough

(reprinted with permission from *Triquarterly*, 1973)

The 'postmodernist' tendency in literature and literary criticism has been characterized as a 'breakthrough', a significant reversal of the dominant literary and sociocultural directions of the last two centuries. Literary critics such as Leslie Fiedler, Susan Sontag, George Steiner, Richard Poirier, and Ihab Hassan have written about this breakthrough, differing in their assessments of its merits and dangers but generally agreeing in their descriptions of what is taking place. What these critics see happening is the death of our traditional Western concept of art and literature, a concept which defined 'high culture' as our most valuable repository of moral and spiritual wisdom. George Steiner has recently drawn attention to the disturbing implications of the fact that, in the Nazi regime, dedication to the highest 'humanistic' interests was compatible with the acceptance of systematic murder. Others like Susan Sontag and Leslie Fiedler have suggested that the entire artistic tradition of the West is corrupted by a kind of imperialism of hyperrationality which is akin to the aggression and lust for conquest of bourgeois capitalist nations. Not only have the older social, moral, and epistemological claims for art seemingly been discredited, but art has come to be seen as a form of complicity, another manifestation of the lies and hypocrisy through which the bourgeoisie has maintained its power.

But concurrent with this loss of confidence in the older claims of the moral efficacy and interpretive authority of art, there is said to have arisen a new sensibility, bringing a fresh redefinition of the role of art and culture. This new sensibility manifests itself in a variety of ways: in the refusal to take art 'seriously' in the old sense, the use of art itself as a vehicle for exploding its traditional preten-

sions and for showing the vulnerability and tenuousness of
art and language in the rejection of the dominant academic
tradition of analytic and interpretive criticism, which by
reducing art to a set of intellectual abstractions tends to
neutralize or domesticate its potentially liberating energies;
in a generally less soberly rationalistic mode of consciousness, one that is more congenial to myth, tribal ritual, and
visionary experience, grounded in a 'protean', fluid, and
undifferentiated concept of the self which is opposed to the
repressed, 'uptight' Western ego.

In summary, then, two strains can be discerned within
the general complex of attitudes which have become associated with postmodernism : the apocalyptic and the visionary. These two strains may operate separately or in con-
junction – later on it will be necessary to particularize them
further. The first strain is dominated by the sense of the
death of literature and criticism; literary culture assumes a
posture acknowledging its own futility. The second strain,
involving the resurrection of the new sensibility out of the
ruins of the old civilization, expresses hopefulness for
revolutionary changes in society through radical trans-
formations in human consciousness. The more negative of
these strains manifests itself in its purest form in the so-
called 'literature of silence', a literature which breaks with
the traditions of romanticism and modernism by undermining the quasi-religious awe with which these earlier
movements invested the creative imagination. The more
positive strain involves not only a break with the past, but
the attempt to envision and create a revolutionary future.
Avant-garde critical thought has thus allied with radical
social and political criticism, the latter having adapted
concepts of sensibility drawn from aesthetics in order to
support a 'dialectics of liberation'.

I want here to raise some critical questions about the
postmodernist breakthrough in the arts and about the larger
implications claimed for it in culture and society. I want in
particular to challenge the standard description of postmodernism as representing a sharp break with romantic-
modernist traditions. To characterize postmodernism as a
'breakthrough' – a cant term of our day – is to place a
greater distance between current writers and their predecessors earlier in the century than is, I think, justified.

The first part of this essay argues that postmodernism should be seen not as breaking with romantic and modernist assumptions but rather as a logical culmination of the premises of these earlier movements, premises which are not always clearly defined in discussions of these issues. In the second part of the essay I want to argue that the revolutionary claims which have been widely made for the postmodernist new sensibility are overrated, and that when we view it in the context of the current social and cultural situation, postmodernism shows itself to be a reactionary tendency, one which reinforces the effects of technocratic, bureaucratic society.

I

In its exclusively literary sense, postmodernism may be defined as that movement within contemporary literature and criticism which calls into question the claims of literature and art to truth and human value. As Richard Poirier has observed, 'Contemporary literature has come to register the dissolution of the ideas often evoked to justify its existence: the cultural, moral, psychological premises that for many people still define the essence of literature as a humanistic enterprise. Literature is now in the process of telling us how little it means.' This is an apt description of the contemporary situation, but what it neglects to mention is that literature has been in the process of telling us how little it means for a long time, as far back as the beginnings of romanticism and the rise of romantic alienation and despair.

It is clear why we are tempted to feel that the contemporary popularity of anti-art and artistic self-parody represents a sharp reversal. It does not seem so long ago that writers like Rilke, Valéry, Joyce, and Yeats preached a kind of salvation through art. For Rilke, as for Shelley and other romantics, poetry was 'a mouth which else Nature would lack', the great agency for the restitution of values in an inherently valueless world. This belief in the constitutive power of the imagination which supported romantic and modernist writers, their confidence in the order and meaning reposed in high cultural tradition as a means of rescuing themselves from the chaos and fragmentation of a mass, industrialized society, appeared suddenly to have run its course by the mid-fifties. Since then, art and literature have increasingly incorporated a sense of irony and scepticism toward art's traditional pretensions to truth, high seriousness, and the profundity of 'meaning'. Whereas Eliot, Faulkner, and their imitators sometimes seemed to be writing with an eye to providing texts capable of being submitted to the complex critical 'explications' of the New Critics, much of the literature of the last twenty years has been conditioned by the wish to remain invulnerable to critical analysis – the 'opacity' of the New Novel being one case in point.

The conventions of postmodernist art systematically invert the respect for artistic truth and significance which had characterized modernism. In Donald Barthelme's anti-novel, *Snow White*, a questionnaire poses the reader such questions as, 'Has the work, for you, a metaphysical dimension?' Alain Robbe-Grillet writes and campaigns on behalf of a type of fiction in which 'obviousness, transparency, precludes the existence of *higher worlds*, of any transcendence'. Susan Sontag denounces the interpretation of works of art on the grounds that 'to interpret is to impoverish, to deplete the world – in order to set up a shadow world of "meanings".' Leslie Fiedler in an essay on modern poetry characterizes one of its chief tendencies as a revolt against 'the platitude of meaning'. Jacob Brackman, in his brief but illuminating study, *The Put-On*, describes this device in art and social behaviour as an attempt to forestall by ridiculing in advance the raising of the traditional question of what a work of art means: 'We are supposed to have learned by now that one does not ask what art means.' It appears that suddenly the term 'meaning' itself, as applied not only to art but more general experience, has joined 'truth', 'reality', and 'correctness' in the class of words which can no longer be written unless apologized for by inverted commas.

Thus it is tempting to agree with Leslie Fiedler's conclusion in a recent essay that 'the culture religion of modernism' is now dead. The most advanced art and criticism of the last twenty years seems to have abandoned the ethos which guided modernism, an ethos dominated by the respectful emphasis it placed on the concept of artistic *meaning*. A number of considerations, however, render

Fiedler's conclusion misleading. Once examined closely, both modernism's positive faith in literary meanings and postmodernism's repudiation of these meanings prove to be highly ambivalent attitudes – much closer to each other than might at first appear. It is my argument here that 'the culture religion of modernism' has not ended with postmodernism, but rather has reached a further, possibly ultimate stage of its development. Postmodernist anti-art was inherent in the logic of the modernist aesthetic, which in turn derived from the romantic attempts to substitute art for religion.

The nineteenth century's attempt to elevate art to the status of a surrogate religion was a paradoxical development. On the one hand, such a move seemed to increase enormously the cultural prestige and importance of art. But the terms in which the religious function of art was defined actually foreshadowed the twentieth-century reduction of art to triviality and marginality. Consider the following statement by Ortega y Gasset, published in 1925, contrasting the attitude of the avant-garde of his time, that art is 'a thing of no consequence' and 'of no transcendent importance', with the veneration which art had inspired in the previous century:

> Poetry and music then were activities of an enormous calibre. In view of the downfall of religion and the inevitable relativism of science, art was expected to take upon itself nothing less than the salvation of mankind. Art was important for two reasons: on account of its subjects which dealt with the profoundest problems of humanity, and on account of its own significance as a human pursuit from which the species derived its justification and dignity.

Ortega ascribes the great prestige of art in the nineteenth century to the fact that art was expected to provide compensation for the 'downfall of religion and the inevitable relativism of science'. But the downfall of religion and the relativism of science were developments which could not help undermining the moral and epistemological foundations of art. Once these foundations had been shaken – and the romantics experienced an acute sense of their precariousness even as they glorified the creative imagination – art could scarcely lay claim to any firm authority for dealing with 'the profoundest problems of humanity' and for endowing the species with 'justification and dignity'. Ortega's own philosophical writings are profound commentaries on this crisis of authority in modern experience.

From its beginnings, the romantic religion of art-was a highly ambivalent phenomenon. It manifested that 'agonism' or self-conflict with its own impulses which Renato Poggioli, in his *The Theory of the Avant-Garde*, identifies as a defining characteristic of avant-garde thought. The ultimate futility and impotence of art was implicit in the very terms with which the romantics, and subsequently the modernists, attempted to deify art as a substitute for religion. The concept of an autonomous creative imagination, which fabricated the forms of order, meaning, and integration which men no longer believed could be found in external nature, implicitly concedes that artistic meaning is a pure fiction, without any corresponding object in the extra-artistic world. For this reason, the doctrine of the creative imagination contained within itself the premises of its refutation. The religion of art, even at its highest points, carried within itself the grounds of its destruction.

Postmodernism has forced us to recognize to an extent impossible only a few years ago the precariousness of the modernist religion of art and its claims for the creative imagination. We are now in a position to perceive that the very concept of a *creative* imagination contains an inherent contradiction and thus an unavoidable irony. For an order or pattern of meaning which must be invented by human consciousness out of its own inner substance or structure – whether it is thought to come from the private subjectivity of the individual or from some intersubjective *Geist* that is assumed to be common to all minds – is necessarily uncertain of its authority. Textbook descriptions of romanticism stressing the affirmative flights of the romantic priests of art tend to ignore the ambivalence pervading romantic writing. Wordsworth, for example, proclaiming the existence of a spirit in Nature which 'rolls through all things', pauses self-consciously to consider that this might well be 'a vain belief', justifiable only on pragmatic grounds. And his affirmation of this spirit is haunted by his difficulty in determining whether man actually perceives it as an external reality or creates it out of his own mind. The Shelleyan stereotype of the poet as godlike creator who brings forth a new cosmos *ex nihilo* and soars beyond the range of commonsense reality is, from another perspective, only an honorific reformulation of the alternate stereotype of the poet as a marginal person, a hapless trifler or eccentric or a perverse libertine who inhabits a world of autistic fantasy and ignores objective reality. There is a secret and un-acknowledged collaboration between rebellious aesthetes and their philistine detractors which remains an unwritten chapter in the social history of art. For both poetolatry's glorification of the artist as a demi-god and philistinism's denigration of him as an irresponsible social deviant share a common definition of the artist as a special kind of person, one who perceives the world in a way different from that of ordinary objective judgement. But we have only recently begun to see the inner kinship between the doctrines of creative imagination and imaginative autonomy and the myth of the artist's alienation.

These developments which we have been discussing must be traced ultimately back to the great crisis in European culture which became evident toward the close of the eighteenth century. On the philosophical level, the critical philosophies of the seventeenth and eighteenth centuries and the rise of empirical science dissolved the ancient connection between rational, objective thought and value-judgements. Values became increasingly viewed as inherently subjective and 'ideological' (a fate which would to a large extent overtake even objective thought at a later date). There set in the condition which Erich Heller has described as 'the loss of significant external reality', the sense that the objective, knowable world and the realm of meanings and values are irreparably divided. A number of social changes within modern culture have immensely deepened this philosophical scepticism. Industrialism intensified the separation of fact and value by monopolizing objective thought in the form of technology, commerce, and in our own time bureaucracy, administration, and social engineering. In advanced industrial society, 'reason' appears commonly as a *cause* of alienation rather than a potential cure, a value-free, depersonalized, finally aimless and irrational mode of calculation which subserves the goals of arbitrary power. The 'human' agencies of emotion, value-judgement, and creativity are necessarily defined as antithetical to reason and objectivity. Also of great importance is the disproportion in advanced society between the pervasiveness of intellectual analysis and the apparent ability of this analysis to answer questions of pressing human importance. With the proliferation of technological knowledge and the spread of the behavioural sciences, modern man comes to have a sense of being oppressed rather than enlightened by rational 'explanations'. As the machinery of such explanation becomes more and more detached from the ends it was designed to fulfil, there is a growing sense of the uselessness of rational thought, and a further tendency to see this thought as itself tentative, arbitrary, and unreliable. The cognitive agencies of culture come to seem a merely contingent and temporary human invention. These feelings eventuate in the longing to be rid of the burden of rational consciousness. The general dehumanization of the idea of rational objectivity as a consequence of its identification with a soulless technology, a corrupt social authority, and a useless machinery of explanation has played an important role in determining the modern definition of art as a form of imaginative discourse antithetical to discursive reason.

It was the diminished status of rational knowledge, reduced to mere neutral fact, which inspired the romantic invention of imaginative truth as an antidote. But as such interpreters of romanticism as Robert Langbaum, M. H. Abrams, and Harold Bloom have noted, the romantic exploitation of imaginative truth was shadowed by the age's apprehension that any truth containing a value-component (if not all truth) might be no more than an arbitrary construction. Objective facts, for all their unsatisfying inertness, could at least be verified. If imaginative truth were determined from within rather than without, how could a poet know whether one myth prompted by his imagination were truer than any other? There was in the very assertion that poetry endows the universe with meaning – the proposition of Shelley's *Defence* – an implied confession of the arbitrary nature of that meaning. In this way, romantic aesthetics typifies the more general crisis of modern thought, which pursues a desperate quest for meaning in experience while sceptically unable to accept the validity of any meaning proposed. The paradox of the sophisticated modern mind is that it is unable to believe in the objective validity of meanings yet unable to do without meanings. The double status of meaning itself in the arts and in aesthetic theory is one outcome of this paradox. For the last two centuries, Western aesthetic speculation has engaged in a tightrope act in which the significance which must be ascribed to art in order to justify its importance has had to be eliminated from art in order to guarantee its authenticity. Thus we have the numerous self-contradictory attempts in the twentieth century to define art as a kind of nondiscursive communication, a discourse that is somehow both nonreferential yet valid as knowledge.

The double attitude of the romantic aesthetic with respect to meaning repeats itself in postmodernist art in the form of a divided response to the loss of meaning. On the one hand, there is a tendency to view the loss of a significant external reality as a form of liberation, a release from a binding tradition, a determinate moral order, and an *a priori* definition of selfhood. On the other hand, the sense of being liberated from ancient obligations can easily turn into a sense of isolation and betrayal directed at the world's failure to yield an objective teleological order. The literature of radical liberation, which sees the overthrow of traditional humanism as a prerequisite for the triumph of a Politics of Ecstasy, betrays an internal kinship with the sombre, resignedly apolitical 'literature of silence', which dramatizes man's present 'liberation' from external authority as a profound emptiness. The healthy-minded, untroubled postmodernism expressed in such phenomena as happenings, Living Theatre, the music and writings of John Cage, the more beatific poetry of the Beats, the fiction of Ken Kesey and Richard Fariña, and the more hopeful and ebullient strains of the rock and psychedelic movements – this contrasts with the ironic, disillusioned vision of such writers as Barthelme, Robbe-Grillet, Beckett, Borges, the Barth of *The End of the Road*, and the Nabokov of *Invitation to a Beheading*. What links these two strains of postmodernist art together is their common commitment to an apocalyptic view of the world, one predicated on the assumption of the disappearance of significant external reality and the consequent uselessness of traditional ways of making sense of the world, the uselessness of art, literature, and language themselves. But one group sees this situation as a ground for celebration, the other as a ground for pathos.

In Borges's 'The Library of Babel' or Barth's *The End of the Road*, the theme of the death of meaning and the techniques of self-parody and structural involution are used in order to evoke a solipsistic universe in which human consciousness cannot transcend its own myths. These fictions generate a sense of pathos at the absence of a transcendent order. Though no teleology is envisioned as possible, the writer at least *wishes* it were. As Borges's narrator declares, 'Let heaven exist, even though my place be in hell. Let me be outraged and annihilated, but for one instant, in one being, let your enormous library be justified.' The library, containing all possible books and all possible commentaries on and interpretations of experience but none which can claim authority over the others, cannot be justified. But Borges affirms the indispensable nature of justification. As in such earlier modernists as Kafka and Céline, the memory of, or longing for, a significant external reality that would justify human experience persists in the writer's consciousness and serves as his measure of the distorted, indeterminate world he depicts. This kind of postmodernist writing, though it presents the distorted perspective of solipsism as the only possible perspective, nevertheless presents this distortion *as* distortion – that is, it implicitly affirms a concept of the normal, if only as a concept which has been tragically lost. As Georg Lukács has observed, the presentation of distortion as such presupposes an undistorted model as the norm. In this sense, the kind of literature we are considering – and Beckett's works would provide a further example – retains a link with traditional Western rational humanism by virtue of its felt sense of the pathos of this tradition's demise. Such literature may be said to affirm an objective order of values, not by permitting the assumption that such an objective order actually exists, but by assuming that the loss of such an order is a deprivation.

Far different is the attitude expressed in the more celebratory forms of postmodernism. Here there is scarcely any memory of the benefits of an objective order of values in the past and no regret over the absence of such an order in the present. 'Significant external reality' figures only as a symbol of the reactionary authority and predetermination of a repressive past, and its disappearance is viewed as liberation. Dissolution of ego-boundaries, seen in the more austere postmodernist works like *Invitation to a Beheading* as a terrifying disintegration of identity, is viewed as a bracing form of consciousness-expansion and a prelude to growth. The obsessive quest for justification which characterizes Borges's protagonists is dismissed as a mere survival of outmoded thinking. For in a world which simply *is*, there is no point in even raising the question of justification as a problem. The dialectical structure and tension which lend vitality and shape to the works of the more austere postmodernists, drawn from the conflict between the human aspiration for meaning and the bland expressionlessness of reality, give way to a celebration of the undifferentiated. The tragic quest for meaning and justification, for transcendence, gives way to a glorification of *energy*, conceived as pure immanence and process. There is, in a sense, a kind of 'transcendence' that is taken as the object of this liberationist stance, a transcendence of the past, of objective reality, of the commonly understood limits of everyday forms of perception. But this is a transcendence which has, by definition, no goal, no teleology, no definable way of completing itself, and thus it expresses itself as a benign celebration of the infinity of all being.

Susan Sontag, expressing this attitude in criticism, observes of art and the world : 'Both are. Both need no justification; nor could they possibly have any.' The exemplary posture for Miss Sontag becomes the acceptance of the totality without critical discrimination, a posture exemplified in the work of John Cage: 'Cage proposes for our experience,' Miss Sontag says, 'a world in which it's never preferable to do other than we are doing or be elsewhere than we are. "It is only irritating," he says, "to think one would like to be somewhere else. Here we are now." ' Cage himself says : 'We are intimate in advance with whatever will happen,' not because history has any meaning or direction, but precisely because it is so pointless that to *expect* meaning is absurd. Thus distortion, far from being viewed as a deviation from any desired, if unattainable, norm, is taken to be the normal and proper condition of human experience.

Whereas, as we saw, austere postmodernism retains some sense of the conflict between human desire and the external world of circumstance which pervades classical tragic literature, ecstatic postmodernism merges conflicts into an undifferentiated unity of being. Where conflict does enter into the world of this latter kind of art, it is generated not by anything inherent in the nature of reality but by artificial and removable institutional repressions, usually dramatized in the shape of crude stereotypes of technological, institutional repression of sexual energy. Tragedy is thus replaced by sentimental melodrama, typified, for instance, in such oppositions as that between the putatively 'best minds' of Allen Ginsberg's generation and 'Moloch', or between Ken Kesey's 'Big Nurse' and the sexually omnipotent hero, McMurphy, of *One Flew over the Cuckoo's Nest*.

Different in character as the two strains of the postmodernist impulse are, their common intellectual, social, and historical origins establish their family relationship as continuations of the single tradition of romantic and modernist art. Both strains arise out of that conception of the human condition which underlay the romantic concept of spiritual alienation. The division between austere and healthy-minded postmodernism corresponds to the antithesis between the romantic agony of a figure like Byron as contrasted with the visionary ecstasy of a Blake; in the twentieth century, the division appears in the opposition between the 'tragic vision' of the literature of conservative-traditionalist modernism – Eliot, Yeats, Faulkner, etc. – and the radical energy-worship of Dada, Futurism, Surrealism, and, more recently, some of the 'Projective' poets descended from William Carlos Williams. The concept of man binding these antithetical lines of development together is one in which man is totally and irreparably alienated from a significant external reality, an objective order of values. Once this connection is understood, the coherence of postmodernism and its continuity with romantic and modernist tradition is clarified.

One of the clearest proofs of this continuity, yet one that is rarely noted by literary scholars, is the persistence of an 'organicist' theory of art through each of the cultural periods with which we have been concerned. The organicist theory of art bridges the extremes of positive romanticism with its quasi-religious glorification of artistic autonomy and nihilistic or solipsistic postmodernism with its denial of artistic transcendence. From Coleridge and his German predecessors to Robbe-Grillet and Susan Sontag there runs a common theory of art as an autonomous, self-contained entity, 'a thing in the world' and not an interpretive commentary on the world. What alters from one period to the next in successive phases of literary history is not the structure of the definition of art itself but the implications drawn from the definition. Thus, while the romantics and post-modernists share in common an organicist definition of art, they use it in different ways. The romantics did not employ the organicist aesthetic in order to deny referential meaning and teleology to art. Their formulations, however, anticipated the contemporary employment of this aesthetic to that end.

It was Coleridge who made the famous assertion, crucial in the development of modern criticism, that a good poem should 'contain in itself the reason why it is so and so, and not otherwise'. This statement of principle begs the question of what a good poem is since it defines poetic value as conformity to the poem's 'self' yet refrains from characterizing that self. The confusion of this aesthetic principle parallels the confusion of the age with respect to the definition of human nature, and it reflects the deterioration of the ancient integrated worldview. That worldview had been able to say what things are and had not needed to fall back on tautologies of self-reference. Nevertheless, the circularity of Coleridge's organic principle has not prevented it from compelling assent from influential modern authors, critics, and aestheticians, who ignore the fact that the idea rests on a concept of 'self-containment' which neither Coleridge nor anyone after him has succeeded in clarifying. Nor has it been noted that a literal application of the organic principle, which, it must be admitted, Coleridge himself did not choose to make, destroys the possibility of ascribing meaning to a work of art – or else renders the concept of such meaning inconsistent with aesthetic theory. The logical consequence of the organicist principle is to fence off the work of art from intellectual references, meanings, and concepts, things which must be dismissed as 'outside' or 'extrinsic' to the work of art, not 'self-contained' within it. Though Coleridge and his contemporaries did not drive the logic of organicism to such reductive conclusions – they were still powerfully influenced by their classical heritage of *mimesis* – this logic in itself tends toward the view that a work of art finally 'means itself'. From this position it is only a further step to the idea that a work of art has no meaning at all.

In advancing his organic principle, Coleridge did not think of himself as reducing or attenuating the scope of literature. On the contrary, by making the imagination an organic faculty, Coleridge sought to identify the uniquely valuable element of literature, the quality which made it superior to rationalistic discourse and to the positivistic science of his day. What Coleridge could scarcely foresee was that the very terms of his defence of poetry would be convertible into the terms of its refutation; the grounds on which romantic organicism tries to dignify art are identical to those on which later critics would deny art its interpretive function. For the idea of self-contained artistic meaning, though capable of supporting an affirmative theory of artistic transcendence, is equally capable of supporting the bleakest, most naturalistic denial of transcendence.

Consider an example. Emerson, in a famous passage in 'Self-Reliance', asserts : 'Those roses under my window make no reference to former roses or to better ones; they are for what they are; they exist with God today. There is no time to them. There is simply the rose.' This seems a familiar Emersonian celebration of the divine immanence of nature. Considered substantively, however – that is, apart from its affirmative tone – Emerson is expressing the same idea as that given by Robbe-Grillet in the following statement: 'The world is neither significant nor absurd. It *is* quite simply.' Emerson and Robbe-Grillet are talking about the 'organic' or self-significant character of the external world, but the analogy with the work of art is obvious. Neither nature nor art can mean anything – they merely are. Once it began to be thought that nature is simply itself, it was inevitable that art would receive a similar fate. However affirmatively espoused, the aesthetics of self-contained meaning is symptomatic of an intellectual situation in which meaning is being emptied out of the world, so that things appear only in their simple presence.

Organicist theory, then, far from representing a more exalted view of art and its function than that accorded by traditional mimetic theory, is symptomatic of a loss of confidence in art's ability to imitate reality – or in reality's ability to provide material worth imitating. This breakdown in the connection between art and an objective, significant world induces a self-protective, attenuated concept of art, one which protects art from being judged in terms of empirical truth and external ethical norms, criteria which, it is felt, art can no longer meet. That this 'penitent art', as George Santayana termed it, often boasts of its lofty spiritual mission is immaterial. The grounds underlying the organicist defence of art are logically identical to the grounds on which contemporary intellectuals despair of art and deny art's ability to interpret reality : the view that art inhabits a universe stripped of teleology and is doomed only to 'mean itself'.

Twentieth-century restatements of organicism, as in such theorists as Croce, Cassirer, Langer, Frye, and the American New Critics, have effectively extended this theory's latent hostility to the concept of artistic meaning. The present century has witnessed the culmination of the revolt against the ancient idea that a work of art 'says' something, communicates some more or less humanly important 'matter'. There is no more telling evidence of the despairing situation of humanistic intellectuals, whether they are aware of it or not, than the fact that art, according to their most favoured conception of it, is incapable of asserting beliefs, convictions, or hypotheses – or is regarded as inferior art if it makes a point of doing so. According to the main tradition of modern aesthetics, art deals with experience only as myth, psychology, or language – not as objective truth. It is held that art supplies frames of reference which 'organize' or 'order' the randomness of experience into coherent patterns. But this artistic 'ordering' of experience is not seen as capable of being authenticated by anything in the objective structure of the experience itself. Consequently, the artist and the reader are expected to 'believe' in the reality of this aesthetic order only provisionally, as a kind of mythic assent. It is felt that either there are no beliefs one can legitimately risk affirming or else that the belief-affirming modes of expression have been hopelessly discredited. Though they do not admit it, the theorists mentioned above have not succeeded in giving art any stronger cognitive and epistemological foundations than were provided by the 'pseudo-statement' theory of I. A. Richards and the Logical Positivists. This failure of modern aesthetic theory to find an interpretive function for art has helped prepare the ground for the narcissism and self-contempt which mark postmodernist aesthetics.

Twentieth-century aestheticians would dispute the accusation that the theory of artistic autonomy does away with artistic meaning. These theorists popularly distinguish between the 'non-discursive' meaning characteristic of art and the inferior propositional meanings of science, logic, and practical discourse. (See, for example, Susanne Langer's theory of 'presentational symbols'.) Their attempts to reconcile the principle of autonomy, however, with the presence of significant meaning in art have not met with notable success. Organicist theories repeatedly tend toward confused formulations which rescue themselves by contradiction and paradox. Thus the most assiduous American exponent of organic theory, Murray Krieger, attempts to reconcile a 'contextualist' aesthetic with an aesthetic which will permit art to refer to the world by resorting to 'miraculism' as the only possible way out : 'The literary work ... is able miraculously to satisfy both propositions at once, being at once totally thematic and totally aesthetic, answerable to itself only by being answerable to the outside world.' This kind of *credo quia impossibile* in literary criticism could not help undermining the interpretive claims of literature itself. The organicist theorizing of the forties and fifties not only helped to dethrone the ancient theory of art as *mimesis*. Having toppled the older aesthetic, the new theory proved incapable of resisting the attacks on its own scepticism turned against itself. The organicist theory has thus proved vulnerable in recent years to precisely the same kind of attacks which its advocates had once levelled at representational theories of art.

This vulnerability is seen in current attacks on the New Critics by postmodernist spokesmen. It is both ironic and fitting that the New Critics should have been dethroned from critical pre-eminence by the weight of arguments they themselves perfected. The New Criticism engaged in the paradoxical endeavour to defend poetic meaning by arguing that 'a poem should not mean but be'. In this respect they manifested that ambivalence toward meaning which is endemic to modern thinking about art. It requires only a modicum of historical sense to see that when Susan Sontag now indicts New Critical-style interpretation of literature, she does so on the ground of the very crime for which the New Critics had condemned their own critical opponents, namely, 'the heresy of paraphrase'. The New Critics were masters of interpretation who had a profound scepticism of interpretation. Their theory of literature was in conflict with their method. While their close explications of specific texts called attention to the importance of meaning in literature, their theoretical arguments spread or reinforced suspicion of the notion that literature can even be said to have anything so discursive and didactic as a meaning. That the New Critics are in the seventies routinely disparaged as meaning-mongers and hyperintellectualizers reveals the power, and the continuing cultural prestige, of the anti-intellectual scepticism which they helped to further. Here is a significant example of the way in which ideas latent in the modernist tradition have come to be turned against modernism.

If postmodernism, then, has superseded romanticism, modernism, and the culture religion of art, it has done so with weapons forged by these earlier movements. An illustration of postmodernism's love-hate relationship with its cultural precursors is found in Donald Barthelme's *Snow White*, one of the postmodernist works that is most skilful in its deployment of the literary past in a subversive way. A passage from the novel helps show how Barthelme assimilates aspects of modernism so as parodically to undermine them:

'Try to be a man about whom nothing is known,' our father said, when we were young. Our father said several other interesting things, but we have forgotten what they were . . . Our father was a man about whom nothing was known. Nothing is known about him still. He gave us the recipes. He was not very interesting. A tree is more interesting. A suitcase is more interesting. A canned good is more interesting.

Barthelme here parodies the advice which Henry James had offered to the aspiring fiction writer: 'Try to be one of the people on whom nothing is lost.' Barthelme inverts the assumptions about character, psychology, and the authority of the artist upon which James, the 'father' of the modernist 'recipe' for the novel, had depended. In postmodernist fiction, character, like external reality, is something 'about which nothing is known', lacking in plausible motive or discoverable 'depth'. Language forfeits its traditional power to render experience significantly, and meaning itself, as we have seen, comes to be regarded with a mixture of distrust and boredom. James had stressed the importance of artistic selection and ordering, defining as the chief obligation of the novelist that he so order his material as to 'be interesting'. Barthelme subverts these Jamesian principles by introducing a law of equivalence according to which nothing is intrinsically more 'interesting' than anything else. Such a logic destroys the determinacy of artistic selection and elevates canned goods to equal status with human moral choice as legitimate artistic subject-matter.

In place of James's earnest dedication to his craft, Barthelme assumes an irreverent stance toward his own work, conceding the arbitrary and artificial nature of what he creates. Literature retracts any Jamesian claims to deal 'seriously' with the world and reverts – for quite different reasons – to the kind of open confessions of the artificial, make-believe status of the novel which so annoyed James in his reading of Thackeray and Trollope. The writer's very inability to transcend the solipsism of his perception and the circularity of his medium determines both his subject-matter and his structural principles.

It would seem that the Jamesian aesthetic could not be stood on its head more completely. But only a surface consideration of the comparison could be content to leave it at that. James himself, in both his fiction and his criticism, contributed powerfully to the scepticism which Barthelme turns against him. T. S. Eliot wrote that Paul Valéry was 'much too sceptical to believe even in art'. The same thing, in greater or lesser degree, could be said about all the great modernist worshippers at the shrine of artistic form, not excluding James. Consider James's view of the infinite complexity of experience, which is 'never limited, and . . . never complete', and the elusiveness of which he dramatized through the interminable ambiguities of his later fiction. Like Joseph Conrad, James combined an intense dedication to unravelling the secret springs of motive and action with an acutely developed sense of the ultimate futility of such an enterprise. Though it provided the material for infinite conjectures, experience could not finally be formulated with authority.

Moreover, for James, the artistic ordering of experience was haunted with an irreducible perplexity. Jarring with James's insistence on the crucial importance of formal shaping and selection is the curiously subjectivist justification which James accords to this process. He frequently asserts that the orderings of the artist cannot derive from or be determined by the raw material of life itself. As he observes in *The American Scene*:

> To be at all critically, or as we have been fond of calling it, analytically minded . . . is to be subject to the superstition that objects and places, coherently grouped, disposed for human use and addressed to it, must have a sense of their own, a mystic meaning proper to themselves to give out : to give out, that is, to the participant at once so interested and so detached as to be moved to a report of the matter. That perverse person is obliged to take it for a working theory that the essence of almost any settled aspect of anything may be extracted by the chemistry of criticism, and may give us its right name, its formula for convenient use. From the moment the critic finds himself sighing, to save trouble in a difficult case, that the cluster of appearances can *have* no sense, from that moment he begins, and quite consciously, to go to pieces; it being the prime business and the high honour of the painter of life always to *make* a sense – and to make it most in proportion as the immediate aspects are loose or confused.

James says here that there are no objective determinants guiding the act of 'making sense' of the experience treated

by art. The 'mystic meaning' of events is not in the events
themselves, or determined by them, but in the observer.
James perceives that under such a condition there is a
danger the observer will 'go to pieces' unless he takes up
the artist's task of constructing a sense. The circularity of
this position reveals an unacknowledged desperation. James
assigns 'high honour' to the shaping artist and shame to the
observer who succumbs to confusion. One might reasonably
and without contesting James's assumptions, call this esti-
mate into question. The confused person is, at least, regis-
tering a response to the real nature of the situation; the
artist, succouring himself on arbitrary fictions of order, is
guilty of a contemptible self-indulgence. James rests his
claims on the high honour of the artistic process on the
profoundly damaging admission that artistic order is not
grounded in anything outside itself. In effect, James's
assumptions and those of Henry Adams, who in his
Education played the part of the desperately bewildered
observer, are not far apart.

Similarly, the transition from James to his parodist, Barthelme, involves not so great a distance as might be
supposed. James's art and his aesthetic assumptions pre-
figure, if they do not acknowledge, the sense of the loss of
belief in a significant external reality which is the explicit
theme of postmodernism. James's characteristic gesture is
to try to rise above this loss by imposing upon experience
an imaginative, aesthetic order, and he rests his faith in
traditional resources of language and narrative structure as
means to this end. The postmodernist, Barthelme, perceiving
that any such imposed order is arbitrary, cannot take it
seriously as a solution to the problem; he thus takes the
modernist's traditional seriousness – which the modernist
himself could not justify – as a target of parody. In this
fashion, postmodernism exploits the radically nihilistic and
sceptical premises latent in literary thinking since the
romantic period. Whereas modernists such as James, Eliot,
and Wallace Stevens turned to art – defined as the imposi-
tion of human order upon chaos – as an antidote for that
'immense panorama of futility and anarchy which is
contemporary history', as Eliot called his age, the post-
modernists have recognized that under such conceptions of

art and of history it makes no sense to regard art as providing any more consolation than any other discredited cultural
institution, secular or religious. Postmodernism signifies that
the nightmare of history, as modernism defined history, has
overtaken modernism itself. For if history is seen as an
unintelligible flux of phenomena, lacking in inherent significance and structure, then no exertions of the shaping,
ordering imagination can be anything but a dishonest refuge
from truth.

II

Numerous literary and cultural critics have spread the view
that the postmodernist literary sensibility is part of a larger
cultural revolution that is sweeping away the outmoded
bourgeois consciousness with its legacy of egocentric individualism, its obsession with rationality and objectivity, and
its pattern of aggression and guilt. This bourgeois-rationalist-
humanist tradition, grounded on the assumption of a sharp
differentiation between subject and object, mind and body,
fantasy and objective reality, 'high culture' and popular
culture, is said to be giving way to a kind of sensibility that
rejects the elitism of hierarchical thinking and which views
experience not as a rationally classifiable entity but as a
fluid, seamless process. Going by various labels – New
Sensibility (Susan Sontag), Aesthetic Ethos (Herbert Marcuse),
Polymorphous Perversity (Marcuse and Norman O. Brown),
Consciousness III (Charles Reich), etc. – this sensibility presupposes the superiority of visionary experience, expansion
of the boundaries of consciousness, and the release of primal
energies over the kind of thinking which relies on conformity to the 'reality principle'. For the new consciousness,
the reality of the subjective or intersubjective world, the
collective or mythic unconscious, is of a higher order than
the superficial reality of measurable facts with which objective reason deals. This commitment to 'inner space' and
mythic vision, having captured a significant segment of the
contemporary youth culture, is said by Fiedler to approach
the proportions of a 'great religious revival'. With the aid
of the mass media, the efforts of the cultural Left to hasten
political and social revolution by stimulating a revolution
on the level of consciousness, a 'greening of America', have

made a significant imprint on popular thought, deeply influencing the direction of education, social thought, and the arts.

The quest for transcendence by way of the paradise within, not as an escape from outer reality but as a means of transforming outer reality, has become the focus of much contemporary cultural and artistic activity. An art and literature which celebrates the expansion of consciousness has established itself as an alternative to the despair and resignation which mark the more austere forms of post modernism described in the first part of this essay. Psychedelic art, acid rock music, Living Theatre, and the Artaudian Theatre of Cruelty, with their emphasis on orgiastic communion and their attempt to submerge thought in physical action or sensation, are prototypical forms of this art of celebration. In this kind of art, the spontaneous release of sexual and psychic energy is the goal, replacing the endeavour of humanistic art to interpret and make sense of the world. Experience is seen as pure process, 'permanent revolution', and the goal of art is to reflect its endless dynamism.

Critical theories supporting this kind of art define art as Dionysian erotic or physical energy rather than Apollonian interpretation and judgement. 'Writing,' says Richard Poirier, 'is a form of energy not accountable to the orderings anyone makes of it and specifically not accountable to the liberal humanitarian values most readers want to find there.' Literature, that is to say, more closely resembles a physical force ('energy') than a form of thought or rationalized experience ('liberal humanitarian values'). In a similar vein, Susan Sontag describes 'the exemplary modern artist' as a 'broker in madness' whose activity is not subject to judgement according to 'the "human scale" or humanistic standard proper to ordinary life and conduct'. He is 'a free-lance explorer of spiritual dangers' whose task is 'making forays into and taking up positions on the frontiers of consciousness . . . and reporting back on what's there'. A species of vitalism appears to underlie all this – as if artists and intellectuals have to prove to themselves that they are alive. In fact, Poirier positively commends the writer who uses 'language designed to remind himself of how fully alive he is'.

Thus behind much current discussion of the post-bourgeois sensibility which may be about to dethrone the ethos of capitalism, competition, and repression there lies an idea which originated in avant-garde aesthetic theory – the idea of the artist as exemplary revolutionary, the creative imagination as the ultimate revolutionary force. For it is the artist's pioneering explorations on 'the frontiers of consciousness' which shake the rest of mankind loose from conventions and habits and prepare the way for the new order. Much contemporary cultural radicalism can thus be seen as making application of the latent revolutionary socio-political content of a certain kind of aesthetics to contemporary society. If art is seen as a kind of autonomous myth, something that turns its back on objective reality and reason, then art represents the essential form of liberated, anti-bourgeois sensibility. In so far as art refuses to comply with the expectation that it hold the mirror up to nature and present a criticism of life, it has to that degree helped to frustrate and weaken the epistemological realism upon which bourgeois culture is based. The humanistic aesthetic, subjugating art to the extra-aesthetic objective reality which it is supposed to imitate, enslaves the imagination to the order of probable cause and effect. The all but axiomatic opposition in modern aesthetics between discursive and expressive meaning, between language as communicative *sign* vs language as infrareferential *symbol*, comes to correspond to the political distinction between human liberation and enslavement to a tyrannical social order. The work of art, an autonomous universe of pure possibility unchained to the empirical or the normative orders, exemplifies the realm of freedom against that of necessity.

Paradoxically, it is an ostensibly hermetic and conservative concept of art which underlies this radical aesthetic. In earlier romantic and modernist art, the visionary aesthetic was often used to justify a withdrawal into the privileged sanctuary of high art, a fastidious disengagement from mass society. Earlier formalist movements, e.g. the French Symbolists, the English Decadents, T. S. Eliot, Ezra Pound, T. E. Hulme, had associated themselves with conservative social attitudes. The conservatism of these writers, however, came out of a deep distrust of bourgeois industrialism and capitalism. Moreover, the 'traditions' to which these writers sometimes appealed were defined in mythic terms, that is, as a timeless unconscious archetype which opposed the rational consciousness and consecutive logic of modern bourgeois culture. (Eliot's concept of tradition, sometimes mistakenly identified with classical and Renaissance precedents, is in fact of this modernist, anti-rationalist stamp.) The current adaptation of formalist aesthetic ideas for revolutionary goals thus exploits the hostility to bourgeois rationalism already latent in conservative formalism. Though critics like Sontag, Poirier, and Richard Gilman condemn as a 'confusion of realms' efforts to make art an instrument of political purposes, their view of the artistic use of the imagination is identical to that expounded by Herbert Marcuse in *An Essay on Liberation*, who sees the 'aesthetic ethos' as the prototype of the revolutionary consciousness.

The kind of aesthetics in question, of course, would hardly qualify as radical in the sense associated with programmatic Leftist politics. As Fiedler observes, the radicalism of the new sensibility is antithetical to that of conventional Marxism, the Marxists being 'last-ditch defenders of rationality, intrinsically hostile to an age of myth and passion, fantasy and sentimentality'. Indeed, some of the attitudes expressed by radical artists appear downright conservative. John Cage's work, for instance, expresses uncritical approval of the status quo and hostility to doctrinaire revolutionary ideology. Such an attitude qualifies as radical, however, in the sense relevant here: it is predicated on the glorification of a form of undifferentiated, mythic consciousness which is valued in so far as it is subversive of rational categorization. Moreover, Cage's acquiescence to things as they are presupposes that they are presently to be transformed by the dynamics of history and technological development without necessitating exertions of human will.

Radical critics attempt to discredit objective consciousness by showing its essentially historical and contingent character. Objective thought, they argue, far from being the climax of man's struggle, is at best a stage in the evolution of consciousness preparatory to the culminating stage of reunification of sensibility. At worst, objective consciousness is a delusive and dangerous historical myth that has rationalized the interests of class and power and inflicted incalculable destruction in the form of military and economic aggression and psychic repression. Thus Susan Sontag cites 'the damage that Western "Faustian" man, with his idealism, his magnificent art, his sense of intellectual adventure, his world-devouring energies for conquest, has already done, and further threatens to do'. In a similar vein, Richard Gilman asserts that 'the old Mediterranean values – the respect for the sanctity of the individual soul, the importance of logical clarity, brotherhood, reason as arbiter, political order, community – are dead as *useful* frames of reference or pertinent guides to procedure; they are even making some of us sick with a sense of lacerating irony'. To expose in this way the objective pretensions of humanistic rationality as nothing more than a myth is to reveal the subjective rationalization for power and conquest which allegedly underlies this kind of thought. Theodore Roszak sums up the counter-cultural objections to objective thinking as follows : 'objective consciousness . . . like a mythology . . . is an arbitrary construct in which a given society in a given historical situation has invested its sense of meaningfulness and value'. (Roszak does not consider that his endorsement of this view undermines his own conclusions about the counter-culture.) And Miss Sontag, in support of the structuralist thinker Roland Barthes, asserts that 'all explanatory models for fundamental states of affairs, whether sophisticated or primitive, are myths'. Once the mythical status of the belief in objectivity is established, a primary condition for cultural revolution will presumably have been accomplished.

Though the new sensibility is in some of its manifestations hostile to contemporary uses of technology, this mode of thought frequently sees technology as compatible with the new 'life-styles' promoted by the revolution. Thus Fiedler, noting that psychedelic drugs are synthetically manufactured, presents a Marcusean vision of a future in which sensuous pleasure, art, and culture are no longer in alienated opposition to technology but in harmony with it. For Fiedler this merger of sensibility and technology represents a reconciliation of the polar antitheses which have peculiarly marked the history of American culture : the primitive 'Redskin' West vs the rationalistic, mechanized 'Paleface' East : the pastoral Garden vs the Machine. The prototypical American, says Fiedler, will no longer need 'to pursue some uncorrupted West over the next horizon' – that quest born of immaturity and innocence for which Fiedler's critical works of the fifties and sixties had indicted American writing. Rather, newly liberated Americans in the post-humanist society will 'make a thousand little Wests in the interstices of a machine civilization on its steel and concrete back', living 'the tribal life among and with the support of machines'. The goal, then, of cultural revolution becomes not the destruction of technology but its reorientation away from the rationalist ethos and toward the goals of vision and organic consciousness.

A frequent target of radical attack has been the humanities establishment in the universities, held up as typical of the repressive rationalism and elitism which on a larger scale pervades American society as a whole. Susan Sontag's polemics against interpretation and the charges of mandarin Arnoldian traditionalism levelled by such critics as Fiedler, Poirier, and Louis Kampf illustrate the tendency of this kind of criticism to insinuate that the chief ills of modern humanities scholarship, criticism, and teaching lie in their traditionalism, their resistance to innovation, their excessive intellectualism, and their refusal to abandon rigidly defined, patrician canons of artistic taste. According to Fiedler, for example, contemporary criticism has yet to free itself from the hierarchical standards established by the New Critics of the forties and fifties, which Fiedler characterizes as 'the finicky canons of the genteel tradition and the culture religion of modernism, from which Eliot thought he had escaped – but to which, in fact, he only succeeded in giving a High Anglican tone'. Fiedler calls for a new criticism appropriate to the postmodernist view of reality, a criticism more eclectic, subjective, and whimsical in its approach, viewing the literary 'text' not as an objective entity to be analysed but as a fluid nexus of possibilities to be experienced, something which merges with the subjective associations of the critic.

It should be clear from the preceding sketch that the radical position we have been examining tends to reduce all cultural issues, whether literary or social, to the same basic dialectic in which nonrational energy opposes repressive rationalism and traditionalism. This kind of analysis seems to me vulnerable in several respects. To define the repressive nature of contemporary establishments in this way is to misunderstand the relationship between power and intellectual culture. Unlike the situation in commercial, craft, and agrarian societies, social authority and political and economic power in advanced industrial society are relatively independent of intellectual culture. Whereas power and authority once depended on at least the theoretical sanction of moral and intellectual institutions, modern authority is increasingly capable of operating without such sanctions. Manipulating opinion by means of the mass media, or, where that is not practicable, simply ignoring questions of principle, modern forms of power do not need to claim to be legitimized by a worldview or a set of values derived from intellectual culture. Whereas power once justified itself in terms of a single, culturally received interpretation of experience, modern power operates within a culture of radical ideological dissonance; pluralism – as opposed to any traditional absolutist dogma – is the reigning philosophy of the establishment.

Of course modern technological society can scarcely be termed pluralistic with reference to its distribution of wealth and power, but it is highly pluralistic in matters of ideology and style. In this area, modern society is restless, obsessed with novelty, and tolerant of any innovation so long as it does not threaten to disturb the objective distribution of power. Far from representing the last vestiges of tradition, corporate-technological society is hostile to tradition and to the fixity of traditional standards, which are seen as inhibiting growth and progress. As J. H. Plumb observes in *The Death of the Past*, 'Industrial society . . . does not need the past. Its intellectual and emotional orientation is toward change rather than conservatism, toward exploitation and consumption. The new methods, new processes, new forms of living of scientific and industrial society have no sanction in the past and no roots in it. The past becomes, therefore, a matter of curiosity, of nostalgia, a sentimentality.' It is precisely its freedom from any inherited ideological principles which makes it so easy for corporate-technological society to co-opt the ideologies and styles of cultural and artistic revolutionaries and to exploit them for material profit.

The theory of the excessively 'rational' character of

modern establishments proves no less misleading when submitted to examination. In corporate-technological society, processes of production, distribution, and consumption tend to become autonomous, justifying themselves with reference to mere growth and efficiency and expelling considerations of extrinsic social and moral utility. Bureaucratic institutions tend to follow no rationale beyond that of their self-perpetuation and expansion and no values beyond quantitative production and technical efficiency. In short, the type of 'rationality' in which this kind of society specializes is a purely functional or instrumental rationality, that is, a rationality devoted to expediting goals which have not themselves been rationally determined and are not subjected to rational criticism. It is this trivial, dehumanized rationality which cultural radicals take to be the essence of the rational consciousness they condemn. In this faulty analysis, reason, once assumed to be man's chief remedy for human alienation, comes to be seen as one of the chief causes of alienation. This misleading diagnosis of the disease of modern culture as a 'hypertrophy of the intellect', to quote Susan Sontag's phrase, inevitably results in the proliferation of quixotically anti-rationalistic cures for cultural ills.

When we turn to the situation in the humanities and the university departments of literature, we find numerous parallels with the conditions just described in the larger corporate-technological society. It is a commonplace that humanistic studies have enjoyed marked advances in the present century in methodological sophistication and quantitative production. It was such advances that led Randall Jarrell, in a well-known essay several years ago, to label the age an 'age of criticism'. Jarrell's essay anticipated the feeling of fatigue and disillusionment which many had begun to feel and which has since intensified toward the rationalistic, systematic analysis of art. But such labels as Jarrell's are misleading when they are taken to suggest that criticism in the twentieth century has become more genuinely rational in the sense of being more aware of its aims and goals. As criticism has proliferated and its methodologies have become ever more systematic and flexible, there has been no concomitant advance in relation to the more central questions of what art and literature and the study of them are for – what they aim to accomplish. On the contrary, advances on the instrumental level have been accompanied by an increasing incoherence and confusion on the level of substance – a development which parallels the course of the larger corporate-technological society. As criticism has advanced in methodological rationality there has been a corresponding erosion regarding the collective sense of the *rationale* of literary study. The demoralization which has resulted from this in the teaching of literature can scarcely be estimated.

With the deterioration of coherence in the rationale of the humanities, humanistic studies in the universities have largely abandoned the traditional goals of humane education and succumbed to the general bureaucratization and technicization of education which has absorbed the university as a whole. In the modern university, bureaucratic administration increasingly replaces philosophical ideas and values as the central 'meaning' of the university, a development which ideological pluralism enormously intensifies; since no worldview or theory held within the university has the authority to speak for the whole, the whole becomes so diffuse, fragmented, and incoherent that only the mechanics of administration remain as a binding force. The pluralism of the university as a whole is echoed within each of its departments. In literary studies, pluralism manifests itself in the gentleman's agreement that all critical 'approaches', and, by inference, all assumptions about the nature of literature, are potentially valid. The triumph of pluralism is usually heralded as a great victory for free enquiry and in part justifiably so. But it is a truth which has been too often misused to evade questions of definition. By impartially sanctioning a plurality of goals, purposes, and methods as valid objects of humanistic activity, the humanities have protected themselves from having to define their main goals. This protection is purchased, of course, at the price of the intellectual substance and integrity of the discipline.

Finally, pluralism usefully rationalizes the attitude which elevates quantitative 'production' of books, articles, and bibliographies into the chief measure of professional accomplishment, or at least into one of the chief criteria of professional advancement. Almost any scholarly project, critical approach, textual interpretation, or critical judgement qualifies as valid, hence publishable, hence usable in the quest of advancement, so long as a minimal degree of technical competence is attained.

It is clear why the attacks of cultural radicals upon professional humanistic study as vestiges of the genteel tradition are misplaced. With the triumph of pluralism, a new professionalism has emerged in humanistic studies which departs not only from the dogmatic elitism of the genteel tradition but from less class-bound, more general standards of common sense. It is true, of course, that the ritualistic forms of genteel decorum are still often assiduously maintained in common rooms and faculty clubs of many universities. Such survivals do not disguise the fact that the ascendant new professionalism is in its corporate form indifferent to whether high cultural literary values prevail or not. The new professionalism is technocratic in its outlook – that is, oriented towards production and methodology – mirroring the patterns of the larger corporate-technological society in the same way that the genteel professionalism which prevailed earlier in the century had mirrored the patrician-dominated culture of the period before World War I.

Just as the corporate-technological society finds it easy to absorb dissonant and divergent fashions in style and ideology, the new professionalism in the humanities encourages widespread institutional tolerance of new fashions in criticism, and it does not withhold its rewards from those who practise the new critical eclecticism and subjectivism advocated by Fiedler. Bound by few real intellectual standards and by no coherent sense of purpose, the new professionalism is not intrinsically hostile to postmodernist anti-rationalism and other revolutionary styles in literature and culture. Indeed, courses exploiting this kind of subject-matter have become one of the chief means by which universities now lure students and tuition. In the scholarly and critical journals, critical approaches ranging from modestly 'far out' to radically 'hip' are not unwelcome. It may be supposed that the new professionalism will depend more and more on such new critical fashions in order to fill its ever more demanding production quotas.

In recommending an eclectic, subjectivistic approach to

criticism based on an open, indeterminate conception of the literary text, Fiedler fails to notice that something answering to this description has been institutionalized for some time. Theories of the inexhaustible ambiguity and 'polysemous meaning' of literary texts have popularized the view that these texts have no determinate meaning, that their meaning is a function of the speculation brought to them by readers and critics. This theory of interpretation in an extreme form has been promoted by Northrop Frye, among others, who asserts that 'all literary works without exception' are 'like a picnic to which the author brings the words and the reader the meaning'. Though not subjectivistic in its intent, Frye's view points clearly in that direction in its implications (conflicting oddly with Frye's aim of establishing a scientific basis for criticism). As Frederick Crews points out, the assumption governing Frye's theories is that 'each critic is free to adopt the "approach" that suits his fancy, and most of the approaches prove to be little more than analogical vocabularies lending an air of exactitude to whatever the critic feels like discussing . . . What does it matter whether we call ourselves Thomists or Aristotelians or phenomenologists, provided we don't take our method too solemnly or show impatience with our neighbour's?'

Influenced by critics such as Frye, Fiedler, and the 'radical historicists' whom E. D. Hirsch attacked in his book, *Validity in Interpretation*, many now conceive interpretation as the application to the text of 'analogical vocabularies', myths reflecting the interests of the interpreter but having no more determinate relation to the text than any alternate set of myths. In acceding to this prestigious view, the new professionalism in literary study makes its accommodation, in its own way, with the postmodernist view of the indeterminancy of truth, the impossibility of an objective point of view. Moreover, this open-ended conception of interpretation, by relaxing the rules of evidence and inference which formerly inhibited free critical improvisation, proves highly congenial to the production demands of the new professionalism.

In humanistic culture and in the larger society, the condition is the same. The establishment has renounced humanistic standards, and its rationality turns out on inspection to be a pseudo-rationality. Hence the conception of revolution sponsored by cultural revolutionaries, consisting of a release of nonrational energies and a violent break from the humanistic tradition, is bound to backfire and reinforce the powers it aims to subvert. This is but to say that the conception of cultural revolution favoured by the avant-garde over the last century has come to a dead end. Advanced industrial society has outstripped the avant-garde by incorporating in its own form the avant-garde's main values – the worship of change, dynamic energy, and autonomous process, the contempt for tradition and critical norms. With the technocratic and bureaucratic transformation of the old bourgeois values into the values of the age of consumption, the arch antagonist against which the avant-garde revolted and against which it defined itself has all but disappeared. Yet cultural radicals continue to cling to the threadbare dialectic which opposes vital energy to the rigidities of reason and tradition, even though this way of conceiving revolution is irrelevant to a technological, consumption-oriented society. Those critics like Philip Rahv who compare the contemporary avant-garde unfavourably with that of the earlier years of the century miss the point when they diagnose the problem as a case of the present generation's susceptibility to the attraction of 'trendy' popularity. What such critics fail to realize is that the contemporary avant-garde is operating according to the same general aesthetic and cultural principles which motivated their predecessors. What has changed is the situation, in particular the nature of the opposition, which renders once defiant gestures merely 'trendy'.

Throughout the nineteenth century, when neo-classical and Christian standards retained a lingering influence over culture, artistic defiance of received traditions and conventions in the name of the autonomy of the imagination possessed a significance which can scarcely be duplicated by similar gestures today. The element of risk with which Susan Sontag tries to endow artistic activity when she characterizes the exemplary modern artist as a 'broker in madness' and 'a free-lance explorer of spiritual dangers' is sharply diminished by the loosened social and cultural context in which such radical gestures must be performed. Bold transgressions of conventions and standards lose their meaning in a situation in which conventions and standards are routinely disregarded to the point where no one is sure whether they exist at all. In an age obsessed on every level with breakthrough, experimentation, and the almost daily invention of new environments and new identities, the conception of art as a risky form of spiritual improvisation earns little distinction. This kind of artistic revolt becomes assimilated into the trend which Lionel Trilling has described as 'the acculturation of the anti-cultural, or the legitimization of the subversive'.

If we have reached, then, the point of no return for avant-garde anti-rationalism, which ends up reinforcing the logic of the establishment, it is perhaps time to reconsider our ways of defining radicalism and revolution, in art and culture. This poses the most serious dilemma of all, however, for we find ourselves stranded, it seems, between a feckless anti-rationalism on the one hand and a decadent and useless traditional humanism on the other. Is it wholly necessary, however, to conclude that the humanist alternative is forever and finally dead? The indictment against it, against Western 'Faustian' man and his aggressiveness, his arrogance, his infinite belief in his own infallibility, and the destruction these qualities have wrought, must obviously be taken very seriously. But the indictment should note too the relevant fact that Faust, after all, repented his sins and was punished for them and that the moral standards by which we condemn Faust are also part of the Western rationalist heritage. To indict the hubris of rationalism without noting that the critical terms of the indictment derive from this same rationalism, is to fall victim to the affectation of self-laceration. If it is true that humanistic values originated in support of the interests of a particular social class, it is also true that some of these values are not necessarily tied to class, but are part of a more universal human heritage.

A radical movement in art and culture forfeits its radicalism and impoverishes itself to the degree that it turns its back on what is valid and potentially living in the critical and moral traditions of humanism. In a society increasingly irrational and barbaric, to regard the attack on reason and objectivity as the basis of our radicalism is to perpetuate the nightmare we want to escape.

Bibliography

This bibliography lists general studies, not works on particular authors; for studies of these see, among other sources, the series 'Critical Appraisals' (Calder and Boyars) and 'Writers of the Seventies' (Warner, New York). Creative works are also not included, but the following anthologies of short fiction are relevant and useful: F. R. Karl and Leo Hamalian, *The Naked i: Fictions for the Seventies* (New York, 1971); Philip Stevick (ed.), *Anti-Story: An Anthology of Experimental Fiction* (New York, 1971); and Jo David Bellamy, *Superfiction: Or the American Story Transformed* (New York, 1975).

NOTE: Several important journals have concentrated on modern, contemporary and postmodern fiction. *Modern Fiction Studies, Contemporary Literature* and *Journal of Modern Literature* have extensively covered modern fiction, and have produced special issues on many of the contemporary novelists represented here. Also see *Twentieth Century Literature* and *Critique*, and in England *Critical Quarterly* and *New Review*. *Triquarterly* has produced special issues on postmodernism (see especially issue No. 26 (Winter 1973)); so has *New Literary History* (espec. vol. 3,1 (Autumn 1971)) and *Boundary* 2. Also see the newspaper-magazine *Fiction* and the English equivalent *Bananas*.

MODERN STUDIES OF THE NOVEL

Robert Alter, *Partial Magic: The Novel as a Self-Conscious Genre* (Berkeley, 1975).

Morton Bloomfield (ed.), *The Interpretation of Narrative: Theory and Practice* (Cambridge, Mass., 1970).

Wayne Booth, *The Rhetoric of Fiction* (Chicago, 1961).

Malcolm Bradbury, *Possibilities: Essays on the State of the Novel* (London and New York, 1973).

Jonathan Culler, *Structuralist Poetics* (London, 1974).

John Halperin (ed.), *The Theory of the Novel: New Essays* (New York and London, 1974).

Barbara Hardy, *The Appropriate Form: An Essay on the Novel* (London, 1964).

W. J. Harvey, *Character and the Novel* (London, 1965).

William O. Hendricks, *Essays on Semiolinguistics and Verbal Art*

(The Hague, 1973).

Frederic Jameson, *The Prison-House of Language* (Princeton, N.J., 1972).

Gabriel Josipovici, *The World and the Book: A Study of Modern Fiction* (London, 1971).

Frank Kermode, *The Sense of an Ending: Studies in the Theory of Fiction* (New York and London, 1967).

David Lodge, *Language of Fiction* (London and Berkeley, 1966).

J. Hillis Miller (ed.), *Aspects of Narrative* (New York, 1971).

Louis D. Rubin, *The Teller in the Tale* (Seattle and London, 1967).

Robert Scholes and Robert Kellogg, *The Nature of Narrative* (New York and London, 1966).

Robert Scholes, *Structuralism in Literature* (New Haven, Conn., 1974).

Philip Stevick, *The Chapter in Fiction: Theories of Narrative Division* (Syracuse, N.Y., 1970).

Philip Stevick (ed.), *The Theory of the Novel* (New York, 1967).

Harold Toliver, *Animate Illusions: Exploitations of Narrative Structure* (Lincoln, Neb., 1974).

STUDIES OF CONTEMPORARY AND POSTMODERN FICTION

Irving Adelman and Rita Dworkin, *The Contemporary Novel: A Checklist of Critical Literature on the British and American Novel Since 1945* (Metuchen, N.J., 1972).

Bernard Bergonzi, *The Situation of the Novel* (London, 1970).

Bernard Bergonzi (ed.), *Innovations* (London, 1968).

Jerry H. Bryant, *The Open Decision: The Contemporary American Novel and Its Intellectual Background* (New York, 1970).

Michel Butor, *Inventory: Essays*, ed. Richard Howard (New York, 1968; London, 1970).

Raymond Federman (ed.), *Surfiction: Fiction Now and Tomorrow* (Chicago, 1975).

Leslie Fiedler, 'Cross the Border – Close That Gap: Postmodernism', in *Sphere History of Literature in the English Language, Vol. 9: American Literature Since 1900* (London, 1975), ed. Marcus Cunliffe.

John Fletcher, *Claude Simon and Fiction Now* (London, 1975).

David D. Galloway, 'Postmodernism', *Contemporary Literature*, XIV, 3 (Summer 1973), pp. 398–405.

William H. Gass, *Fiction and the Figures of Life* (New York, 1970).

James Gindin, *Postwar British Fiction: New Accents and Attitudes* (London, 1962).

Elizabeth Hardwick, 'Reflections on Fiction', *New York Review of Books*, February 13, 1969, pp. 12–17.

Ihab Hassan, *Radical Innocence: Studies in the Contemporary American Novel* (Princeton, 1962). *The Dismemberment of Orpheus: Toward a Postmodern Literature* (New York, 1971). *Paracriticisms: Seven Speculations of the Times* (Chicago, 1975).

Jack Hicks (ed.), *Cutting Edges: Young American Fiction for the 70s* (New York, 1973).

Frederick R. Karl, *A Reader's Guide to the Contemporary English Novel* (London, rev. ed., 1963).

Alfred Kazin, *Bright Book of Life: American Novelists and Story-tellers from Hemingway to Mailer* (New York and London, 1974).

Frank Kermode, *Modern Essays* (London, 1971).

Marcus Klein (ed.), *The American Novel Since World War II* (New York, 1967).

Jerome Klinkowitz, *Literary Disruptions: The Making of a Post-Contemporary American Fiction* (Urbana, Ill., 1975).

Richard Kostelanetz (ed.), *Contemporary Literature* (New York, 1964).

David Lodge, *The Novelist at the Crossroads, and Other Essays on Fiction and Criticism* (London, 1971).

Thomas McCormack (ed.), *Afterwords: Novelists on Their Novels* (New York, 1969).

Vivian Mercier, *A Reader's Guide to the New Novel from Queneau to Pinget* (New York, 1971).

Iris Murdoch, 'The Sublime and the Beautiful Revisited', *Yale Review*, XLIX (December 1959), pp. 247–71. *The Sovereignty of Good* (London, 1970).

Raymond Olderman, *Beyond The Waste Land: The American Novel in the 1960s* (New Haven, Conn., 1972).

Richard Poirier, *The Performing Self* (New York and London, 1971).

Alain Robbe-Grillet, *For a New Novel: Essays on Fiction*, trans. Richard Howard (New York and London, 1965).

Nathalie Sarraute, *The Age of Suspicion*, trans. Maria Jolas (New York and London, 1963).

Robert Scholes, *The Fabulators* (New York, 1967).

Sally Sears and Georgiana W. Lord (eds.), *The Discontinuous Universe: Selected Writings in Contemporary Consciousness* (New York and London, 1972).

George Steiner, *Language and Silence* (London, 1967). *Extra-territorial* (London, 1972).

Wylie Sypher, *Loss of the Self in Modern Literature and Art* (New York, 1962).

Tony Tanner, *City of Words: American Fiction 1950–1970* (London, 1971).

James Vinson (ed.), *Contemporary Novelists* (London and New York, rev. ed., 1976).

Richard Wasson, 'Notes on a New Sensibility', *Partisan Review*, XXXVI, 3 (1969), pp. 460–77.

Tom Wolfe and W. E. Johnson (eds.), *The New Journalism* (London, 1975).

Notes on Authors

IRIS MURDOCH, born in Dublin in 1919, was educated at Oxford and Cambridge and was for several years a Fellow of St Anne's College, Oxford, and a university lecturer in philosophy before she became a full-time writer. Her novels include *Under the Net* (1954), *The Bell* (1958), *A Severed Head* (1961), *The Red and the Green* (1965), *The Nice and the Good* (1968), *Bruno's Dream* (1969), *An Accidental Man* (1972), *The Black Prince* (1973) and *Henry and Cato* (1976). She has written plays and criticism, including *Sartre: Romantic Rationalist* (1953) and *The Sovereignty of Good* (1970).

PHILIP ROTH, born in Newark, New Jersey, in 1933, went to the University of Chicago, and now teaches literature part-time at the University of Pennsylvania. One of the leading Jewish novelists of the postwar period, he published *Goodbye, Columbus*, a novella and five stories, in 1959 to win the National Book Award. He has since published many novels, novellas and satires, including *Letting Go* (1962), *Portnoy's Complaint* (1969), *The Breast* (1972), *The Great American Novel* (1973), and *My Life As a Man* (1974). His criticism is collected in *Reading Myself and Others* (1975), which includes the essay reprinted here.

MICHEL BUTOR was born in 1926 at Mons en Baroeul, France; he studied philosophy at the Sorbonne, taught in several countries, including England, and now is Professor of Comparative Literature at the University of Geneva. His fiction includes *L'Emploi du Temps* (trans. as *Passing Time*) (1957), *La Modification* (*Second Thoughts*) (1957), and *Degrés* (*Degrees*) (1960). His essays published in France as *Repertoire I, II,* and *III* (1960, 1964, 1968) are part-reprinted in translation in *Inventory: Essays* (1968), ed. Richard Howard.

SAUL BELLOW won the Nobel Prize for Literature in 1976. He was born in Quebec in 1915 of immigrant Jewish background; his family moved to Chicago when he was nine and he studied at Chicago, Northwestern and Wisconsin Universities; he still teaches at Chicago. His novels include *Dangling Man* (1944), *The Victim* (1947), *The Adventures of Augie March* (1953), *Henderson the Rain King* (1959), *Herzog* (1964), *Mr Sammler's*

Planet (1970) and *Humboldt's Gift* (1975). He has also written plays and short stories, and a good number of essays.

JOHN BARTH, born in 1930 in Maryland, educated at Pennsylvania State University, has taught at the University of Buffalo and now at Johns Hopkins. His novels are *The Floating Opera* (1956), *The End of the Road* (1958), *The Sot-weed Factor* (1960), and *Giles Goat-Boy* (1966). *Lost in the Funhouse* (1968) is 'fiction for Print, Tape, Live Voice'; and his *Chimera* (1972) consists of three novellas going back to the beginnings of myth and narration.

DAVID LODGE was born in 1935, studied at University College, London, and is now Professor of English at the University of Birmingham. A novelist and critic, he is author of *The Picturegoers* (1960), *Ginger, You're Barmy* (1962), *The British Museum is Falling Down* (1965), *Out of the Shelter* (1967) and *Changing Places* (1975). His criticism includes *Language of Fiction* (1966) and *The Novelist at the Crossroads* (1971), from which the essay here is taken.

FRANK KERMODE is King Edward VII Professor of English in the University of Cambridge. A leading critic of Renaissance and modern literature, his works include *Romantic Image* (1957), *Puzzles and Epiphanies* (1963), *The Sense of an Ending* (1967), and the Fontana collection *Modern Essays* (1971), which contains studies of several contemporary novelists.

JOHN FOWLES, born in 1926, studied French at Oxford, served in the Royal Marines, and now lives in Dorset. He is author of *The Collector* (1958), *The Magus* (1966), *The French Lieutenant's Woman* (1969) and *The Ebony Tower* (1975), a collection of linked stories.

B. S. JOHNSON was born in 1933 in Hammersmith, went to King's College, London, and in addition to fiction wrote poetry, plays and television scripts, as well as directing in television. His novels include *Travelling People* (1963), *Albert Angelo* (1964), *The Unfortunates* (1969) and *Christie Malry's Own Double-Entry* (1973). *Aren't You Rather Young to be Writing Your Memoirs?* (1973) is a collection of short stories with an introduction reprinted here. Brian Johnson died in 1975.

DORIS LESSING was born in Persia in 1919, and lived in Southern Rhodesia from 1929 until 1949, when she moved to England. She has published many books, of plays, verse, and documentary, as well as volumes of stories. Her novels include *The Grass is Singing* (1950), the *Children of Violence* sequence, commencing with *Martha Quest* (1953), *The Golden Notebook* (1962), and *Briefing for a Descent into Hell* (1971).

PHILIP STEVICK is Professor of English at Temple University, Philadelphia. A leading American critic of fiction, he has published essays in many journals. He is author of *The Chapter in Fiction* (1970) and editor of the invaluable anthology *The Theory of the Novel* (1967). He also edited *Anti-Story* (1971) and is currently working on a book on contemporary fiction.

GERALD GRAFF is Professor of English at Northwestern University in Illinois. He is on the editorial board of the magazine *Triquarterly* from which his essay is taken.